Bipartisan Foreign Policy

Myth or Reality?

Bipartisan Foreign Policy

Myth or Reality?

CECIL V. CRABB, JR.

Department of Political Science
Vassar College

ROW, PETERSON AND COMPANY

Evanston, Illinois   White Plains, New York

Acknowledgments

During the summer of 1951 I was privileged to work in the Office of Congressional Relations in the Department of State, where I gathered much data and gained many valuable insights into the problems associated with bipartisan foreign policy. Then and later I talked with numerous officials in the government in both the executive and legislative branches about the subject dealt with in this book. I am especially grateful for the generous assistance given me by Miss Louise White and Messrs. George Gray and Phillip Claxton in the Office of Congressional Relations, who suggested fruitful avenues of research and stimulated my thinking about new facets of the subject. I also wish to thank former Assistant Secretary of State for Congressional Relations, Jack McFall, for taking time from his heavy schedule to discuss his experiences with me. Nothing in this book, of course, should be construed as representing the official viewpoint of the State Department or the opinions of these or any other officers serving with it, except where State Department policy has been plainly indicated in the documentation.

I am indebted to many others who have shared (knowingly and unknowingly) in the preparation of this book. It was mainly from my former teacher and friend, Professor D. F. Fleming of the Political Science Department at Vanderbilt University, that I acquired training in subjecting popular idols and sacred cows to rational analysis. Professors Carl B. Swisher and Malcom Moos at Johns Hopkins University also made valuable suggestions when they read portions of this book in manuscript form. My colleagues in the

Political Science Department at Vassar College have discussed with me many points included in this book, and from them I have received many constructive criticisms. My father read the entire manuscript and offered a number of valuable suggestions for its improvement. Professor Richard Snyder, of the Department of Political Science at Northwestern University, also read early drafts of the manuscript and offered many cogent comments invaluable in later revisions. Mrs. Ruth Ashman provided indispensable typing assistance in the preparation of successive drafts of the manuscript. In acknowledging the co-operation of all these friends, however, I wish to emphasize that I alone, of course, am responsible for all errors of fact and judgment.

Finally, I am most deeply indebted to my wife, Harriet, to whom this book is affectionately dedicated. Without her unstinting help and ceaseless encouragement at every stage, it could never have been completed.

CECIL V. CRABB, JR.

Poughkeepsie, New York

Table of Contents

Introduction

... I raise the fervent prayer that we may ever strive for
an unpartisan American foreign policy—not Republican, not
Democratic, but American—which substantially unites our
people at the water's edge in behalf of peace. . . .
—Senator Arthur H. Vandenberg,
New York Times,
November 4, 1947.

... The bipartisan foreign policy has been hiding outrageous
betrayals of American principles, a disgraceful abandonment
of our vital interests, a vicious undermining of our economic
and financial solvency, and the flagrant neglect of even the
minimum requirement for an impregnable national defense.
—Senator William Jenner,
Congressional Record,
May 14, 1950, p. 3349.

For over a decade the United States has attempted to conduct its foreign affairs upon a "bipartisan" basis. The principle was initiated by the Roosevelt administration in its

wartime studies of the problem of collective security after World War II. The principle was employed later by Presidents Truman and Eisenhower as serious foreign policy problems arose during the years that followed. At intervals during the decade after World War II, an extraordinary degree of unity prevailed between the Democratic and Republican parties in the sphere of foreign relations. Unity reached a notably high plane with respect to the formulation and adoption of the United Nations Charter. After 1945 the two parties collaborated to formulate policies designed to promote economic and military stability in Western Europe. But unity has not always prevailed in foreign relations since World War II. The Far Eastern policies of the Roosevelt and Truman administrations and the Middle Eastern policies of the Eisenhower administration, for example, ultimately generated partisan storms of intensity seldom reached in American diplomatic history.

A major theme of this book is that the bipartisan approach to foreign relations has neither met the expectations of its most dedicated adherents nor justified the strident cries of its severest critics. It has not fulfilled the hopes of its strongest advocates because partisan discord has prevailed toward several important problems in American foreign affairs. Indeed, as we shall see more fully in later chapters, the rather uncritical acceptance of the bipartisan principle may have in fact fostered disunity. The bipartisan principle has not borne out the dire predictions of its most passionate foes because it has unquestionably made possible forceful demonstrations of national unity in the face of grave and recurrent external crises. At crucial intervals in the postwar decade it has been a vital element in the successful containment of Soviet Russia's imperialistic expansions.

More than a decade's experience with the bipartisan principle indicates that the verdict on how well the principle has served this country must be a mixed one. The advantages to be gained by pursuing a bipartisan approach to foreign relations have been widely recognized. The same cannot be said, however, for the disadvantages. Most infrequently do the writings and speeches of persons seriously concerned with American foreign policy indicate any awareness that the bipartisan principle may have disadvantages as well as advantages. The harmful consequences realized from following the principle seem to have escaped the attention both of the general public and of commentators on the American politico-governmental system. Support for the principle seems almost universal within the United States and—what is much more a matter for serious concern—almost completely uncritical.

A second theme of this book is that the disadvantages of a bipartisan approach to foreign affairs may at times outweigh any advantages the approach may possess. More often than not the impact of these disadvantages upon the American political and governmental system is subtle and long range, rather than direct and immediate. But the fact that the disadvantages are not readily apparent does not reduce their ultimate importance. No attempt will be made to enumerate these harmful consequences in this Introduction, since they are analyzed in detail in later chapters. At this point we can do no more than suggest some of the areas in which their impact is most likely to be felt: in the pattern that has emerged throughout American history for the control of foreign relations within the government; in the operation, usefulness, and future of the American two-party system; in the realm of executive-congressional relations, with respect to both foreign and domestic affairs; and, as would be anticipated, in the substance and effectiveness of American foreign policy.

A third theme of this book is that the difficulties of conducting foreign relations upon a bipartisan basis have seldom been recognized, much less assessed systematically. The explanation for this fact derives in major degree from an inability or unwillingness—probably a little of both—on the part of individuals within the government who are involved in the foreign policy process to agree upon a precise definition of "bipartisan foreign policy." The concept has various, and sometimes quite contradictory, meanings. This fact in itself has produced considerable bickering between the two political parties as serious foreign policy problems have arisen since World War II. In addition to ambiguity inherent in the concept, other obstacles hinder the maximum application of the bipartisan principle. Without attempting to list them here (Chapters 7 and 8 treat them in detail), we may observe that until there has been some attempt to classify and analyze these obstacles, there can be little progress toward their eventual elimination.

In summary, then, the purpose of this study is to analyze the concept of bipartisan foreign policy systematically, with particular emphasis upon those aspects of the subject that have been neglected by other writers. To accomplish this, the study has been divided into two parts. In the first part, Chapters 1 through 6, a factual foundation is laid, beginning in Chapter 1 with the historical reasons why the unprecedented emphasis upon the bipartisan principle emerged during the period of the Second World War. The five chapters that follow present case studies of important developments in American postwar foreign relations in which efforts were made to follow this principle.

The second part of this study, Chapters 7 through 9, is devoted to an analysis of the nature of the bipartisan concept and to an exploration of its implications for the American politico-governmental system. Chapters 7 and 8 treat the factors that will largely determine whether bipartisan co-operation is achieved. In Chapter 9 a balance is struck:

the assets and liabilities of bipartisan foreign policy are evaluated.

As we have already observed, the problem of definition is one of the major difficulties in the way of conducting foreign relations on a bipartisan basis. Space is not available here to enter into a lengthy treatment of definition. The problem is dealt with comprehensively in Chapter 7. Here it must suffice to point out that bipartisanship may be thought of as *a goal to be reached* (unity in foreign affairs) or as *the means for reaching this goal*. When the former meaning is intended, "bipartisan foreign policy" may be loosely interpreted to mean policy supported by majorities within each political party. When used in the latter sense, the reference is frequently to a "bipartisan approach" to foreign affairs or to the "bipartisan process," in which case the emphasis is upon certain practices and procedures designed to bring about the desired unity.[1]

Neither of these ideas alone can serve as a sufficient definition of bipartisanship. Both are central to the definition. For it is clear that certain kinds of "unity"—when, for example, the opposition party is coerced into silence—are the antith-

---

[1] Throughout the postwar period the terms "bipartisan," "nonpartisan," and (occasionally) "unpartisan" have been used interchangeably to describe the kind of foreign policy desired. "Nonpartisan" was preferred by Senator Vandenberg and by former Secretary of State Hull. One commentator writes that Hull implied by "nonpartisanship" that "both parties were equally responsible for foreign policy." See Arthur Krock, "Bipartisanship—Theory and Fact," *New York Times Magazine,* March 14, 1954, p. 32. For Vandenberg's views, see Arthur H. Vandenberg, Jr. (ed.), *The Private Papers of Senator Vandenberg* (New York: Houghton Mifflin Company, 1952), p. 550.

But in spite of the preference for "nonpartisanship" by such eminent authorities, the term "bipartisanship" seems more accurate and is, accordingly, used throughout this study. The initial portion of Chapter 7 deals at length with the difficulty of defining bipartisanship. But a study of two-party relations from 1943 to 1956 leaves little doubt as to the ultimate objective sought. It was, to quote from Senator Vandenberg, a "meeting of the minds [toward foreign affairs]. Thus we achieved substantial unity." *Idem.*

Bipartisanship thus suggests more forcefully than the two negative terms the idea of *positive co-operation* between the two major parties *in the formulation of crucial foreign policy decisions.*

esis of bipartisanship. Unity is the overriding goal, but it must be achieved by the use of acceptable procedures and machinery.

For the present, then, bipartisanship will be defined as *the attempt to achieve unity in foreign affairs through the use of certain techniques and practices acceptable to both political parties.*

At the outset it is necessary to emphasize the fact that bipartisanship is being given a somewhat more precise and restricted meaning than it possesses in everyday usage. This has been done for two reasons. First, the working definition offered here substantially accords with the conceptions of bipartisanship entertained by those most closely associated with American foreign policy in the postwar era. Second, uniform usage throughout this study is desirable if the writer and the reader are to be on common ground with the makers of the policies.

Quite clearly the question of bipartisanship in foreign affairs is intimately related to numerous other problems connected with both foreign relations and the American politico-governmental system as a whole. Ideally, an extended inquiry into bipartisanship should entail a thorough study of such issues as the roles of the President and Congress in foreign relations, the internal organization and operation of Congress, and the nature and operation of the American party system—to list but a few of the important related questions. In a comparatively short study, limitations of space do not permit as full a treatment of such problems as might be theoretically desired. Often the most that can be done is to mention the interrelationship, without attempting a thorough evaluation of it.

Among these associated problems, none is perhaps so intimately connected with bipartisanship in foreign affairs as the issue of executive-congressional relations. Relations between the presidency and Congress *as institutions* are bound to have a direct and often decisive bearing upon the relations between the party in power and the opposition, if for no other reason than that the President is automatically the leader of his party and that his leadership extends into the sphere of legislation. While the two problems—relations between the parties and relations between the executive and legislative branches—are intimately connected, only confusion can result from regarding them as identical problems. Harmony may prevail between the two branches of the government concerned with foreign affairs; but this fact alone will not guarantee bipartisan co-operation in the foreign policy realm. Thus during both the Greek crisis in 1947 (Chapter 3) and the Korean War in 1950 (Chapter 5), Congress overwhelmingly approved policies proposed by President Truman. Yet both of these examples have been cited time and again by leading Republicans as foreign policy undertakings that lay outside the area of bipartisan collaboration.

As a rule, interparty relations must be viewed as a problem that is broader than the problem of institutional relations. Naturally, harmonious relations between the two branches of the government concerned with foreign affairs will contribute to the dominant objective of bipartisanship: national unity in behalf of the nation's foreign policy objectives and commitments. Yet institutional harmony may itself be a product of favorable interparty relations. The history of American foreign policy since 1945 clearly establishes the fact that congressional leaders are likely to co-operate more readily with a president's foreign policy program when there has been a previous record of collaboration between spokesmen for each party in the stage of policy formulation.

Interparty relations present a broader problem than executive-congressional relations for another reason: the goal of bipartisan foreign policy—national unity in foreign affairs—extends beyond the halls of Congress. The most formidable obstacles to reaching this goal are often not found in Congress at all, but derive from political conflict throughout the country at large, especially during national elections. Elections afford the greatest opportunity available for disrupting the stability and continuity of foreign policy, and it is important to recall in this connection that President Roosevelt's desire to initiate bipartisan collaboration stemmed in large part from his fear that the election of 1944 would seriously jeopardize the allied war effort and America's efforts to assure peace in the postwar world.

Although its importance to the problem of bipartisanship cannot be ignored, extended inquiry into executive-congressional relations must be left to other writers. The emphasis throughout this study is upon party relationships as they bear upon foreign affairs. These relationships cannot of course be studied *in vacuo*. Wherever the context requires it, reference is made to corollary problems. Works cited in the References at the end of each chapter and in the Bibliography at the end of the book will guide the reader to a more detailed study of such problems.

More than a decade has elapsed since President Roosevelt and Secretary of State Cordell Hull, together with such congressional leaders as Senators Arthur H. Vandenberg and Tom Connally, attempted to generate bipartisan support for the United Nations as an instrument of international peace and security. A decade, to be sure, is insufficient time to permit final conclusions concerning the implications of bipartisanship for the United States. Some of these implications have now become reasonably clear; others are not likely to be fully understood for years to come. Still, the time is overdue for some kind of an assessment of these implications. It is hoped that this study will contribute to that end.

ONE

Bipartisanship and American Experience in Foreign Affairs

In 1923, almost a generation before the Second World War, a perceptive student of American foreign relations, Ray Stannard Baker, observed that

America has never yet devised a sound or efficient technique of diplomacy. . . . Nearly every important treaty the country has been called upon to make has become a bone of contention between the Executive and the Senate. It is certain that in years to come if we are to go forward in the new paths and stand for a clear-cut world policy, we must devise some method of speaking to the world promptly and with an undivided voice. Our present system leads to utter weakness, muddle and delay; it forces both sides to play politics, and instead of meeting the issue squarely, to indulge in a vast controversy over the prerogatives of two coordinate branches of the Government. The deadlock between the Executive and the Senate every time we face a really critical foreign problem is intolerable. It not only disgraces us before the nations, but in some future world crisis may ruin us [12, p. 718].[1]

Although this commentator was referring to the partisan storm engendered within the United States by the League of Nations issue following the First World War, he might just as accurately have been referring to numerous other foreign

[1] References numerically listed will be found at the end of each chapter.

9

policy issues which have confronted the American government throughout its diplomatic experience. Since the foundation of the Union, partisan discord and friction, personal animosity, and rivalry between the President and Congress have more often than not characterized efforts by the United States to deal with foreign policy problems. Efforts to follow the principle of bipartisanship in foreign affairs since World War II must be analyzed against a background of recurrent disunity and instability in the sphere of foreign relations.

This is not to suggest that disunity has always prevailed. During war, for example, both political parties and both branches of the government have usually succeeded in keeping conflict to a minimum. Moreover, sporadic attempts have been made throughout American history to reduce the strong likelihood of disunity by trying to promote closer liaison between the parties and the branches of the government concerned with foreign policy. These early efforts, however, were unusual, and often they had little or no effect in preventing internal conflict when serious foreign policy issues arose.

What are the major sources of this conflict within the American government? Disunity may derive basically from two courses (and frequently from both at once): institutional disharmony between the President and Congress, and animosity between the two political parties. With respect to almost every major issue which arose in external affairs before World War II, conflict from one or both of these sources was usually present in varying degrees of intensity. It is neither necessary for our purpose, nor possible within the space available, to present a detailed history of American foreign relations or even to discuss every instance when disunity within the government interfered with the formulation and execution of foreign policy decisions. Instead, in order to establish a background against which the reader may evaluate postwar efforts to conduct foreign relations upon a bipartisan basis, it will suffice to concentrate upon selected examples from American diplomatic experience that illustrate the sources of disunity within the American government.

In creating this background we have divided our study into three parts. First, we shall look briefly at some of the underlying causes of disunity between the President and Congress over foreign affairs. Then we shall consider the impact of partisan discord upon American foreign relations. Finally, we shall note some of the efforts made by foreign policy makers before World War II to promote unity within the government—efforts that foreshadowed the contemporary emphasis upon bipartisan foreign policy.

1. Institutional Conflicts in Foreign Affairs

Responsibility for foreign affairs in the American system of government is divided between the President and Congress, and in certain instances between the President and the Senate alone. The Constitution requires that the Senate ratify treaties by a two-thirds vote and that it confirm appointments of diplomatic as well as other civil officers. Congress must raise and support the armed forces and "declare war." More generally, it appropriates money for the conduct of foreign affairs. In addition, it may investigate the operation of the government in the foreign policy field. These are, in summary, the major techniques by which one or both houses may influence American foreign relations. In recent years Congress has come to possess another power that may, in an age of almost instantaneous communication between distant parts of the world, prove an even more effective means of influencing foreign affairs than its constitutional prerogatives. This is the opportunity available to legislators (individually, in committees, or through the action of one or both houses) to shape public opinion. Future chapters will illustrate the extent of this power in greater detail. Here we need only refer to the Truman administration's difficulties with Congress over American foreign policy in the Far East.

Despite the fact that Congress has certain powers in foreign affairs, American diplomatic experience has clearly elevated the President into a position of leadership and initiative in the foreign policy field. Some authorities on the American Constitution have contended that the founding fathers intended the Senate at least (if not Congress as a whole) to be a full "partner" with the Executive in the management of foreign relations. It seems clear enough that the founders were intensely suspicious of strong executive power and that they desired the Senate to become a kind of "council of state" to advise the President when important matters arose in external affairs.

But we are not here concerned with what the Constitution may or may not have originally intended. We must accept what American history has established as fact, that the role of the President in foreign relations overshadows that of Congress and of the Senate alone. The predominant position of the President has been recognized by the Supreme Court (24). Today it is difficult to take issue with Abbot Smith's view that

The President's activities in foreign affairs are such as almost to give him the power of war and peace; certainly the effective limitations on his power are political in nature and not constitutional; he would be ill-advised to move faster than the sentiment of the country will allow, but his constitutional disabilities alone will never actually prevent him from getting the nation practically into a state of war [21, p. 229].

Congress has not often willingly accepted a subordinate position in foreign affairs. Throughout the nineteenth century especially, a kind of running skirmish took place between the Presidency and Congress, as each sought to extend its own powers and to establish itself in a position of leadership. Today the pre-eminent role of the Executive seems to be generally conceded, even though institutional conflict within the government has by no means ended. Without attempting to trace chronologically the conflict between the President and Congress over foreign affairs, we may note certain recurrent sources of friction between them that contribute to disunity and instability in the sphere of foreign relations.

THE TREATY-MAKING PROCESS

The customary form of agreements between governments is a treaty. It follows then that the branch controlling the treaty-making process will likely have a decisive voice in determining American foreign policy. As we noted above, the Constitution provides that the President shall make treaties "by and with the Advice and Consent of the Senate. . . ." Treaties receive the "consent" of the Senate if they are ratified by a two-thirds vote of the members present. But under what circumstances may the Senate give its "advice" upon treaties to the President? Before negotiations are opened with other countries? While they are in progress? Or after a treaty has been drawn up and signed? What obligation exists upon the President to follow advice given him by the Senate? These and other questions associated with the treaty clause of the Constitution have been productive of almost endless misunderstanding between the President and Senate concerning the prerogatives of each in the treaty-making process. Hostility was particularly intense during the nineteenth century—so much so that Secretary of State John Hay remarked that "A treaty entering the Senate is like a bull going into the arena; no one can say just how or when the final blow will fall—but one thing is certain: it will never leave the arena alive" (22, p. 53).

Rivalry between the President and the Senate over the exact meaning and scope of the treaty clause appeared early in American history. President Washington, for example, in an evident attempt to gain the "advice" of the Senate upon a proposed treaty, encountered such procrastination and frustration at its hands that he swore eloquently that he would never make such an effort again. Occasionally, presidents after Washington requested the Senate to give its advice in respect to a treaty before negotiations took place with foreign countries. Not infrequently such action had unmistakable political motivations, as when President Polk requested the Senate to approve a reduction in American claims to the Oregon Territory, whose exact boundary was in dispute between the United States and Great Britain. Elected to the presidency upon the militant platform of "Fifty-four forty, or fight!" Polk came to the conclusion that the United States had a doubtful claim to Oregon above the forty-ninth parallel. Consequently he sought to enlist the Senate in extricating himself from the untenable position he had assumed with Great Britain, by asking that body to approve in advance a revision of American claims. In his message to the Senate, Polk declared that "Should the Senate, by the Constitutional majority required for the ratification of treaties, advise the acceptance of this proposition, or advise it with such modifications as they may, upon full deliberation, deem proper, I shall conform my actions to their advice" (12, p. 588). Many of Polk's political opponents regarded his request as a departure from precedent and firmly believed that the President was seeking to shift the onus for a reduction of American claims onto the Senate. Thus Daniel Webster observed disdainfully that "In the general operation of government, treaties are negotiated by the President and ratified by the Senate; but here is the reverse—here is a treaty negotiated by the Senate, and only agreed to by the President" (12, p. 588).

Sweeping claims of the Senate's right to participate actively and from an early stage in the negotiation of treaties, however, were voiced at intervals for the next century. One of the most far-reaching assertions of this right was heard during the period of the Paris Peace Conference following World War I, when certain Republican senators proposed sending eight of their number to France to acquaint themselves firsthand with President Wilson's negotiations. Moreover, it was in this period that Wilson's political opponent, Senator Lodge, accused him of departing from the Constitution by failing to include senators among the American delegates to the Paris Peace Conference (13, p. 304).

But in spite of repeated attempts by the Senate to interpret the "advice and consent" clause broadly and dynamically, the prevailing view after a century and a half of American diplomatic experience is that the President (in practice, officials under his supervision) negotiates treaties and submits them for ratification by the Senate. The Senate may of course reject them outright; it may add crippling amendments and reservations; it may refuse to act on them; or it may approve them. Throughout the entire process of treaty making, however, the President maintains the upper hand. At any stage he may withdraw a treaty from consideration by the Senate, refuse to accept amendments and reservations, or refuse to proclaim a treaty as law even after it has been ratified. If he finds the Senate particularly obdurate—or, more charitably, whenever he thinks the national interest demands it—he may effectively by-pass the Senate altogether by reaching an understanding with other nations through an "executive agreement." Although denunciations against such agreements are heard in the Senate periodically, they have now generally been viewed as within the prerogatives of the President and have, in certain instances, been sanctioned by Congress itself.

American diplomatic history seems to have confirmed the view that the Senate's role in treaty making is largely negative and passive. The initiative rests with the President. The Senate can neither make policy nor can it effectively block agreements that the President may think justified. Within recent years numerous senators themselves have substantially conceded the Senate's secondary role. Senator Arthur Vandenberg, for example—who came to epitomize bipartisanship in the postwar period—advised the Senate in 1948:

> I think the Senate is entitled, at any time it pleases, to use the advice clause of the Constitution to tell the Executive what it thinks concerning foreign affairs. But I think it would be a tragic and unfortunate thing if the habit ever became general or too contagious because I respectfully submit, . . . only in those instances in which the Senate can be sure of a complete command of all the essential information prerequisite to an intelligent decision, should it take the terrific chance of muddying the international waters by some sort of premature and ill-advised expression of its advice to the Executive [5, p. 107].

APPOINTMENTS IN THE DIPLOMATIC FIELD

Along with its prerogatives in the treaty-making process, the Senate also is required to confirm diplomatic appointments. Conflict between the Executive and the Senate has arisen over such appointments, especially when the Senate has attempted to utilize its powers to influence the substance of foreign policy. During the nineteenth century, for example, on several occasions the Senate contended that this power entitled it to specify the purposes for which appointments should be made and the policies individuals so confirmed were to carry out. An interesting example occurred when Van Buren (himself a former senator and minister to England) was President. Wishing to authorize the newly appointed minister to Peru to negotiate a commercial treaty with Ecuador, Van Buren informed the Senate of this purpose, when he sent the appointee's name to be confirmed, as follows: ". . . I bring this subject to the notice of the Senate that, if it shall be deemed proper to raise any question, it may be discussed and decided before and not after the power shall be exercised" (12, p. 592).

But as with the Senate's role in treaty making, its ability to influence foreign policy directly through its power of confirmation has declined within recent years. Resourceful presidents have devised various means of evading Senate control over their actions. They have made "interim appointments" when Congress was not in session, thereby presenting the Senate with a *fait accompli;* even if the Senate eventually refused confirmation, the appointee may have already devoted weeks or months to his assignment. Furthermore, presidents have relied with increasing regularity upon "personal representatives" to carry out diplomatic missions. Such individuals may be persons who either already hold some governmental position or who hold none at all. Wilson relied heavily upon Colonel House during World War I. In effect, House exercised many functions of the State Department, and neither he nor the President bothered to keep the State Department informed of his activities (23, pp. 247–54). Similarly, during World War II Harry Hopkins operated in much the same capacity for President Roosevelt. In time, Hopkins was referred to in the press as Roosevelt's "personal foreign office." Early in 1941 he was sent to England where he played a crucial role in cementing Anglo-American relations and in providing a channel of direct liaison between Roosevelt and Churchill.[2]

We may conclude that the Senate's power to confirm diplomatic appointments affords very little opportunity to influence action in the foreign policy field.

CONTROL OVER THE MILITARY ESTABLISHMENT

Conflict between the two branches of the government over control of the armed forces has provided a recurrent and troublesome source of disunity in American diplomatic experience. Perhaps more than at any time in modern history, today a nation's influence in world affairs is determined in direct ratio to its military strength. With the world divided into two antagonistic power blocs, the importance of the military establishment for American foreign policy has risen to unprecedented proportions. Thus President Truman's policy of containment presupposed the existence of sufficient armed strength to prevent the spread of militant communism. More recent declarations of American policy—"creating situations of strength" and "negotiating from strength" —have also required sufficient military forces to safeguard the vital interests of the nation. It is difficult to foresee a time when the United States will not be required to keep powerful

[2] The importance of Hopkins' mission to Britain early in 1941 can be gauged by the following quotations from Robert E. Sherwood's *Roosevelt and Hopkins*. Hopkins, Sherwood wrote, was regarded in Washington as "Roosevelt's own personal Foreign Office." When he arrived in England, Prime Minister Churchill "ordered the unrolling of any red carpets that might have survived the Blitz." While in Britain Hopkins privately assured leaders of the British government that "the Americans are with us. . . ." Hopkins quoted the famous passage from the Book of Ruth, "Whither thou goest, I will go . . ."—assurance which, Lord Beaverbrook stated, was more valuable to Britain than all the war material the United States had sent throughout previous months. A British editor revealed that in an "off-the-record" speech at Claridge's, Hopkins had "left us with the feeling that although America was not yet in the war, she was marching beside us, and that should we stumble she would see we did not fall" (**20**, pp. 283, 285, 305, 328, 536).

armed forces available to enforce its foreign policy objectives.

The Constitution designates the President as commander in chief of the military establishment, but it also gives Congress the right to declare war and to raise and maintain the Army and Navy. Do these powers confer upon Congress the right to control *the use* of the armed forces to support the nation's diplomatic interests? Is the President limited in his management of foreign relations by an obligation to respect the right of Congress to declare war, to the extent that he cannot take steps that might lead to war? Does the legislative branch possess the right to instruct the Executive regarding military strategy in time of war? Neither the Constitution nor the debates in the Constitutional Convention provides clear answers to these questions. There seems to be no question but that the founding fathers desired Congress to exercise ultimate control over the armed forces by its power to declare war. Before the era of the blitzkrieg, nations customarily gave notice of their intention to begin hostilities, so that the expectation existed that Congress might debate the wisdom of going to war. Early presidents sometimes hesitated to take forceful action in external affairs because war had not been declared and because they did not want to usurp powers possibly belonging to the legislative branch.

Alexander Hamilton very early understood the limited control over foreign relations that Congress possessed through its powers to declare war. With regard to President Jefferson's initially timid actions in the face of attacks upon American shipping by the Barbary pirates in 1801, Hamilton wrote with disgust that "the first thing . . . which excites our surprise, is the very extraordinary position, that though Tripoli had declared war in form against the United States, and had enforced it by actual hostility, yet there was not power, for want of *the sanction of Congress*, to capture and detain her crews." Hamilton totally rejected the view which he felt Jeffersonians were following—what he called "one of the most singular paradoxes ever advanced by a man claiming the character of a statesman"—that "between two nations there may exist a state of complete war on the one side—of peace on the other" (9, p. 133). But whatever may have been the original intention of the Constitution, American diplomatic history amply confirms the fact that, in the words of Quincy Wright, the power of Congress to declare war "has never prevented war when the President wanted one" (26, p. 235).

Limitations of space prevent us from doing more than call attention to selected instances of conflict between the President and Congress over the use of the armed forces. In 1826 President John Quincy Adams proposed to send delegates to a conference in Panama sponsored by the newly independent countries of Latin America. This course clearly risked war with Spain, since Spain had not yet recognized the independence of her former colonies. Adams' proposal caused strong misgivings in Congress, where it was widely felt that the President was invading the power of Congress to declare war. But even at this early date the President also had supporters in the legislature. Senator Johnson of Louisiana expressed what has come to be the prevailing view of the President's powers when he observed that "The President has, at all times, the power to commit the peace of this country, and involve us in hostilities. . . . And this distrust and jealousy of the Executive will destroy all power to do good, and all power to act efficiently" (9, p. 127).

A similar issue arose in the 1840's after Texas declared her independence from Mexico and expressed a desire to be annexed by the United States. Vigorous opposition to annexation was heard in the Senate (the Texas question quickly became embroiled in the overriding slavery issue), partially on the ground that the annexation of Texas would amount to a declaration of war against Mexico. Numerous resolutions were introduced into the Senate denouncing the proposed treaty of annexation, the theme of most of which was that "the treaty-making power does not extend to the power of making war, and . . . the President and Senate have no right to make war, either by declaration or adoption" (9, p. 128). The entire episode is highly significant in showing President Polk's unwillingness to be deterred by congressional opposition from ordering American troops to occupy territory adjacent to the Rio Grande River, thereby making war with Mexico inevitable.

Again, during the Venezuelan boundary dispute with Great Britain in 1897, the issue was whether President Cleveland, in pursuing a belligerent policy toward Britain, was risking war without the consent of Congress. Vocal opposition to Cleveland's policy was heard in both houses, but one of Cleveland's defenders, Senator Daniel of Virginia, supported his policy with these words:

That the Executive could not commit Congress or the country [to war] by his action is readily admitted. But it may as well be stated at the same time that the country has never refused yet in all its history to stand by a President who was guarding its rights and interests [9, p. 130].

The most dramatic use by a president of his powers as the Commander in Chief to defend the nation's vital interests in more recent years was of course President Truman's intervention in the Korean War in 1950. An overwhelming majority of the members of Congress from both parties supported the President's action, although many legislators thought the President should have asked Congress for a declaration of war. One of President Truman's strong supporters, Senator Douglas of Illinois, explained that such a request had not been made for two reasons: insufficient time had existed to make the request without jeopardizing the defense of South Korea, and procedures in Congress were too slow to permit it to consider such a request speedily. Commenting generally upon the scope of the President's authority over the armed forces, Douglas declared:

the acts of the President in helping to protect southern Korea from Communist aggression were in thorough harmony with the legislative intent of the framers of the Constitution, in line with sound historical precedent, in conformity with international law and the rules of the United Nations, and in the best interests of our own ultimate security and the peace of the world [8, July 5, 1950, pp. 9792–94].

It is possible to take issue with Douglas' interpretation of the intention of the founding fathers; but there can be no doubt that he was expressing a view that precedent and American diplomatic tradition amply support. We may summarize the point being discussed here by saying that there are few, if any, effective limits upon the power of the President to utilize the armed forces to support the nation's foreign policy objectives.

Thus far we have discussed the ability of Congress to influence foreign policy in the short run. We have observed that these powers seldom constitute a serious barrier to the President's leadership in the foreign policy field. Nevertheless, Congress does have the power to influence the *long-range direction and effectiveness* of American diplomacy. As we shall see more fully in the chapters that follow, virtually every important foreign policy undertaking in the postwar period has entailed troop commitments, substantial appropriations, or both. Without the funds necessary to carry out American diplomatic objectives, and lacking the potential power of an effective military force, the President would be gravely handicapped in the exercise of his duties in the foreign policy field, and especially in the paramount duty to safeguard national security. Funds come from Congress through its power of appropriation, and the size of the military establishment is determined in the long run by Congress, too. Consequently, collaboration between the two branches of the government directly concerned with foreign affairs is well-nigh indispensable for the nation's survival.

Appropriations and the Foreign Policy Process

The power of Congress to influence foreign policy decisions has grown most impressively in its control over appropriations. In both domestic and foreign policy, Congress must authorize expenditures and appropriate funds for the operation of the government. Throughout the greater part of American history, as long as the United States was pursuing a substantially isolationist policy, control over the purse strings did not give the legislative branch a particularly decisive voice in the foreign policy process. Occasionally, one or both houses have threatened to deny funds a president needed for some diplomatic undertaking; or less frequently, Congress has attempted to determine policy by appropriating funds and requesting the President to use them for a specified purpose. One example of an attempt by Congress to influence the substance of foreign policy occurred during the administration of John Quincy Adams, who requested funds to send delegates to a conference of the Latin American countries in Panama. Eventually Congress granted the necessary appropriations, but not before the House attached a rider to its bill prescribing instructions to be followed by the American delegates to the conference. Certain members of Congress, however, viewed this as an unwarranted intrusion into the jurisdiction of the President over foreign relations. Thus Daniel Webster believed the rider was unconstitutional, since it represented an attempt by the House to usurp a function "which, from its nature, belongs to the Executive and not to us" (18, p. 150).

A somewhat different tactic was followed by the House in the 1840's toward the question of sending an American minister to Mexico. Many representatives believed that the United States had insufficient commercial interests in Mexico to justify establishing diplomatic representation there. During House debate on this issue, forceful claims of congressional authority over this matter were voiced, as when Representative Linn of New York declared that

The power of this House, as a coordinate branch of the Legislature, over our foreign intercourse, is rather incidental than direct or express; and yet may, as it should, be both potent and controlling. Accordingly, from the origin of the Government to the present time, this House has exercised this power, in the negative form, of either confining the appropriations within the limit of its own judgment and discretion, or of withholding them from particular branches of the [diplomatic] service . . . [18, pp. 151–52].

But in spite of such claims, the House rider was ultimately withdrawn and the necessary funds were provided.

As foreign policy problems have grown more complex and as the United States has assumed a more active role of world leadership, control of appropriations has become one of the most important means available to Congress to influence foreign policy decisions. Particularly since the Second World War, foreign policy undertakings have required vast sums of money for their execution. It is necessary only to think of the Greek-Turkish aid program, the Marshall Plan, various programs of arms aid to Europe and other areas threatened by Communist domination, and the Point Four Program of technical assistance to underdeveloped countries to realize that none of these projects would have been possible without active congressional support. There is irony in the fact that certain *indirect* powers available to Congress have become more and more important, while Congress' *direct* constitutional prerogatives in foreign affairs have become less and less important. The crucial role now played by Congress in foreign affairs by virtue of its control of appropriations was assessed in a recent report by the House Foreign Affairs Committee as follows:

the major foreign policy programs of our country involve heavy expenditures of public funds, so that the responsibility for the purse as it relates to our foreign policy cannot be separated from the root and substance of that policy. Thus, the Congress has become a significant, regular, and necessary participant in the conduct of the foreign affairs of this country . . . [18, p. 159].

It may yet be too early to assert that Congress has finally achieved a level of partnership with the President in foreign affairs.[3] Even in the postwar period, presidents have on occasion publicly committed the United States to certain actions and left Congress little alternative but to approve the policy contemplated and to grant the funds required for its implementation. Examples of this are President Truman's public declaration of aid to Greece in 1947, as analyzed in Chapter 3, and his commitment to send arms aid to Europe after the formation of NATO, as discussed in Chapter 4. But such instances have been exceptional. As in the past, the President retains the initiative in foreign affairs; and in the short run, congressional control over appropriations does not serve as an effective restraint upon executive leadership. Presidents may virtually ignore Congress for brief periods of time;[4] but they will do so only by taking the risk that

[3] For examples of such assertions, see Nobleman (18).
[4] Presidents normally have limited funds available that they can use when necessary in the absence of a specific authorization by Congress. Thus in the late 1920's when President Hoover contemplated sending United States delegates to a disarmament conference (a move opposed by certain vocal elements in Congress), a State Department officer admitted candidly to the House Foreign Affairs Committee that the lack of funds was no barrier to the President's proposal—"if we have any money in our State Department emergency fund, it comes out of that. That is the only way . . . there is no law against it" (25, p. 135).

their policies may be repudiated or drastically modified
when they are finally compelled to seek funds for their sustained implementation.

2. *Partisan Conflicts in Foreign Affairs*

Thus far we have discussed institutional conflicts between
the two branches of the government as each has attempted
to exert its influence in the foreign policy process. Serious
threats to the stability and consistency of American foreign
policy more often arise from partisan discord over foreign
relations. When controversies arise within the government,
it is frequently difficult to find their precise origin. Disharmony between the Executive and Congress will doubtless tend to deepen and sharpen existing differences between
the parties, and vice versa. Can the difficulty which President
Wilson experienced with the Senate over the Treaty of Versailles, for example, be viewed as principally a conflict between Democrats and Republicans, or between the Executive and the Senate? While both elements were clearly
present, most commentators on the period of the First World
War identify the root of the conflict as partisan and personal
animosities between Wilson and the Republican majority in
the Senate. For example, Thomas A. Bailey wrote: "Blind
partisanship, as much as any other single factor, ruined the
League of Nations in the United States." He felt that close
to four-fifths of the opposition to the League stemmed from
"nothing more than unreasoning hatred of Wilson" (1,
p. 38). Institutional and political conflicts are almost always
intertwined. The judgment of Laves and Wilcox during the
Second World War would apply with equal validity to the
broad stream of American diplomatic experience: ". . . the
achievement of over-all *government* policies (as distinct
from *legislative* and *executive* policies) is extremely difficult

unless the party relationships are just right between the two ends of Pennsylvania Avenue . . ." (15, p. 913).

It is not our purpose to explore the over-all impact of political parties upon the American system of government. It must suffice to observe that parties have perhaps been responsible for more far-reaching changes in the American constitutional system than any development since the foundation of the Union. As is well known, the founding fathers neither anticipated nor desired the emergence of political parties within the United States. But in spite of such warnings as those contained in Washington's "Farewell Address" and Madison's essay in *The Federalist,* No. 10, by the end of Washington's tenure as president, parties had established themselves as an integral part of the American system. From an early date, the influence of parties was felt in the realm of foreign affairs, and it may be said that the impact had both positive and negative consequences for American foreign policy. The impact was constructive in that parties often nullified (or if not nullified, then mitigated) some of the harmful effects deriving from the constitutional doctrine of checks and balances. As the acknowledged leader of his party, an incumbent president has traditionally worked closely with party leaders in Congress to generate broad support within the government for his legislative policies, both foreign and domestic. The realization that decisions in foreign affairs inevitably have political consequences has frequently served to bind the members of the majority party in behalf of a common program. A forceful president can utilize numerous techniques—patronage, persuasion, access to public opinion, contacts with state and local party leaders, and promises of support in forthcoming campaigns—to unite members of his party behind his program, thereby minimizing the risk that institutional conflict will develop on important questions of public policy.

But the rise of political parties has also produced harmful consequences for American foreign relations by fostering divisiveness and instability at home when important diplomatic issues arise. Virtually every major problem in the history of American diplomacy that has arisen during a time of peace has fomented some degree of partisan discord. A perceptive student of the treaty-making process has concluded that

If the framers of the Constitution had realized that the members of the Senate would be divided into political parties to one of which the President would also belong, and that two-thirds of the members of the Senate would very seldom belong to the same party as the President, they would hardly have put the power of defeating treaties in the hands of one more than one-third of the members of the Senate present. From the time political parties first appeared, Senators in voting on treaties have inevitably felt the pressure of political motives. The temptation to defeat a treaty made by a President belonging to another political party was certain to be present. Either the treaty, if completed, might redound to his and his party's political advantage or the defeat of his foreign policy would produce an impression of ineffectiveness and thus be of advantage politically [13, pp. 12–13].

Political controversy over foreign affairs has been part of the American scene since the earliest days of the Republic. A dramatic example of such conflict was the intense public debate generated by the Jay Treaty with England in 1794. This treaty ultimately produced a heated partisan contest. Riots broke out across the country, including one in which Alexander Hamilton, a strong defender of the treaty, was stoned. So bitter was the opposition of Jeffersonians to the treaty that John Jay was hanged in effigy by his critics. Nevertheless, the treaty was ratified in the Senate by a straight party division. Holt comments that

defeat of the treaty was only prevented by the fact that it happened to be one of those rare occasions when two-thirds of the members of the Senate were of the same party as the President. The tendency to vote on treaties according to party lines operated as completely as conditions permitted [13, p. 18].

Within a decade (long enough for the Jeffersonians to assume control of the government) partisanship erupted again when President Jefferson attempted to purchase the Louisiana Territory from France in 1803. Long an advocate of a strict construction of the Constitution, Jefferson had strong doubts concerning his right to acquire this territory, but after prolonged negotiations with France he agreed to purchase it, thereby doubling the land area of the United States. A recent diplomatic historian has commented that

Division of opinion on the purchase was for the most part along party lines. Members of the Federalist party . . . foresaw certain doom for their party in the incorporation of new western and southern territory. They were opposed, therefore, to the acquisition of Louisiana, and especially to the article of the treaty promising the incorporation of the inhabitants into the Union [19, pp. 97–98].

The dominant issue of national politics from the early 1800's down to the Civil War was, of course, the slavery question. Almost every important foreign policy problem in this period became intertwined with the slavery controversy. One such problem (to which we have made reference above) was the annexation of Texas. Even before Jackson left the White House, considerable sentiment had developed within both the United States and Texas in favor of annexation. But the move was violently opposed by most of the nonslave states on the ground that addition of this territory to the Union would vastly increase the power of the "slavocracy." The treaty of annexation submitted to the Senate in June, 1844, failed to receive the necessary two-thirds vote—a development which caused the Texas representative present in Washington to write that party considerations influenced many of those, who voted against the ratification, to oppose it. The question of the annexation of Texas to this Government has . . . become strictly a party question between the [D]emocrats and [W]higs in the pending contest for the next Presidency [13, p. 58].

After the Civil War, partisanship was felt particularly with regard to westward expansion and the acquisition of territory outside the United States. Thus in Johnson's administration the opposition of radical Republicans well-nigh guaranteed that treaties for the purchase of certain West Indian islands from Denmark and for the establishment of reciprocal commercial agreements with Hawaii would be rejected. In regard to the treaty with Hawaii, the dedicated expansionist William H. Seward commented, in a vein familiar to contemporary Americans, that

Each of the political parties seems to suppose that economy and retrenchment will be prevailing considerations in that election [1868] and the leaders of each party therefore seem to shrink from every suggestion which may involve any new national enterprise, and especially any foreign one [13, p. 104].

The Democrats finally won the presidency under Cleveland, and hostility between the parties continued without abatement toward several foreign policy issues. Thus in 1888 a treaty providing for the settlement of disputes between the United States and Great Britain over fisheries in the northeast was subjected to a concerted attack by the Republican majority in Congress. Sir Charles Tupper, one of the British negotiators of this treaty, wrote concerning its rejection by the Senate:

The United States Senate having a Republican majority, which was unwilling to give the Democratic party any advantage in the impending presidential election, rejected the treaty. "We cannot allow the Democrats to take credit for settling so important a dispute," a leading Republican senator told me at the time . . . [13, p. 121].

The frankly partisan motivations that guided the action of the Senate were admitted freely by both political parties. Justifying his opposition to the treaty, one Republican senator observed that "there is not a Democrat on that side of the Chamber who would have supported it if it had not come from a Democratic administration" (13, p. 149).

In view of the deep-seated differences prevailing between Democrats and Republicans before the turn of the century toward Manifest Destiny and expansionism, it is perhaps something of a wonder that political discord did not interfere with the prosecution of the Spanish-American War. Democrats as a whole opposed expansionism in foreign affairs, while Republicans favored it. Imperialism thus became the dominant foreign policy issue during the period of the Spanish-American War, although it was heavily overlaid with such domestic controversies as those over free silver, corporate monopolies, and electoral reforms. Ironically, Senator Henry Cabot Lodge, who was later to lead the fight against Senate ratification of the Treaty of Versailles, lamented Democratic opposition to the treaty of peace with Spain. In contrast to his later position on the Treaty of Versailles, Lodge observed that rejection of the Spanish-American treaty by the Senate would reflect upon "the whole country in the eyes of the world, and would show we are unfit as a nation to enter into great questions of foreign policy" (13, p. 166). In the end, Lodge's fears proved groundless. Largely for reasons that we shall investigate more fully later in this chapter, the Senate ratified the treaty by a vote of 57 to 27, although the vote was substantially along party lines. Holt concludes that "the vast majority of Republicans supported the treaty of the Republican President and two-thirds or more of the Democrats opposed it" (13, p. 169).

The most spectacular and far-reaching instance of partisan considerations shaping American foreign policy is found in the controversy over the Treaty of Versailles following World War I. "Throughout the entire proceedings," writes Holt, "runs the theme of party politics which ultimately decided the action of the Senate" (13, p. 249). Limitations of space do not permit us to devote more than cursory attention to the Treaty of Versailles and to the partisan storm that raged around it in the United States after its negotiation. A strong case can be made for the view that this treaty in fact substantially met the demands of Senate Republicans, most of whom had in the years preceding World War I expressed their desire for some kind of international security organization to preserve world peace. Commentators holding this view ascribe Senate opposition chiefly to two factors: personal animosity toward President Wilson, and a desire to prevent the Democratic party from winning further prestige from the war and its aftermath. The opposite contention came from Senator Lodge and his supporters, of course, who argued that only the inflexibility of Wilson and his unwillingness to make reasonable concessions kept the United States out of the League of Nations.

A more moderate view is that the rejection of the Treaty of Versailles by the Senate must be attributed to a variety of factors, and that responsibility must be allocated (though not necessarily equally) to both sides. The Senate Republican majority made little attempt to conceal its partisan approach to the treaty and its overriding concern with the election of 1920.[5] Wilson was little inclined to recognize the

[5] Evidence of the undisguised partisanship of Republicans toward this issue abounds. For example, after Wilson presented the Treaty of Versailles to the Senate, the Republican majority reorganized the Foreign Relations Committee to assure the dominance of their own viewpoints. Senator Lodge wrote that "this was a strong committee and such as the existing conditions demanded" (12, p. 700).

Before the treaty reached the Senate, Lodge revealed in an interview that Re-

Senate as a "partner" in the process of treaty making. He was unwilling to accept the numerous amendments and "reservations" to the treaty proposed by his political opponents, thereby assuring its rejection by the Senate.

Senate rejection of the Treaty of Versailles constituted probably the most important stimulus to bipartisanship in foreign affairs after World War II. President Roosevelt and Secretary Hull were determined to avoid a repetition of Wilson's battle with Republican senators, and to that end they sought minority party co-operation in the solution of foreign policy problems while World War II was still in progress. Senate rejection of the treaty had taught a valuable lesson.

From World War I down to the late 1930's the United States played a passive role in world affairs. Committed to a policy of "isolationism," the United States required clear evidence of aggressive intent by Germany, Italy, and Japan before it awoke to the fact that the nation was not isolated from world affairs. Almost too late, the United States attempted to help its European and Far Eastern allies by "aid short of war" and by preserving the façade of neutrality while arming its merchant shipping, sending materials to its overseas friends, and proclaiming a Western security zone within which Axis warships would be sunk. Throughout the pre-World War II period, President Roosevelt encountered strong partisan resistance from Republicans (and from a few isolationist Democrats) in his efforts to support the free-world coalition against Axis aggression without bring-

publicans proposed to deal with the treaty by attaching crippling amendments so that the onus for failure to secure ratification would fall on Wilson. He stated, "If President Wilson does not see fit to return it to our allies that is his responsibility" (13, pp. 264–65).

Equally impressive is the so-called "round robin" which Lodge caused to be sent to the Republican majority, committing members of the GOP to consider the League of Nations only after peace terms had been decided upon with the Central Powers.

ing the United States into the war. So formidable was isolationist sentiment in Congress that the President on numerous occasions chose to by-pass that body altogether in
achieving his goal of protecting national security, as when
in 1940 he exchanged fifty overage destroyers with Great
Britain for bases in the Western Hemisphere. Here Roosevelt resorted to an "executive agreement" because of the
virtual certainty that a treaty authorizing this exchange
would not receive the necessary two-thirds majority in the
Senate. As one student of American foreign relations has
written of this crucial period,

The views and the actions of President Roosevelt in the period
between 1937 and 1941 were certainly not in harmony with those
of the prevailing group in Congress and so there was no solid
basis for collaboration, indeed very little on which to agree, in
the field of foreign affairs [3, p. 42].

Forced to deal with a Congress that was as a whole insensitive to the dangers confronting the nation, Roosevelt was required to take extraordinary steps on his own authority or
to allow national security to be seriously jeopardized.

3. Rudiments of Bipartisanship

Recognition among officials in both branches of the government that institutional and partisan disharmony may
jeopardize the formulation and execution of sound foreign
policy decisions has by no means been limited to the period
following World War II. Although the term "bipartisanship"
did not come into currency until the end of World War II,
certain practices foreshadowing bipartisanship in foreign relations may be discerned very early in the history of the Republic. Such practices were employed at intervals down to
the Second World War to impart unity and stability to for-

eign relations. The principal difference between these practices and bipartisan foreign policy in the postwar period is that in the former case they were utilized sporadically—and often ineffectively—to generate the desired unity. A further difference between earlier periods and the postwar era, as we shall see more fully below, was that considerable hostility to these practices existed within Congress and among members of the party out of power.

During the War of 1812, President Madison sought to prevent disharmony between the Executive and Congress and between the parties over the negotiation of a peace treaty with England. Accordingly, he requested Senator James A. Bayard and Speaker of the House Henry Clay to participate in the negotiations. Both accepted the assignment. But in doing so (in contrast to more recent custom) both also resigned their seats in Congress, since, to quote from Senator Bayard's letter of resignation to the governor of Delaware, acceptance of the President's request was "an implied and virtual resignation of my seat in the Senate." A commentator on this period has written that Bayard and Clay believed that their appointment had put them in a compromising position by placing upon them

a double duty: To their colleagues at the Conference, to respect any confidences that might there be confided to them, and with their associates in Congress, to disclose all matters within their knowledge. Accordingly, both resigned from Congress before entering formal duties as Commissioners [12, pp. 596–97].

Earlier in this chapter reference was made to President Polk's attempt to generate support in the Senate for his reduction of American claims to the Oregon Territory. Before he opened negotiations with Great Britain, Polk discussed the Oregon question with a number of influential senators. Once more, individual senators called attention to a lack of propriety in the method of this attempt by the President to generate unified support within the government for his policies. Vigorous efforts by the President and Webster, his Secretary of State, to win prior Senate approval to a revision of American claims was, in the view of many senators, highly irregular. The Webster-Ashburton Treaty, said Senator Benton, was in effect "ratified out of doors" (13, p. 62).

President Grant frequently resorted to certain practices that foreshadowed the principle of bipartisanship in foreign relations. After the Senate rejected the Johnson-Clarenden Convention by a vote of 54 to 1 (the convention attempted to settle certain American claims for damages against the British growing out of the Civil War), Grant and Hamilton Fish, his Secretary of State, met with influential senators—especially Charles Sumner, the powerful chairman of the Senate Foreign Relations Committee—before further efforts to settle this issue were undertaken. After prolonged negotiations between the governments concerned, the claims were finally settled to the satisfaction of the Senate in 1872 (19, pp. 315–19).

Few major foreign policy issues arose in the period from the Civil War to the Spanish-American War. There was no compelling need for unity in the foreign policy field. But the Spanish-American War had been preceded by years of partisan conflict over the acquisition of foreign territory. In general, Republicans were expansionist, while Democrats tended to oppose an imperialistic foreign policy. Against this background of partisan conflict President McKinley had to negotiate a treaty of peace after the Spanish-American War that would be acceptable to two-thirds of the Senate. The atmosphere within the government was distinctly unfavorable for such a treaty, which, in Holt's words,

came at a moment when no important treaty had been approved by the Senate for more than twenty-five years. It contained a radical departure from the traditional policy of the United States which the President requested the senators, of whom more than a third were political opponents, to approve [13, p. 165].

The "radical departure" to which Holt refers was the acquisition of the Philippine Islands, a move that for the first time gave the United States an important stake in Far Eastern affairs.

Seeking to create the most favorable circumstances possible for the reception of his treaty in the Senate, McKinley requested three senators (one of whom was a Democrat) to act as negotiators of the treaty with Spain. As events turned out, the treaty passed the Senate (57 to 27) by one vote more than the necessary two-thirds majority. No doubt, as Senator Hoar observed at the time, "the treaty would have been lost, if Senator Gray, one of the Commissioners who made it, who earnestly protested against it, but afterwards supported it, had not been a member of the Commission" (12, p. 598). Perhaps the most interesting aspect of this example is not so much that the treaty eventually passed; rather it is that widespread opposition existed in the Senate to McKinley's use of members of that body as treaty negotiators. Senator Hoar, for instance, condemned the practice both at the time and throughout the years which followed because it "places the Senator so selected in a position where he cannot properly perform his duties as a Senator. . . . If that practice continues, it will go far . . . to destroy the independence and dignity of the Senate" (10, pp. 29–30). In later years other senators alluded unfavorably to McKinley's practice of sending members of the Senate to negotiate treaties, principally because such action tended to obscure the issues involved and to cause appeals for its ratification by the Senate to be based upon the comity many senators consider that they owe each other. Thus one senator recounted that in debate over the treaty ending the Spanish-American War, the senior senator from Maine (Hale) had been placed in a most embarrassing position because his colleague from Maine, Senator Frye, had helped negotiate the treaty.

A kind of rudimentary bipartisanship was followed during the First World War, when both political parties agreed to declare a political truce for the duration of hostilities, as reflected in the slogan current at the time: "Politics is adjourned." Hoping to preserve something of this truce in the postwar period, Wilson followed precedent when he designated a Republican, Henry White, to accompany him to Paris to negotiate the treaty of peace. White had been a diplomat and had earned from Theodore Roosevelt the designation of "the most accomplished diplomatist this country has ever produced." The British statesman, Lord Curzon, called White the "dearest, best, and most lovable of men." Outstanding as White's personal characteristics and prior diplomatic experience might have been, however, he in no sense represented the viewpoints of dominant Republicans in the Senate, particularly Senator Lodge. Possessing few methods for influencing the actions of Senate Republicans led by Lodge, White was little more than a figurehead in terms of providing any useful liaison between the President and the Senate. His effort by cablegram to gain from Senator Lodge the "exact phraseology of amendments modifying the League of Nations Covenant which Senate considers important . . ." produced nothing but greater antagonism between the President and his Republican critics. Lodge viewed White's request as a "trap" laid by the President with White's connivance, to commit Senate Republicans to support the League. Allan Nevins, White's biographer, regards this ill-fated attempt to generate unified support within the government for the League of Nations as one of the crucial stages in the rejection of the Treaty of Versailles by the Senate (17, pp. 397–404). It must be concluded that no matter how lofty White's intentions and how impressive his background, he failed utterly to avert conflict between the President and the Irreconcilables in the Senate. One commentator writes that White "knew from his constant private correspondence with Lodge of the Senator's personal opposition [to the League], but there is no record that he either suspected the danger [of its rejection] or warned Wilson of it" (**13**, p. 273).

The lessons of White's failure were learned by later policy makers. After World War II, Democratic presidents were usually careful to choose individuals to provide liaison who could command support within their party's legislative councils and who could be presumed generally to reflect their party's viewpoint about world affairs.

Practices foreshadowing bipartisanship in foreign affairs were utilized sporadically in the period between the two world wars. President Harding appointed senators to represent the United States at the Washington Naval Conference in 1921–22. Secretary of State Hughes was determined to gain widespread support in the Senate for a reduction in naval armaments, and "he felt he needed both Chairman Henry Cabot Lodge of the Senate Committee on Foreign Relations and Oscar Underwood, the ranking member of the minority on the committee, as official delegates" (**23**, p. 265). When in the late 1930's the United States began to abandon its historic policy of isolationism, the need for unity within the government became increasingly clear. Shortly after his appointment as Secretary of State, Cordell Hull set about eliminating ardent partisans from the State Department, on the theory that "our foreign affairs should not be the football of domestic politics. . . ." Furthermore, from time to time during the years preceding the outbreak of World War II, Secretary Hull conferred with former President Hoover on important foreign policy issues. Although there was still no systematic attempt to follow the principle of bipartisanship, President Roosevelt in 1939 informed Congress that "these perilous days demand cooperation between us without traces of partisanship" (14, pp. 180-81, 202). The next year he appointed two Republicans to the Cabinet—Henry Stimson as Secretary of War and Frank Knox as Secretary of the Navy. Both strongly believed in avoiding partisanship in order not to jeopardize national security (6, p. 8).

We have devoted this chapter to establishing a background against which efforts to follow the principle of bipartisanship after World War II may be more intelligently understood. First, we dealt with the problem of how the Constitution divides responsibility in the foreign policy field, observing that while both the President and Congress have certain prerogatives, the President has emerged as the national leader in foreign affairs. Then we looked at examples of conflict between the President and Congress in the sphere of foreign relations. These examples revealed that historically, conflict has prevailed between them but that the President has at his disposal certain techniques that can, at least in the short run, effectively nullify congressional restraints on his powers. In the long run, however, it is clear that Congress has an influence—when troop commitments and large sums are demanded, a profound influence—upon the course of American foreign relations. We also observed that in addition to institutional conflicts, partisan disagreements can and have disturbed the continuity and effectiveness of American foreign relations. Such disputes have been present in American history from the late seventeenth and early eighteenth centuries down to the present day. Occasional, and often ineffectual, efforts have been made throughout American history to eliminate these conflicts; and in these efforts certain practices foreshadowing bipartisan procedures in the postwar period may be identified. Yet at no time before the Second World War was there any sustained effort to follow a bipartisan approach to foreign relations. Not until the United States emerged as the leader of the Western coalition was there a conviction that the barriers to unity described in this chapter might constitute grave threats to national survival and, after 1947 at least, the survival of the entire free world.

With this background in mind, we turn in the next chapter to a detailed consideration of the first of several case studies in which the bipartisan principle was followed toward foreign policy problems in the postwar era. We begin these case studies by considering American efforts to create an international organization to preserve world peace.

References

1. Bailey, Thomas A., *Woodrow Wilson and the Great Betrayal*. New York: The Macmillan Company, 1945.
2. Borchard, Edwin M., "Treaties and Executive Agreements," *American Political Science Review,* **40** (August, 1946), 729–39. An informative treatment of the constitutional validity of executive agreements.
3. Bradshaw, Mary E., "Congress and Foreign Policy Since 1900," *Annals of the American Academy of Political and Social Science,* **289** (September, 1953), 40–48.
4. Brookings Institution, *Governmental Mechanism for the Conduct of United States Foreign Relations*. Washington, D.C., 1949. A source of detailed background on the difficulty of avoiding conflict in American foreign affairs.
5. Brown, Ben H., Jr., "Congress and the Department of State," *Annals of the American Academy of Political and Social Science,* **289** (September, 1953), 100–107.

6. Byrnes, James F., *Speaking Frankly*. New York: Harper and Brothers, 1947.

7. Cheever, Daniel S., and Haviland, H. Field, Jr., *American Foreign Policy and the Separation of Powers*. Cambridge, Mass.: Harvard University Press, 1952. Gives a detailed background on the difficulty of avoiding conflict in American foreign affairs.

8. *Congressional Record* (daily edition).

9. Corwin, Edward S., *The President's Control of Foreign Relations*. Princeton, N.J.: Princeton University Press, 1917.

10. Fleming, D. F., *The Treaty Veto of the American Senate*. New York: G. P. Putnam's Sons, 1930.

11. ———, *The United States and World Organization, 1918–1920*. New York: G. P. Putnam's Sons, 1932. The Senate position in respect to the Treaty of Versailles is appraised on pages 475–87.

12. Haynes, George H., *The Senate of the United States*, Vol. 2. Boston: Houghton Mifflin Company, 1938. The evolution of the treaty clause in the Constitution may be found on pages 571–79. Washington's difficulties with the Senate are discussed on pages 583–84. Pages 585–86 recount Jackson's attempt to secure prior Senate approval of a treaty with the Choctaw Indians in 1830.

13. Holt, W. Stull, *Treaties Defeated by the Senate*. Baltimore: The Johns Hopkins Press, 1933. The evolution of the treaty clause in the Constitution is discussed on pages 1–14.

14. Hull, Cordell, *The Memoirs of Cordell Hull*, Vol. 1. New York: The Macmillan Company, 1948.

15. Laves, Walter H. C., and Wilcox, Francis O., "Organizing the Government for Participation in World Affairs," *American Political Science Review*, 38 (October, 1944), 913–30.

16. Lodge, Henry Cabot, *The Senate and the League of Nations*. New York: Charles Scribner's Sons, 1925. Gives Senator Lodge's position on the League of Nations and the Treaty of Versailles.

17. Nevins, Allan, *Henry White*. New York: Harper and Brothers, 1930. Perhaps the most definitive treatment of Henry White's efforts to act as a bridge linking Wilson and the Republicans.

18. Nobleman, Eli E., "Financial Aspects of Congressional Participation in Foreign Relations," *Annals of the American Academy of Political and Social Science,* 289 (September, 1953), 145–64.

19. Pratt, Julius W., *A History of United States Foreign Policy*. New York: Prentice-Hall, 1955. A readable and up-to-date history of American foreign relations. Chapter 14 contains an extended treatment of the Oregon controversy and the conflict between Polk and the Senate occasioned by it. The Senate's position in respect to the Treaty of Versailles is analyzed on pages 512–23. Chapters 37 through 42 give details of the conflict between Roosevelt and Congress during the period immediately preceding World War II.

20. Sherwood, Robert E., *Roosevelt and Hopkins,* Vol. 1. New York: Bantam Books, 1948.

21. Smith, Abbot, "Mr. Madison's War," *Political Science Quarterly,* 57 (June, 1942), 229–46.

22. Stuart, Graham H., *American Diplomatic and Consular Practice*. New York: D. Appleton-Century Company, 1936.

23. ———, *The Department of State*. New York: The Macmillan Company, 1949.

24. *United States* v. *Curtiss-Wright Export Corporation,* 299 U.S. 304 (1936). Here the Court held that the President must possess a "degree of discretion and freedom from statutory restriction [in foreign affairs] which would not be advisable were domestic affairs alone involved."

25. Westphal, Albert C. F., *The House Committee on Foreign Affairs*. New York: Columbia University Press, 1942.

26. Wright, Quincy, "International Law in Relation to Constitutional Law," *American Journal of International Law,* 17, 234–44.

TWO

Planning the United Nations: High Tide of Bipartisanship

On July 28, 1945, the Senate of the United States ratified the United Nations Charter by a vote of 89 to 2 (3, p. 8190). Senate ratification climaxed over three years of intensive study and preparation by the State Department in collaboration with committees of Congress and influential party leaders both inside and outside the government. The purpose of this study was to lay the groundwork for a world security organization that could preserve international peace after World War II. Ever mindful of the partisan conflict which had riven the American body politic when the Treaty of Versailles had been submitted to the Senate by President Wilson after World War I, President Roosevelt and Secretary of State Cordell Hull were determined that the issue of collective security in the postwar period should not again become embroiled in domestic politics. To that end, beginning in the spring of 1942,[1] the Roosevelt administration initiated State Department studies of the problem of maintaining international peace through collective action. The plans ulti-

[1] Records consulted by the author in the Office of Congressional Relations, Department of State, indicate May 27, 1942, as the date when Republicans and Democrats first conferred on postwar problems.

mately worked out were embodied with little significant change in the United Nations Charter, drafted at the San Francisco Conference on International Organization in May and June, 1945.

The virtual unanimity displayed by the Senate when it ratified the charter may be attributed partially to the fact that by July, 1945, the Second World War had not yet been won; war has traditionally united the American people in support of the foreign policies pursued by the incumbent administration. Yet this is an incomplete and superficial explanation, since it ignores several much more fundamental reasons why preliminary studies of the United Nations within the United States marked the high point in party collaboration in foreign affairs during the years that followed. To appreciate fully the revolution in American foreign relations wrought by Senate ratification of the charter, and to understand more intelligently the operation of the bipartisan principle in foreign affairs under almost ideal circumstances, it is necessary to examine more closely the reasons why this phenomenon occurred.

First, there were the procedures and machinery established—after pressure had been exerted upon the Roosevelt administration by influential congressmen [2]—to facilitate collaboration between spokesmen for both parties in these studies from the earliest stage of policy formulation. The first bipartisan consultations on this issue were held in May,

[2] The initiative for conducting these preliminary studies of the United Nations on a bipartisan basis apparently did not come entirely from the executive branch. Former Senator Tom Connally of Texas, ranking Democrat on the Foreign Relations Committee during the latter part of the Roosevelt administration and throughout the life of the Truman administration, writes: "One month after Pearl Harbor, I asked [Secretary of State] Hull to send State Department representatives on a regular basis to Capitol Hill. . . . Several Republican members led by [Senator Arthur H.] Vandenberg had complained to me that they were not getting sufficient information from the State Department. I wanted the entire committee, not only the Democrats, kept advised of the world situation" (4, p. 261).

1942, three years before the San Francisco Conference. Thereafter, consultations were continued at regular intervals and broadened to include an ever-growing circle of Republican and Democratic party leaders. The major channel of liaison between the parties was the Senate Foreign Relations Committee, which held both informal, exploratory conferences and formal meetings to consider draft proposals from State Department officials.

An important stage in establishing bipartisan liaison on a more systematic basis took place on March 22, 1944, when Secretary Hull requested the Foreign Relations Committee to form a small representative group to explore more thoroughly the problem of maintaining peace in the postwar era. This "Committee of Eight," consisting of an equal number of Democrats and Republicans, received the first State Department draft of the proposed United Nations on April 25 (4, p. 268). In the months that followed, the Committee of Eight met weekly, and despite an evident desire by the State Department to communicate draft proposals to Britain and Soviet Russia, the committee subjected them to prolonged and careful scrutiny. Before it would agree to the circulation of drafts among the Allies, the committee demanded that drafts be clarified to eliminate any suggestion that the United Nations constituted a "world government," to remove any implication that the UN contemplated the establishment of a "world police force," and to make more emphatic the requirement that important decisions taken by the Security Council could be subject to "veto" by any of the Great Powers (4, p. 267).

An important feature of the bipartisan approach to this problem was the fact that prolonged and intensive consultations between representatives of both parties were held and major decisions were agreed to *before* these decisions were made public or discussed with other countries.

A second characteristic of bipartisanship in this period was the care exercised by the Roosevelt administration to work through the acknowledged leadership of the opposition party. Failure to follow this practice had seriously jeopardized the chances for Senate acceptance of the League of Nations after Wilson went to Paris in 1918–19. The only Republican on the five-man American commission to the Versailles Peace Conference was Henry White, a nominal Republican. Wilson's formidable opponent in the Senate, Henry Cabot Lodge, said that Wilson had appointed himself four times—and Henry White! After 1945, as we shall see more fully in later chapters, the Truman administration's frequent neglect of this principle vastly complicated the task of achieving unity in foreign affairs. Not only was the designated Republican party leadership within Congress brought into the preliminary planning of the United Nations, but the Administration also sought the advice of prominent GOP spokesmen outside the government as well. Before the San Francisco Conference, bipartisan consultations within Congress had been extended to include (in addition to the Committee of Eight) members of the House Foreign Affairs Committee, the elected political leadership of both houses, and members of Congress who had expressed a keen interest in postwar problems. Especially influential among members of Congress who had not been included in early bipartisan studies were the sponsors of the so-called "B2H2 resolution," which sought to define American relations with the proposed United Nations. The State Department and Committee of Eight opposed this resolution as too sweeping (it provided, for one thing, that occupation armies should be placed under UN command) and as being premature in its enthusiastic support for an organization whose structure and powers were as yet undefined (6, pp. 41–65). Outside the government, the Roosevelt administration solicited the opinion of such prominent Republicans as former President Herbert Hoover, Harold Stassen, Charles Evans Hughes, Thomas E. Dewey, and John Foster Dulles.

By neglecting the views of no significant faction within the opposition party, Roosevelt and Hull effectively forestalled the complaint (heard later during the Truman and Eisenhower administrations) that the incumbent administration was consulting only with members of the minority party known *in advance* to be sympathetic to its views. Even more important, this effort to get a thorough sampling of opinion prevailing within the GOP had the result of preventing a rift between two sections of the party: those members who were concerned with foreign affairs in their legislative duties but who might not be politically influential; and the party leadership outside Congress, which often had little responsibility for, and little knowledge of, foreign policy questions.

A third factor of major importance in uniting the Senate behind the United Nations Charter was the frequency with which the Roosevelt administration in this period utilized members of Congress from both parties as negotiators and observers at international conferences. Two Republicans represented the United States at the Bretton Woods International Monetary Conference in July, 1944. Two other Republicans attended the International Civil Aviation Conference in Chicago in November and December, 1944. The United States delegation to the San Francisco Conference in the spring of 1945 contained an equal number of Republican and Democratic congressmen, plus advisers from both parties. Members of the opposition party were thus asked to share in implementing a number of foreign policy decisions they had helped formulate over a period of years. Their views were accorded equal weight with other members of the delegation at the charter negotiations. "In arriving at their conclusions on all matters," Secretary of State Stettinius reported to the Senate Foreign Relations Committee after the charter had been drafted, "the Delegation retained complete freedom of action and judgment while at the same time agreeing that, in case of differences of opinion, the position of the Delegation should be determined by majority vote" (5, pp. 49, 208). This procedure, Stettinius concluded, enabled both branches of the government to work constructively together "with no thought of partisanship" in drafting the UN Charter at San Francisco.

Important as such contributory factors were, even more fundamental was the fact that from an early date both major parties had reached a consensus on the course of action that the national interest demanded toward this issue. "Collective security" to preserve peace in the postwar world was a logical outgrowth not only of Roosevelt and Hull's prewar and wartime policies, but also of the Democratic party's approach to foreign affairs during the previous generation. The question that would likely decide the fate of the nascent United Nations as an effective instrument for peace was whether the charter was to become a substantial issue in American domestic politics. For despite the emphasis on bipartisanship during preliminary studies of the world organization to be established, without the enthusiastic support of a Republican majority in the Senate, the charter might well, for the second time within a generation, precipitate an acrimonious conflict between isolationist-minded and internationalist-minded citizens. It was one thing for Republican spokesmen like Senators Vandenberg and Austin to endorse the principle of collective security; but without considerable support from other GOP leaders and from rank-and-file party members, these early efforts at bipartisanship would likely produce no lasting unity.

Accordingly, a crucial stage in the quest for enduring

bipartisan support of the United Nations Charter occurred in September, 1943, when Republican party leaders assembled at Mackinac Island, Michigan, to decide upon certain important planks in the party platform for the presidential election in 1944.[3] Here high-ranking spokesmen for the GOP agreed to support the so-called "Mackinac Declaration" drafted by Senator Vandenberg. This document was "a declaration that for the first time united the Republicans in favor of responsible participation in a postwar international co-operative organization, and which became the basis of the 1944 party platform's plank on foreign policy" (6, p. 37). By the Mackinac Declaration the Republican party pledged itself to "responsible participation by the United States in postwar cooperative organization among sovereign nations to prevent military aggression and to attain permanent peace with organized justice in a free world" (6, p. 58).

The declaration had a threefold purpose: to bind all factions within the Republican party to a designated course of action on foreign affairs (intentionally left somewhat ambiguous) in order to assure maximum party unity during the forthcoming elections; to forestall a move by a group of Republicans in Congress to commit the GOP to a platform even more "internationalist" than the policies being drafted by the Roosevelt administration; and, if possible, to defeat the President's bid for a fourth term by capitalizing on the evident desires of the American people for peace and justice in the postwar era (6, Chap. 3, *passim*).

But whatever political motivations may have led to its issuance, the Mackinac Declaration resulted in two important consequences for the attempt to generate public support for the United Nations Charter. It permitted Demo-

[3] The conference at Mackinac Island included all the Republican governors, fifteen members of Congress appointed by the GOP leadership, and ten members of the GOP National Committee (6, p. 55).

crats and Republicans to collaborate thereafter *in pursuit of a commonly shared goal.* And it effectively *averted a threatened rift within the opposition party* over the issue of how best to maintain international peace and American security after the Second World War. Bipartisanship in this instance became essentially a search for the *means* to implement a policy objective that both parties now shared—the maintenance of world peace through collective action among the Great Powers. And by uniting the major factions within the Republican party behind a declaration whose exact meaning was deliberately left vague, even the *appearance* of disunity was avoided, since both internationalist- and isolationist-inclined Republicans could interpret the Mackinac Declaration as embodying their own particular demands.

The ultimate test of the bipartisan approach to the United Nations during this period occurred during the elections of 1944. Could the gains recorded since 1942 in bringing both parties into substantial agreement on the question of an international security organization survive a national election? Or would there be a repetition of 1920, when partisan animosities over the League of Nations issue nullified Wilson's efforts at Paris and prevented the United States from entering the first attempt in recent history to prevent war by collective action? Only once during the 1944 campaign did a serious split between the Democrats and Republicans impend on a foreign policy issue. A rift was avoided when John Foster Dulles, foreign affairs adviser to GOP presidential nominee Governor Dewey, was invited to confer with State Department officials on drafts of the proposed United Nations. This move evidently convinced Governor Dewey that there existed an underlying unanimity between both parties and effectively forestalled further partisan controversy over the issue (4, pp. 268–69).

Since 1945 the bipartisan co-operation that resulted in

Senate ratification of the UN Charter by an overwhelming vote has been widely regarded as a model of constructive party collaboration in formulating a major foreign policy. So firmly were the foundations laid that neither then nor since has there appeared in Congress any noteworthy sentiment for abandoning the principle of collective security or for compelling American withdrawal from the United Nations. Scattered and relatively ineffectual voices have been heard advocating such a course, but in the main it is probably true that congressional support for the UN and the principles upon which it was built were even stronger in 1955 than they had been in 1945.

Why did the bipartisanship that produced such impressive support for the United Nations often fail to materialize as other foreign policy questions arose after the war? The answers to this question are complex and will be discussed in more detail in subsequent chapters. But a partial explanation at least can be found in the fact that the problem of planning the United Nations was a *unique* problem in foreign affairs, and that its very uniqueness contributed heavily to the resultant unity achieved. We need but remember three things to appreciate the dissimilarity between this problem and those that arose in American foreign relations in the years which followed: that Senate ratification of the charter was preceded by three years of intensive study, that no significant appropriation from Congress was required to implement decisions reached in this instance, and that the UN Charter did not at this stage raise any troublesome constitutional issues such as the prerogatives of the Executive versus those of Congress to control the armed forces. Twenty-five years of history had prepared the way within the United States for favorable Senate action on the UN Charter. More than three years of intimate collaboration between spokesmen for both major parties produced decisions designed to make the UN a reality. By the nature of the case, issues that tended to complicate the achievement of bipartisanship after 1945—taxing and spending, crisis diplomacy, exposés of Communists and fellow travelers in high government circles, an evident lack of confidence by the opposition party in the judgment and even the patriotism of executive officials—these issues had not arisen to plague the efforts of those who sought common ground in 1945. Their absence had the effect of launching the first great bipartisan undertaking in an atmosphere of relative interparty harmony and good will.

References

1. Bailey, Thomas A., *Woodrow Wilson and the Lost Peace.* New York: The Macmillan Company, 1944. A brief account of Wilson's failure to generate genuine bipartisan support for the League of Nations is given on pages 92–105.
2. Carelton, William G., *Revolution in American Foreign Policy.* Garden City, N.Y.: Doubleday and Company, 1954. An analysis of the changes brought about in American foreign relations by United States ratification of the United Nations Charter.
3. *Congressional Record,* Vol. 91.
4. Connally, Tom, *My Name Is Tom Connally.* New York: Thomas Y. Crowell, 1954.
5. Senate Foreign Relations Committee, *Hearings on the Charter of the United Nations,* 79th Congress, 1st Session, July 9–13, 1945.
6. Vandenberg, Arthur H., Jr. (ed.), *The Private Papers of Senator Vandenberg.* Boston: Houghton Mifflin Company, 1952.

THREE

The Genesis of Containment

We turn now to a consideration of the manner in which American policy makers attempted to apply the bipartisan principle to relations between the United States and Western Europe in the postwar period. Four important milestones in American diplomacy toward Europe have been selected for detailed treatment: the Greek-Turkish aid program, the European Recovery Program, the North Atlantic Pact, and the military defense of the North Atlantic area. These cases furnish opportunities to learn more about the exact nature of the bipartisan approach, as well as the problems that arise in applying the approach in different kinds of foreign policy situations.

Space does not permit a recapitulation of the events following World War II that ushered in the cold war in the spring of 1947. Here it must suffice merely to note that by the latter date, tension and discord characterized relations among the Great Powers. Prolonged and usually fruitless negotiations between the West and the Soviet Union over such fundamental issues as global disarmament, control of nuclear weapons, peace treaties for Germany and Austria, and relaxation of Soviet control in Eastern Europe, as required by the Yalta Declaration, had resulted in growing hostility between East and West. Communist machinations in Iran, Western Europe, the Near East, and China, along with the steady consolidation of Soviet power in occupied Europe, constituted overwhelming evidence to Western governments that the Kremlin had not abandoned its ultimate goal of world conquest and was determined to exploit postwar instability for its own ends.

As early as March 5, 1946, in a speech at Fulton, Missouri, Winston Churchill told an American audience (presumably with the prior knowledge of President Truman) that "an Iron Curtain has descended from Stettin to Trieste." Churchill urged a "fraternal association" of the English-speaking people to resist further Communist expansion (8, Mar. 6, 1946). But at this time, less than a year after V-J Day, Churchill's proposal found little support in American public opinion. Not until the fruitless foreign ministers conference in Moscow almost a year later did the Truman administration abandon further efforts to reach an accord with the USSR on outstanding international problems. Thereafter, the Administration adopted a policy of firm resistance to Communist expansionism. "Containment," as the new policy came to be called, ultimately demanded unprecedented economic and military assistance from the United States to countries threatened by Soviet imperialism and called for the largest peacetime military establishment in American history.

Not only did American foreign policy undergo a marked reorientation in this period, but an important change also took place in domestic politics. In 1946, for the first time in twenty-seven years the American people elected a Republican majority in both houses of Congress. During the tenure of the Republican-controlled Eightieth Congress, the Truman administration had little choice but to work closely with the legislative branch in formulating foreign policy decisions that both parties could support. At a time when vast foreign aid programs and military commitments were demanded, Republican control of Congress meant that any important foreign policy development had to be evolved on a bipartisan basis or it would not be approved. Co-operation between the two parties in foreign affairs had become indispensable if the United States was to cope adequately with urgent foreign policy crises.

1. The Greek-Turkish Aid Program

The first of these crises arose early in 1947. Addressing a joint session of Congress on March 12, President Truman enunciated a foreign policy principle soon to be known as the "Truman Doctrine." The key sentence in the President's message was, "I believe that it must be the policy of the United States to support free people who are resisting subjection by armed minorities or outside pressures" (3, pp. 1980–81). This sweeping proclamation, called by the *Omaha World Telegram* "the most breath-taking statement ever made in time of peace by an American President or statesman" (8, Mar. 13, 1947), became the foundation stone of American foreign policy toward Europe and constituted America's official declaration of cold war against the Soviet empire.

The immediate occasion for the President's speech was the politico-military situation prevailing in Greece. Throughout the closing months of World War II and into the early postwar period, Communist-led Greek guerrillas had sought to overthrow the legitimate government of Greece; they had been thwarted in their objective only by the presence of British troops. By 1947, Britain, faced with near bankruptcy, could no longer maintain her military occupation of Greece. Britain informed Washington on February 24 of her intention to evacuate Greece by March 31. This presented the United States with an urgent crisis. The problem, as expressed by Senator Vandenberg, was that "the fall of Greece, followed by the collapse of Turkey, could precipitate a chain reaction which would threaten peace and security around the globe" (12, p. 347). Even if the worst did not happen, however, a Soviet base of operations in Greece would constitute an intolerable military threat to the Mediterranean area and to the free world at large. The Truman administration therefore decided that an appropriation of 400 million dollars was needed to contain Communist expansion in Greece and at the same time to bolster the defenses of nearby Turkey. But American assistance must be forthcoming immediately, lest in the interval between British evacuation and action by Congress the Greek revolutionaries (well supplied by the Balkan Soviet satellites) should overthrow the existing government.

The gravity of this situation colored all efforts by the Administration to approach the problem on a bipartisan basis. Within the limited time available, the Administration undertook the most intensive consultations between spokesmen for both parties witnessed since the San Francisco Conference. Two meetings were held at the White House—one on February 27, at which members of the two congressional committees concerned with foreign affairs were present, and the other on March 10, when the Administration reviewed the Greek crisis with congressmen who had not been invited to the earlier meeting (including Speaker of the House Joseph Martin). At the first of these meetings the President had requested that he be "invited" to address Congress in order to present his program of aid for Greece and Turkey (5, p. 318; 12, pp. 338–39).

Despite these two White House conferences, it soon became apparent after the President's speech that his program faced formidable opposition on Capitol Hill. So widespread was congressional apprehension and skepticism about the President's proposal that the State Department, at the suggestion of Senator Vandenberg, solicited written questions from members concerning the nature and scope of the Greek-Turkish aid program. By March 28, over four hundred inquiries had been received, from which the department selected a hundred-odd "typical" questions about the program. A document containing these questions and the State Department's answers was then circulated on Capitol Hill (7, pp. 341–86).

Hearings conducted by both the Senate Foreign Relations Committee and the House Foreign Affairs Committee, however, revealed that opposition to this program had, if anything, become even more formidable. Under-Secretary of State Dean G. Acheson (substituting for Secretary of State George Marshall who was then at the Moscow foreign ministers meeting) presented the Administration's case at both hearings and submitted to prolonged and searching interrogation by committee members. The principal objections at both hearings (foreshadowing militant and prolonged opposition in floor debate) centered on three issues: that the program by-passed the United Nations and perhaps foredoomed that body in its infancy to impotency in the face of a threat to world peace; that the program would establish a precedent for other, more costly, foreign aid projects; and that the program was a bellicose act that might provoke Russia into war (7, pp. 32–60, *passim*).

The last two of these objections were answered by saying that however unprecedented such aid might be and no matter how Russia could interpret the program, the United States had no alternative but to adopt it or risk further Soviet penetration into an area vital to the defense of the free world. But the first objection presented a more difficult problem. To overcome it, two steps were required. First, Warren Austin, American delegate to the Security Council of the UN and former GOP senator from Vermont, addressed a letter to Congress stating that the program was consistent with the principles of the United Nations. Then the program was amended by the Senate Foreign Relations Committee to provide that aid to Greece and Turkey might be terminated if either nation requested it or if either the General Assembly or the Security Council of the UN found the program "unnecessary or undesirable" or if the President felt the program no longer served the national interest (2, p. 249; 12, pp. 345–46).

The Foreign Relations Committee unanimously approved the program on April 3, but Senate debate did not begin until April 8. Here Senator Vandenberg argued that congressional failure to appropriate the requested funds would "give the green-light to aggression everywhere. . . ." Any evidence of vacillation by the government on this issue, Vandenberg warned, would "display a decisive weakness which involved far greater jeopardy than a sturdy display of United States strength" (3, p. 3198). The chief Democratic spokesman for foreign affairs in Congress, Senator Connally of Texas, expressed his gratification that "our foreign relations are upon a non-partisan basis and have the support of both Democrats and Republicans." With Vandenberg, Connally believed that in the absence of this program the "total collapse" of the Greek government was inevitable (3, pp. 3274–76). During Senate debate a letter was read from Secretary Marshall, who urged Congress to approve the program as a matter of the utmost urgency. Despite an evident lack of enthusiasm for the measure on the part of leading Republicans and a few Democrats, the Greek-Turkish aid program was approved after two weeks of debate by a vote of 67 to 23, with seven Democrats and sixteen Republicans voting in the negative.

Although the House Foreign Affairs Committee approved the program by unanimous vote, it was delayed by the Rules Committee for one week. When debate began in the House, Representative Eaton (the new chairman of the Foreign Affairs Committee) described the program as "one of the most fundamental and far-reaching enactments ever proposed in the history of our Congress." Eaton viewed the 400-million-dollar request as vital to the "safety and security of the nation"; he too cited a letter from Secretary Marshall urging favorable action at an early date. The House debate continued for three days, but on May 9 the House joined the Senate in approving the program by a vote of 287 to 108.

It was unfortunate, wrote Senator Vandenberg, that "such important decisions have to be made on a crisis basis" (12, p. 340). Hurried summonses to the White House, alarming reports from the State Department, repeated pleas to Congress for hasty legislative approval—these were the characteristics of bipartisanship in the Greek-Turkish aid program. In spite of the fact that Senator Vandenberg had been consulted from an early date about the crisis prevailing in Greece, the frenzied sequence of events that led to congressional authorization of this project prompted him to admonish the Administration that he wanted to be in on the "take-offs" as well as the "crash landings" in foreign affairs (8, Mar. 14, 1947, dispatch by James Reston). A number of prominent leaders of the GOP in Congress, however, had apparently not been consulted about this program *before* the President's speech, the most influential of them being Senator Taft of Ohio. As time passed, Senator Taft expressed his lack of enthusiasm for bipartisan foreign policy. He cited the Greek-Turkish aid program as but one instance among many in which Republicans "were hardly called in" until "policy itself had been formulated and was ready to be announced. They were merely asked to go along" (8, Aug. 1, 1947).

Ultimately, however, one consideration above all others—the threat to the security of the non-Communist world posed by the situation in Greece—sufficed to override disagreements between the two parties over the adequacy or inadequacy of bipartisan consultations in this instance and over such closely related domestic questions as taxing and spending consequent upon the policy. The *St. Louis Post-Dispatch* editorialized: "Congress may ponder and debate but the President's address has committed the nation to all-out diplomatic action just as a declaration of a shooting war must necessarily follow when the President asks for it" (8, Mar. 13, 1947).

2. *The European Recovery Program*

Act II in the drama of American foreign policy toward Western Europe opened only a few weeks after Congress approved the Greek-Turkish aid program. Its theme was the provision of long-range economic aid to the non-Communist countries of Europe to assist in their economic recovery. American assistance to Europe had begun even before the end of World War II, commencing with UNRRA and continuing through 1946 when Congress granted a two-billion-dollar loan to Britain and extended several millions more in various emergency and interim foreign aid programs. But by 1947 this aid had brought little genuine recovery to Europe. Increasingly the conviction had grown within the executive branch and Congress that further European aid must be granted only after a careful study of both the area's needs and American resources. The United States, said Senator

Vandenberg, "could not longer afford to underwrite futility" (12, p. 391).

By mid-1947 Europe's economic plight had grown desperate. Communist movements, especially in France, threatened to gain political ascendancy. The ill-fated Moscow foreign ministers meeting held in the spring had convinced Western nations that the Kremlin was determined to exploit conditions of postwar economic and political dislocation to advance the aims of international communism. Europe, moving rapidly down the path of economic stagnation, was "largely a vacuum—a military vacuum, an economic vacuum, and a moral vacuum" (6, p. 100). It was against this background that Secretary of State Marshall delivered an epoch-making speech at Harvard University on June 5, committing the United States to a long-range program of economic assistance to promote European recovery—a program soon designated as the Marshall Plan.

The Marshall Plan, first envisioned by Secretary Marshall (6, p. 105; 12, pp. 374–75) [1] and discussed at an early date with Senator Vandenberg and John Foster Dulles (who, as a leading Republican adviser on foreign affairs, participated in the Moscow foreign ministers conference), contained several fundamental conditions. The recipient nations were to make a detailed study of their needs and their own resources for meeting these needs. American aid must be utilized to achieve lasting recovery and not merely to provide "relief" for Europe. Each nation was expected to make the maximum effort of which it was capable to provide for its own requirements. By July, sixteen European governments had conferred and had submitted their requests for assistance to the State Department. The program envisioned was to extend over a period of four and one-quarter years, and ini-

[1] Senator Connally, however, credits Dean Acheson with originating the Marshall Plan (5, p. 323).

tially 29 billion dollars was requested. This amount, however, was subsequently reduced to 22.5 billion and then again to 17 billion as a result of strong pressure from the Senate Foreign Relations Committee (5, p. 323).

Meantime, the Republican-controlled Eightieth Congress —pledged to reduce taxes and to balance the national budget —showed little initial enthusiasm for the Marshall Plan. As the minimum, Republicans demanded a thorough study of the program and of America's ability to finance it. So widespread was this sentiment that studies constituting "the most concentrated, yet broad-scaled stocktaking in the nation's history" (12, p. 377) were required before Congress would act favorably upon the program. Private, nonpartisan citizen groups, the executive departments, research organizations, and committees of Congress all joined to explore the implications of Marshall's proposal. Among these groups was the Herter Committee, officially called The House Select Committee on Foreign Aid, which visited Europe during the summer and fall. Its members returned to the United States (with seventeen trunks of data) convinced of the urgent need for American assistance. One of its major recommendations—that the Marshall Plan be administered by an agency outside the State Department—was ultimately incorporated into the program approved by Congress.

To provide temporary relief to Europe during the winter of 1947–48, Congress accepted an Administration-sponsored bill granting 587 million dollars in stopgap aid (3, pp. 11344, 11405, 11430). On December 19, the closing day of a special session held late in the fall, President Truman asked Congress to approve the 17-billion-dollar appropriation required for the Marshall Plan; 6.8 billion was requested for the first fifteen months of the program. But Congress adjourned without taking action on this request.

Before Congress reconvened in January, the Administration worked closely with Senator Vandenberg to amend the program to meet existing Republican objections. At this stage, the principal demand was that the Marshall Plan should be established on a year-by-year basis, since one Congress cannot bind another. After receiving a letter from Senator Vandenberg, Secretary Marshall agreed to modify the Administration's original program to take account of this objection by putting aid requests on the customary annual basis (10, p. 57). Meantime, in the face of increasing Republican and right-wing Democratic opposition to the Marshall Plan, the Truman administration and its supporters on Capitol Hill prepared to utilize every resource at their command to push it through Congress.[2]

At Senate Foreign Relations Committee hearings that opened on January 8, Secretary Marshall justified the European Recovery Program as "dictated by the highest consideration of national interest." Without it, "our national security will be seriously threatened" (10, p. 1). Marshall strongly opposed the Republican view that administration of the program should be taken from the State Department. "There cannot," he maintained, "be two Secretaries of State" (10, p. 9). Following Marshall, an impressive array of Cabinet officers testified in a similar vein to the program's urgency and necessity, with Secretary of Defense James Forrestal calling the Marshall Plan "insurance against war" (10, p. 480). In the days that followed, the Administration and leaders of the GOP in Congress continued to differ over the administration of the Marshall Plan. Only after the Brookings Institution, a leading private research organization, had studied the program thoroughly and recommended that a separate agency headed by an appointee of Cabinet rank be

[2] Senator Vandenberg, as early as November, had written: "If the resistance which is showing up to the little stop-gap European relief bill . . . is any criterion, our friend Marshall is certainly going to have a hell uv a time down here on the Hill . . ." (12, p. 380).

established, did the Administration and leading Republicans arrive at a compromise on this issue (12, p. 388).

Senate debate on the Marshall Plan opened on March 1 when Senator Vandenberg reported the bill to the floor on behalf of a unanimous Foreign Relations Committee. In an hour-long address, Vandenberg reminded the Senate of "the fate of Czechoslovakia." Czechoslovakia had succumbed to a Communist *coup d'état* on February 25, 1948, a fact that impressed vividly upon the minds of many congressmen Europe's vulnerability and that contributed substantially to the ultimate approval of the Marshall Plan (8, Mar. 14, 1948, dispatch by James Reston). Vandenberg observed that the Marshall Plan "strives to help stop World War III before it starts." The Plan, Vandenberg emphasized, was the "final product of 8 months of more intensive study by more devoted minds than I have ever known . . ." (4, pp. 1915 ff.). For two weeks the Senate debated the bill, ultimately rejecting an amendment offered by Senator Taft designed to cut 1.3 billion dollars from the first year's appropriation. On March 14, the Marshall Plan was approved by the substantial Senate vote of 69 to 17 (4, p. 2793).

In the House, despite overwhelming support by the House Foreign Affairs Committee, the Marshall Plan encountered formidable opposition from a minority of right-wing Republicans and Democrats, some of whom labeled the program "a bold Socialist blueprint" (4, p. A-1749), an effort to give Europe America's deserved "tax cut" (p. A-119), a "huge unconscionable waste of American money and resources" (p. A-9521), and a move which "will ultimately ruin and wreck our economy" (p. A-3337). While this small group of critics could do little to prevent ultimate House approval, the House itself rejected the views of both the Administration and the Senate Foreign Relations Committee by voting to include Spain among the recipient nations.

House-Senate conferees subsequently eliminated this provision, agreed to a separate administrative agency (the Economic Cooperation Administration), provided for the establishment of a congressional "watchdog committee" on foreign aid to review the Marshall Plan after one year, and provided that aid to Europe should be granted on an annual basis. Both houses accepted the conference report on April 2 (4, p. 4053).[3]

Since a bill involving appropriations must in effect go through Congress twice—once as an authorization to spend and again as an appropriation measure—approval by Congress on April 2 did not complete legislative action. In the early summer, the Appropriations committees of each house drafted bills providing the necessary funds. In the process, the House Appropriations Committee reduced the authorized first-year installment by approximately 25 per cent. After long and arduous hearings on the matter, the committee had concluded that "the architects of this world-wide relief program have no definite plan and no definite program," in the words of Chairman John Taber on the House floor (4, p. 7168).

This unexpected threat to a program which had been the subject of almost a year's intensive study raised serious doubts both at home and abroad regarding the stability of American foreign policy and the good faith of the American government. In an unprecedented move, Senator Vandenberg asked to be called as a witness before Taber's committee, where he strongly condemned the committee's ill-advised approach to a complex and grave foreign policy issue. If it persisted in its action, Vandenberg argued, the United States would be regarded as "capricious, unreliable, and

[3] The ECA administrator, Paul Hoffmann, was a prominent businessman chosen at the instigation of Senator Vandenberg who, along with other leading Republicans, desired that the administrator "come from the outside business world with strong industrial credits and *not* via the State Department" (12, p. 393).

impotent" by its allies in the cold war (12, p. 396). Again on the Senate floor, Vandenberg violated a long-standing Senate custom by publicly condemning Taber's committee for reversing "the overwhelming intent of Congress." The consequence of this action, he argued, was to encourage "the alien critics who plot to have these peace plans fail" (12, pp. 397-98). Vandenberg's earnest plea moved Congress to restore all but approximately 400 million dollars of the first Marshall Plan installment authorized earlier in the year.

What light does an examination of the Greek-Turkish aid program and the Marshall Plan throw upon the problem of conducting foreign relations upon a bipartisan basis? With respect to the former, two facts are particularly striking: the almost complete neglect of bipartisan procedures by the Truman administration and, at the same time, the impressive display of unity between the two parties as a result of Congress' overwhelming endorsement of the aid program. In the judgment of the President and his advisers, the Greek crisis presented the United States with a grave threat to its own security and that of the free world. In contrast to the problem of creating virtually unified support for the United Nations Charter or the provision of long-range economic assistance to Western Europe, the Greek crisis by its very nature permitted little time for consultations between the Truman administration and the Republican majority in Congress. It is true that hurried conferences were held at the White House at which the President explained the action he intended to take toward the situation in Greece. But these conferences were in no way regarded by leading Republicans as fulfilling their definition of bipartisan foreign policy.

In spite of existing Republican dissatisfaction over the nature of procedures used, however, a high degree of unity within the government toward this issue was eventually manifested. What, then, was the source of this unity? The answer is to be found in the words of Senator Vandenberg, who wrote: "If we turned the President down . . . we might as well either resign ourselves to a complete Communist encirclement and infiltration or else get ready for World War No. Three" (12, p. 342). The alternatives were simple and readily apparent to all concerned: either the Republican majority in Congress would accept the President's leadership by approving his program, or else it would risk a serious weakening of the anti-Communist alliance by accepting Soviet penetration of the vital Mediterranean area. The choice, in brief, was co-operation between the two political parties or possible diplomatic disaster. Under these circumstances there could be little doubt which course the Republican majority in Congress would prefer.

As we shall see more fully in later chapters, this case was similar in many respects to other major problems in American postwar foreign relations, especially in the Far and Middle East. We may generalize about situations of this kind by saying that the necessity for large appropriations to promote the diplomatic interests of the nation, or the political composition of Congress, or both, may make bipartisan collaboration highly desirable, if not sometimes indispensable. Yet even when there exists substantial dissatisfaction over the bipartisan procedures utilized, this fact alone will not prevent the opposition party from supporting vigorous executive leadership in meeting a serious and obvious threat to national security. Procedures satisfactory to both parties doubtless contribute to unity. The Greek crisis, however, strongly suggests that in the last analysis, unity may be more a product of the external problem prevailing than of bipartisan liaison.

The Marshall Plan as a case study in American postwar foreign affairs provides us with an opportunity to draw still other conclusions about the bipartisan principle as it was applied toward a different kind of foreign policy problem. We may note at the outset that the Marshall Plan was regarded by Senator Vandenberg and other leading Republicans (though not by Senator Taft) as not only proof of the necessity for bipartisan co-operation in foreign affairs, but as an example of the highest type of American statesmanship (12, p. 398). By the end of the program there was no doubt that its major objective—restoring economic and political stability to Europe—had been substantially realized.

Along with the preliminary studies of the United Nations earlier and of the North Atlantic Pact which came later, the Marshall Plan must be regarded as a case study of bipartisan co-operation under well-nigh optimum conditions. As had been the case with the early studies of the UN, ample time was permitted for numerous and thorough studies of this program before it was submitted to Congress for approval. And while Europe's economic situation was steadily deteriorating, by contrast with events in Greece and China in this period, there was comparatively little urgency to the Marshall Plan, and hence no necessity for the Administration to present Congress with a *fait accompli*.

In addition, there were certain factors present in this instance that contributed substantially to the unity achieved. First, as we have noted, the Truman administration made numerous major concessions to accommodate Republican demands, the principal one being the establishment of a separate agency to handle the program. The Administration also accepted another Republican demand—that the program be implemented upon the assumption that its renewal would be determined by the extent to which Europe made effective use of the funds provided (12, pp. 287–88). But almost equally important were certain minor concessions— "window dressing," Senator Vandenberg termed them (12, pp. 388–89)—designed to gain the broadest support possible for the Marshall Plan in Congress. The net effect of both major and minor concessions, as with wartime studies of the United Nations earlier, was to create the impression on Capitol Hill that bipartisanship involved a *joint creative effort* to formulate foreign policy decisions both parties could enthusiastically support.

Another important feature of bipartisanship here was the care with which the Truman administration and its Republican supporters in Congress undertook a thorough study of the program. They sought to draw up a concrete program only *after* all interested individuals and groups had been accorded an opportunity to air their views. More than ninety witnesses had appeared at the Senate Foreign Relations Committee hearings from January 8 to February 5. These hearings, together with the numerous studies undertaken by other public and private agencies, probably represented the most comprehensive effort in the entire postwar period to gauge American public opinion before a major foreign policy decision was reached.

A third characteristic of bipartisanship in this case, and one that goes far to explain why the Marshall Plan was annually renewed without undue opposition from Congress, was the provision requiring periodic reappraisal of the program by a designated congressional committee. Thus not only were consultations to be held in the initiating stage of the program, they were to continue throughout the life of the program. This requirement of a continuing legislative review was a procedure sorely lacking in other foreign policy programs adopted before and after the Marshall Plan— most notably in respect to the Far and Middle Eastern problems. The year-by-year review of the Marshall Plan was not solely an executive responsibility, nor was it left to evolve upon a basis of crisis diplomacy when existing policy had clearly proved inadequate.

Fourth, the major deficiency of the bipartisan approach —the Administration's neglect of the key Appropriations committees—did not become apparent until the summer of 1948, when the House Appropriations Committee reduced the authorized funds by one-fourth. Although the committee's unwillingness to be guided by the overwhelming sentiment of Congress in this instance did little ultimate damage to the program, opposition from the Appropriations committees recurred time and again. Throughout the life of the Marshall Plan there was no assurance that the powerful Appropriations committees in each house would accept agreements worked out between the Administration and the two committees concerned with foreign policy. Experience with the Marshall Plan clearly calls attention to the strategic role of the Appropriations committees in the legislative process. The exclusion of spokesmen for these committees from bipartisan consultations on major foreign policy problems is a serious obstacle to the achievement of unity in foreign relations. With regard to the Marshall Plan these committees were in effect presented with a policy already determined, which they were expected to approve without substantial change. Since the members of these committees tend to be among the most politically influential in Congress, elementary prudence would seem to demand that they be consulted in advance on foreign policy decisions calling for substantial funds.

Finally, we may note that this case illustrates certain political liabilities for the opposition party [4] that appear to be inherent in a bipartisan approach to foreign affairs. Since a later chapter will deal more systematically with the assets

[4] As used throughout this study, the term "opposition" or "minority" party refers to the party which does not control the executive branch. While control of the executive branch and one or both chambers of Congress has been divided between the two major parties thirteen times since the Civil War, ambiguity may perhaps be averted by referring to the "majority party" as the one in control of the White House and *usually* in control of Congress. The two periods covered by this study when this condition did not prevail were 1947–48 and 1955–56.

and liabilities of bipartisanship, here it must suffice merely to call attention to a dilemma that confronted the GOP majority in Congress when it evaluated the Marshall Plan. The Republican party had pledged itself in the congressional elections of 1946 to a fiscal policy involving reduced taxing and spending by the national government. Yet members of the GOP in Congress eventually collaborated with a Democratic administration to approve the largest peacetime foreign aid budget in American history. By so doing, Republicans deprived themselves of an important election issue (Fair Deal spending), and at the same time permitted the Truman administration to achieve one of its crowning successes in the foreign policy field. It may well have been true that the alternative might have proved even less politically desirable. Rejection of the Marshall Plan would have strongly implied a calloused indifference to the plight of countries threatened by Soviet penetration and would have confirmed fears voiced in some quarters that the GOP had learned nothing about the indivisibility of peace since the First World War. Either way—by enabling Democrats to score an impressive victory in the foreign policy field or by reasserting its traditional isolationist leanings—the Republican party stood to gain little political advantage from supporting the Marshall Plan.

References

1. Byrnes, James F., *Speaking Frankly*. New York: Harper and Brothers, 1947. A convenient treatment of the deterioration in East-West relations in the period immediately following World War II.

2. *Congressional Quarterly,* 1947, Vol. 3. Page 250 contains a convenient summary of opposition arguments in the Senate on the Greek-Turkish aid program, and the House debate is summarized on pages 252–56.

3. *Congressional Record,* Vol. 93.

4. *Congressional Record,* Vol. 94.

5. Connally, Tom, *My Name Is Tom Connally.* New York: Thomas Y. Crowell, 1954.

6. Dulles, John Foster, *War or Peace.* New York: The Macmillan Company, 1950.

7. House Foreign Affairs Committee, *Hearings on Assistance to Greece and Turkey,* 80th Congress, 1st Session, March 20–April 9, 1947.

8. *New York Times.*

9. Senate Document No. 205, 80th Congress, 2nd Session. Pages 313–15 contain a complete breakdown of the Marshall Plan allocation for fiscal year 1949.

10. Senate Foreign Relations Committee, *Hearings on European Recovery Program,* 80th Congress, 2nd Session, January 8–15, 1948.

11. Senate Foreign Relations Committee–House Foreign Affairs Committee, *The European Recovery Program,* Senate Document No. 111, 80th Congress, 1st Session, 1947. Gives full background information on United States aid to Europe before 1948 and the origin of the Marshall Plan.

12. Vandenberg, Arthur H., Jr. (ed.), *The Private Papers of Senator Vandenberg.* Boston: Houghton Mifflin Company, 1952.

13. X [George F. Kennan], "The Sources of Soviet Conduct," *Foreign Affairs,* 25 (July, 1947), 566–83. A clear exposition of the doctrine of containment.

FOUR

The Defense of Western Europe

1. The North Atlantic Pact

When the Senate Foreign Relations Committee held public hearings on the Marshall Plan early in 1948, elder statesman Bernard Baruch had proposed that the United States "mutually guarantee the nations entering into this union against aggression. By guarantee I mean a firm promise to go to war in joint defense if any of them are attacked" (7, p. 556). Baruch's recommendation was premature, but within less than a year it had become a reality when the North Atlantic Pact was signed in Washington on April 4, 1949. The original signatories were the United States, the United Kingdom, France, Italy, Belgium, the Netherlands, Luxemburg, Portugal, Denmark, Norway, Ireland, and Canada.[1] This treaty, said John Foster Dulles, was "our most important international decision since the promulgation of the Monroe Doctrine" (6, Mar. 13, 1949).

As a case study to illustrate operation of the bipartisan principle in foreign affairs the North Atlantic Treaty is unique, since the main impetus for its negotiation came originally from the Republican-controlled Eightieth Con-

[1] In addition to the original signatories, Greece and Turkey joined NATO later. Yugoslavia was drawn into the organization by signing defense agreements with these two countries in 1953.

gress—and, more specifically, from Senator Vandenberg. Yet after the elections of 1948 the Democratic-controlled Senate ratified the treaty. Concurrently with congressional study of the Marshall Plan in the first half of 1948, the nations of Western Europe, spurred by the Communist *coup* in Czechoslovakia in February and the Berlin blockade in March, were taking steps to assure their mutual defense. This movement culminated in the Brussels (Western Union) Pact that provided for both common defense effort and joint military planning.

Even before Congress had approved the Marshall Plan, numerous legislators expressed their interest in a closer military association between the United States and Europe (9, pp. 474–75). Senator Vandenberg especially gave this matter much thought, and while not wishing to by-pass the United Nations as the established organ for dealing with questions of international security, he became convinced that Article 51 of the charter permitted the "inherent right of individual and collective self-defense . . ." (9, p. 403). Vandenberg pursued this matter informally with Under-Secretary of State Robert Lovett. Their twofold purpose was to draft a Senate resolution favoring the abolition of the veto in the Security Council of the United Nations on all matters affecting the pacific settlement of disputes and to establish a collective security agreement for the North Atlantic community. Weeks were required to produce a one-page statement embodying these objectives. But this statement—later to form the basis for the Vandenberg resolution in the Senate —was approved by the Truman administration and by Republican leaders late in April.

By early summer a six-point resolution had been introduced by Senator Vandenberg (8, pp. 8–9). Controversy behind the closed doors of the Senate Foreign Relations Committee centered on the first three points of the resolution, which provided for agreements to eliminate the use of the veto in the Security Council on questions involving international security, the development of regional self-defense measures, and—the key phrase of the resolution—a recommendation that the United States associate itself in a regional security pact by constitutional processes. The issue most in need of further clarification at this stage (and it was an issue that proved troublesome in later Senate debate on the treaty) was the question of "automatic war." The Foreign Relations Committee demanded, and received from Senator Vandenberg and Under-Secretary Lovett, assurances that any defense pact contemplated would not jeopardize the traditional powers of Congress to declare war (9, p. 408). With this assurance the committee approved the Vandenberg resolution unanimously, and on June 11 the Senate concurred by the substantial majority of 64 to 6.

Within the month, preliminary discussions were undertaken with the nations of Western Europe, and throughout these discussions there was continual liaison between the State Department and the Foreign Relations Committee. In the words of Under-Secretary Lovett, "an extraordinary collective effort between the legislative and executive branches" ultimately produced a document acceptable both to the signatory powers and to spokesmen for the major parties within the United States. The collaborative bipartisan process that brought this result was further described by Lovett when he testified before the Foreign Relations Committee in public hearings on the treaty:

It would have been quite impossible for the Department of State . . . to have dealt with the multitude of confusing problems without somebody to go to and discuss the various alternatives with complete frankness and complete security. . . . By that I do not mean that we were not given restraints from time to time, or questioned very pointedly, which served the purpose of clarification, but when a line was agreed on . . . we could go back to work and know that we were going to be backed up, and that is of tremendous importance in negotiation . . . [8, p. 247].

Among the "confusing problems" that arose, two are of major importance to our study. There was the issue noted earlier—the fear prevailing in Congress that the treaty would deprive the United States of its freedom of action by committing it to automatic war if Europe were attacked. To allay prevailing fears, the Foreign Relations Committee insisted that early State Department drafts of Article 5 of the treaty be revised to permit a signatory nation to take "such action as it deems necessary" if an attack occurred, thereby leaving the United States (and other signatories) free to go to war or not as conditions required. Second, the committee insisted upon the insertion of a clause affirming that the treaty's provisions would become operative only if "carried out by the parties in accordance with their respective constitutional processes." This provision, at least by indirection, reaffirmed the power of Congress to declare war (8, pp. 245–46; 9, p. 476).

The North Atlantic Pact was signed on April 4, 1949. After a sixteen-day public hearing, the Senate Foreign Relations Committee unanimously approved the treaty and submitted it for Senate debate on July 5. In a two-hour address, "his last full-dress foreign policy speech," Senator Vandenberg urged his colleagues to ratify the treaty as "the best available implement to discourage armed aggression and thus stop another war." Seeking to win the support of a strong economy bloc in the Senate, Vandenberg reminded his colleagues that "The surest way—the only largely effective way—for us to cut our budgets in the years to come is to find a dependable formula for peace" (3, pp. 8891, 8897). The Foreign Relations Committee, added Senator Connally (now chairman of the committee in the Democratic-controlled Eighty-first Congress), had "furnished some of the stone and mixed some of the mortar to complete its symmetry and strength." Re-emphasizing that the treaty did not impair American constitutional traditions, Connally asserted that "The treaty does not involve any commitment to go to war nor does it change the relative authority of the President and Congress with respect to the use of the armed forces" (3, p. 8814).

Opponents of the treaty, led by Republican Senators Taft, Wherry, and Watkins, crystallized their objections into three reservations which they sought to append to the treaty. The gist of the first and third of these made it clear that the pact entailed no moral commitment to furnish American arms and equipment to Europe for the purpose of strengthening its defenses. The second would have required congressional approval before American military units could be assigned to participate in the European defense effort. All reservations, however, were defeated by decisive Senate majorities on July 21; and on the same day the Senate ratified the North Atlantic Pact by a vote of 82 to 13.

As a case study in the successful application of the bipartisan principle to an important foreign policy problem, the North Atlantic Pact closely parallels the United Nations Charter and, in one respect at least, the Greek-Turkish aid program. The parallel with the charter can be seen not only in the overwhelming Senate majorities that eventually ratified both documents, but also in the well-nigh ideal circumstances under which the bipartisan approach operated. Here Republicans could feel that their influence had been decisive in securing modifications in early State Department drafts of the treaty to conform to the evident apprehensions of their party about this project. The initiative for the treaty had actually come from the recognized foreign policy spokesman of the Republican party, Senator Vandenberg—

a fact that contrasted sharply with other important foreign policy developments in the postwar era, when bipartisanship too frequently meant that the party out of power was merely notified of impending developments or asked to ratify an executive decision.[2]

But the analogy with the UN Charter can be pushed too far. A significant difference in this case—and here the parallel is much more with the Greek-Turkish aid program— was that once negotiations between the United States and European signatories had been initiated, the Senate was in the familiar dilemma of being required to ratify the treaty or, in an hour of international conflict and danger, of repudiating the President's leadership in world affairs and of inflicting a grievous blow to American prestige. Thus when Senator Vandenberg was asked in Senate debate "what would happen in the event the Senate refused to ratify the pact?" he replied, "Failure of ratification would end the momentum of peace in a cold war in which we are now winning" (3, p. 8898). Even the opposition of Senator Taft and other Republicans to the treaty was explained by Vandenberg on the ground that these opponents realized their attacks would not seriously jeopardize the treaty's eventual ratification by the Senate (9, p. 498).

Similarly, the Republican insistence upon eliminating from the treaty any implication that its ratification meant automatic war was more of a textual modification than a substantive change. It may have derived, subconsciously at least, from a lingering protest in Congress against the facts of international life which Republicans and Democrats alike did not relish but which they recognized as being inescapable. As a group, GOP leaders probably knew, in the words

[2] This was to a large degree true of the Mutual Security Program which followed the North Atlantic Pact and of bipartisanship as it was applied to American foreign policy problems in the Far East in the postwar period.

of Senator Lodge (Republican of Massachusetts), that the defense pact added nothing to the obligation the United States would have to assume "in case of an armed attack which might occur without a treaty being in existence." Congress, said Senator Margaret Chase Smith (Republican of Maine), "would have an unequivocal moral obligation to declare war immediately on the attacker of one of the signers of the pact" (3, p. A-2089).

Harmonious resolution of the problem of automatic war was important, then, more as a matter of maintaining amiable two-party relations than as a modification of existing American foreign policy. To a substantial degree, the Senate had no choice but to ratify the pact, since after negotiations with the signatories had opened, the United States could not permit the implication to be drawn that it was indifferent to the military and political fate of Western Europe. The redeeming feature, however, was that numerous GOP leaders had co-operated with the Truman administration in bringing about this commitment.

The North Atlantic Treaty was the last important bipartisan undertaking in foreign affairs under the Truman administration. The gradual disappearance of bipartisan co-operation from foreign policy issues first became evident in American diplomacy toward the Far East, as will be pointed out in Chapter 5. But within a few months, sharp partisan differences characterized debate on the Administration's proposals to strengthen Europe's defenses. The Greek-Turkish aid program had established a precedent for American arms aid to nations faced with Communist attack. Then the Marshall Plan followed with a long-range program of economic assistance to aid in European recovery. After that, the United States had signed, and the Senate had ratified, the North Atlantic Pact to protect the security of the North Atlantic community. These programs all received substantial bipartisan support. The North Atlantic Pact, however, comes closer than any of them to paralleling the kind of bipartisan collaboration that had produced the United Nations Charter. One fact alone keeps it from serving as a model of bipartisan co-operation in foreign affairs: it was during discussions of the pact within the government that the seeds were sown for one of the most intensely partisan controversies on a foreign policy issue seen during the entire postwar period. That issue was the provision of American military assistance to the NATO area.

2. The Mutual Defense Assistance Program

On July 25, 1949, President Truman submitted to Congress a request for 1.45 billion dollars in foreign aid to be used principally to furnish military equipment to the signatories of the North Atlantic Treaty. The President stated that the "adoption of the program at this time is essential to reach the objectives of the United States in foreign affairs." He admonished Congress that any sign of "weakness and irresoluteness on our part now would seriously jeopardize all gains we have made so far" in preserving the economic and military security of the non-Communist world (3, pp. 10122–24).

But the reception accorded the President's request by Congress was cool—even, with some members, avowedly hostile. This lack of enthusiasm can be traced to the period immediately preceding Senate ratification of the North Atlantic Treaty. As we saw earlier in this chapter, the Senate had been apprehensive about the degree to which ratification of the treaty committed the United States, explicitly and morally, to furnish arms aid to the NATO countries. This was a question many senators had tried to have clarified before the vote over ratification, but without success. When pressed for a clarification, Administration spokesmen had been equivocal. They wished neither to assert that Senate acceptance of the treaty necessarily implied a commitment to rearm Europe, nor to deny that an arms-aid program would subsequently be presented to Congress.[3] The Administration evidently did not want to make the ratification of the treaty dependent upon subsequent legislative approval of a military assistance program.

Even before the treaty had been submitted for Senate ratification, it was known in Congress that the Administration had prepared drafts of a military assistance program. These drafts had been drawn up without significant consultation between the Administration and Senator Vandenberg or other leading Republican figures (9, pp. 503–6). The proposal was first known as the Mutual Defense Assistance Program (or MDAP); after the Korean War, when economic and military foreign aid were consolidated into one program, it was called the Mutual Security Program (or MSP). In spite of repeated Republican demands that the Administration make known its plans for furnishing arms aid to Europe, it was not until April 21, two weeks after the treaty had been signed, that Senator Connally revealed to a closed meeting of the Senate Foreign Relations Committee that MDAP would entail over one billion dollars in increased foreign aid (6, Apr. 24, 1949). As Senate debate on the treaty progressed through the late spring and early summer, it was generally known in Congress that the Adminis-

[3] Thus when Secretary of State Acheson was asked at the Senate hearings if a vote for ratification obligated a senator to vote for an arms-aid program, he evasively replied: "[A vote for ratification] requires each member of the Senate, if you ratify this treaty, when he comes to vote on the military assistance program, to exercise his judgment less freely than he would have exercised it if he had not been for this treaty." But Under-Secretary of State Robert Lovett told the committee on May 2 that the United States was not obligated to furnish arms and equipment to NATO—"there was no commitment on the part of this country or any other participant in the talks [between the United States and the other NATO signatories] to do a specific thing in the way of supply" (8, pp. 16, 23, 243).

tration had formulated a program of military assistance without seeking the views of Republican leaders, that this program had been discussed with other countries, and that it would involve a substantial increase in foreign aid appropriations over an extended period of time. Yet when opponents of the treaty argued, as did Senator Taft, that "I am absolutely opposed to providing arms for Europe," they were assured by Senator Connally that "we have not committed ourselves to any particular type of military-assistance program" (3, p. 8814).

Given the feeling prevalent among leading Republicans that the Administration had not been completely candid in acquainting Congress with the kind of financial obligation the United States would assume under the treaty, it is not difficult to understand that the initial reception to the President's request was almost uniformly unfavorable—even among Republicans and Democrats who had in the past supported the Administration's major foreign policy undertakings. MDAP, said Senator Vandenberg, was "too big"; he viewed it as a major departure from bipartisan foreign policy (6, July 31, 1949). In a statement to the press he asserted that the program had to be rewritten and curtailed, and that in the meantime only interim arms aid should be furnished to NATO (9, p. 503). For the first time in the postwar period, a serious rift impended within the Foreign Relations Committee, where Senators Vandenberg and Dulles (who was given an interim appointment to the Senate for the period July to November, 1949) served an ultimatum that they would not accept MDAP unless it were redrafted. Within a short time their views were supported by a majority on the committee.

The committee entertained two fundamental objections to the program as submitted by the President. The first was that it had been drafted almost unilaterally by the United

States and that there existed no defense machinery among the NATO countries to allocate arms aid to maximum advantage. The second objection was, in Senator Vandenberg's words, that MDAP was a "war lord bill" (9, pp. 507–8), giving the President virtually unlimited power to dispose at will of American arms and equipment allocated under the program. Other less serious objections concerned the degree to which MDAP would impair Europe's own efforts to defend herself and the strongly held conviction in Congress that forces "in being" were less important to Europe's defense than the NATO "potential" in case of attack (9, pp. 512–13). Despite this disagreement between the Administration and its one-time foreign policy supporters on the Foreign Relations Committee, the State Department continued to urge prompt congressional action on the President's original proposal (6, June 16, 1949). Not until August 2, 1949—when, said Vandenberg, the committee "had our telltale show-down on the arms program" in which "I bluntly laid the 'facts of life' before Secretary of State Acheson and Secretary of Defense Johnson"—did the Administration agree to amend its original bill (9, p. 508).

Initial State Department revisions of MDAP, however, were unacceptable to Vandenberg and other influential Republicans in Congress. And when the program was threatened in mid-August by a House move to reduce its funds by one-half, Senators Vandenberg and Dulles undertook to rewrite the program in a form that could be supported by a majority in each house. Their modifications were designed principally to assure that MDAP was closely integrated into a joint NATO defense effort so that American assistance might make its maximum contribution to Western defense, that arms aid might be terminated if either the President or Congress felt its continuation no longer in the national interest, and that only interim aid was to be granted, pending a thorough study of the most effective way of gearing American assistance to Europe's needs and resources (9, p. 514). With these changes, and after a vigorous supporting speech by Vandenberg, the arms-aid bill passed the Senate on September 22 by a vote of 55 to 24 (3, p. 13168).

The hostile reception accorded MDAP in the Senate had been duplicated earlier in the House, where there was perhaps even more opposition to it than in the upper chamber. The House Foreign Affairs Committee had found it necessary to make thirty-four changes in the bill as originally submitted by the President; but even this did not suffice to gain unanimous support for the bill among committee members. Four minority reports had been filed by members of the committee opposing the bill, and their objections closely resembled those heard in the Senate. Typical criticisms were voiced by Representative Lawrence Smith (Republican of Wisconsin) and Representative James P. Richards (of South Carolina, ranking Democrat on the committee). Representative Smith opposed the "military alliance," saying that it "[is] inconsistent with the United Nations Charter and, if adopted, will give it the kiss of death." Representative Richards based his opposition largely on the grounds of economy, arguing prophetically: "Do not fool yourselves. This is not a 1- or 2-year program. . . . It may last 5 years or 10 years or 15 years and it may cost this Nation many additional billions of dollars" (3, p. 11669).

Amendments sponsored by Richards were ultimately accepted by the House; these cut the authorization for arms aid to slightly over 800 million dollars, or approximately half of the amount requested by the President. The large majorities by which the House cut the Administration's proposal evidenced that the degree of bipartisanship prevailing in American foreign affairs had diminished appreciably since the ratification of the North Atlantic Treaty.

And had it not been for a highly disturbing event abroad, it is logical to assume that MDAP would have emerged from Congress with its authorization seriously reduced.

That event was the explosion of the first Russian atomic bomb. When House-Senate conferees met on September 26, 1949, to reconcile conflicting versions of MDAP, they gathered in an atmosphere of grave national concern. Soviet possession of A-bombs (or the means for making them) increased Europe's vulnerability to attack and raised questions about the degree to which American atomic superiority sufficed to deter a Russian attack or repel it if it occurred. News of the Soviet A-bomb impelled the opponents of MDAP to take a more conciliatory position. Accordingly, House conferees acceded to the Senate version of MDAP, thereby agreeing to authorize a total of $1,000,000,000 for NATO; $211,370,000 for Greece and Turkey; $27,640,000 for Iran, Korea, and the Philippines; and $75,000,000 for the "general area of China" (2, p. 360). Final congressional approval came on September 28, when both houses approved the conference report by substantial majorities (3, pp. 13411, 13463).

The progress of atomic science in Russia had substantially given the Administration the appropriation it had requested from Congress. But the animosity which characterized relations between both parties on this issue in the early spring and summer, the truculence with which pro- and anti-Administration groups held to their demands, the bitter and partisan tone of debate in Congress, the widening gap between isolationist- and internationalist-minded members in each party, and the controversy raging concurrently over American foreign policy in the Far East—all of these indicated that if bipartisanship had not altogether vanished, it was rapidly disappearing from American foreign affairs. The full extent of the cleavage between the views of the

Truman administration and influential Republicans was not revealed until almost a year later, however, when Congress debated the question of whether or not to assign American ground forces to the NATO defense system.

3. The Great Debate on American Defense Policy

The closing scene in the drama of American foreign policy toward Europe in the period covered by this chapter opened late in 1950 and occupied the attention of both branches of the government until the spring of 1951. Its theme was the extent to which American military forces were required to bolster the defenses of the North Atlantic community and, if necessary, to repel attack against this militarily vulnerable area. In time, the so-called "Great Debate" resulted in a clarification of American foreign policy. Ultimately both political parties within the United States supported the assignment of a limited number of American divisions to NATO. But in the process of arriving at this policy, the nadir of bipartisanship toward European affairs was reached, and American leadership of the free world was temporarily imperiled because of the acrimonious controversy raging over the problem of American defense strategy.

To be understood in its proper perspective, the Great Debate must be viewed against a background of growing disillusionment within the United States, and even within certain segments of the Democratic party, with the Truman administration's handling of foreign affairs since 1945, and especially with the course of events in the Far East. This disillusionment came to a head late in 1950 when the intervention of Red China in the Korean War threatened United Nations forces with a decisive military defeat. For several months in the latter part of 1950 and the early part of 1951, the military fate of Korea hung in the balance. The United

States found itself with a steadily increasing military budget, mounting casualty lists, and what many Americans considered unco-operative, reluctant allies in Korea who were content to let the United States carry the brunt of the military effort. These events, coming as they did after the loss of China and the controversy over the Mutual Defense Assistance Program, virtually guaranteed that an atmosphere of mutual confidence and respect, which is indispensable to genuine bipartisan co-operation in foreign affairs, could not exist. Consequently, when Congress debated the question of American defense strategy early in 1951, partisan animosity reached a plane only exceeded by the bitterness characterizing debate over American postwar Far Eastern policy.

The opening gun in the Great Debate was fired on December 20, 1950, by former President Herbert Hoover, who delivered a speech via nationwide radio hookup in which he analyzed current defense policies and made recommendations for their improvement.[4] Professing to have received "hundreds of requests" to give his "conclusions to our national policies," Hoover proposed in essence that American defense thinking be reoriented around the concept of making the Western Hemisphere the "Gibraltar of Western Civilization." Primary emphasis would then be given by the United States to building up air and sea power, while the "prime obligation of defense of . . . Europe rests upon the nations of Europe." Future American assistance to Europe must be conditioned upon whether the NATO countries "show they have spiritual strength and unity to avail themselves of their own resources." Toward Europe, Amer-

[4] A number of Hoover's recommendations had been foreshadowed on December 12, when Joseph P. Kennedy (former American ambassador to Britain) told an audience in Charlottesville, Virginia, that American foreign policy was "suicidal" and "politically and morally a bankrupt policy." Kennedy urged that America's "defense line" be limited to the Western Hemisphere (6, Dec. 13, 1950).

ican policy must be one of "watchful waiting without ground military action." Even if Europe were lost to communism, Hoover argued, "Americans have no reason for hysteria or loss of confidence in our security or our future. . . . In American security rests the future security of all mankind" (6, Dec. 21, 1950).

Hoover's recommendations found wide support both in the nation's press and in Congress (6, Dec. 22, 1950). The foremost advocate of his ideas in Congress was Senator Robert Taft, who, since Vandenberg's retirement, had become probably the most influential Republican in the government. Senator Taft delivered a major foreign policy address early in January in which he advocated a modification of American policy toward Europe in line with Hoover's plea for major emphasis upon air and sea power. Taft did concede that ground forces might be sent to Europe if "we can see a reasonable chance" of defending that area from attack. Posing what in time proved to be the dominating theme of the Great Debate—the respective constitutional prerogatives of the President and Congress over the disposition of the armed forces—Taft argued: "We had better commit no American troops to the European continent at this time. . . . There is no legal obligation to send American land soldiers to Europe." If the President or his advisers planned such a move they were "usurping the authority given them by law and their program should be submitted to Congress for consideration before we become obligated" (4, pp. 58-59).

Symptomatic of the lack of unity now characterizing majority-minority party relations in foreign affairs was Taft's sharp and prolonged criticism of the Roosevelt-Truman administrations' diplomacy throughout the postwar period. Appeals for unity and bipartisanship in foreign policy, said Taft (who had on frequent occasions since the Second World War expressed strong doubts about the desirability of bipartisanship), were nothing more than attempts "to cover up the past faults and failures of the Administration and enable it to maintain the secrecy which has largely enveloped our foreign policy since the days of Franklin D. Roosevelt" (4, p. 55).

Within two days after Taft's speech, his supporter, Senator Wherry of Nebraska (GOP floor leader), introduced a resolution embodying the demands of Hoover and Taft. The Wherry resolution read:

Resolved, That it is the sense of the Senate that no ground forces of the United States should be assigned to duty in the European area for the purposes of the North Atlantic Treaty pending the formulation of a policy with respect thereto by the Congress [4, p. 94].

Meanwhile, the Truman administration had lost little time in reaffirming its determination to send American troops to Europe. On December 22 Secretary of State Acheson, who had just returned from Brussels after conferring with the NATO representatives, announced that General Dwight Eisenhower had been chosen as Supreme Commander of all NATO forces. His selection, said Acheson, "completely revolutionized the attitude of [the European] people toward the problems ahead of them. . . ." Close American association with Europe in a common defense effort, said Acheson (not altogether correctly), was "the product of the decisions of all branches of the Government, of Congress, of the people of the United States over a long period of years" (6, Dec. 23, 1950). The gravity of the issue now dividing the nation and the leadership of both parties prompted President Truman to devote the greater part of his State of the Union message on January 8, 1951, to exploring the problem of American defense strategy. "Our own national security," said the President, "is deeply involved with that of other free nations." He continued:

Our national safety would be gravely prejudiced if the Soviet Union were to succeed in harnessing to its war machine the resources and the manpower of the free nations on the borders of its empire.

. . . The Soviet Union does not have to attack the United States to secure domination of the world. It can achieve its ends by isolating us and swallowing up all our allies . . . [4, p. 99].

Consequently, President Truman strongly urged Congress to approve a program of continued economic and military assistance for foreign countries and to extend the draft act so that the American military potential might be increased.

By early January the major issues in the Great Debate had been clearly revealed. A large number of Republicans, led by Taft and Wherry and supported by right-wing Democrats, demanded, at a minimum, that the Administration's plans for American military participation in the NATO defense effort be approved by Congress and, at a maximum, that the Administration abandon its proposal to station American ground forces in Europe. A majority of Democrats, supported by a number of Republican moderates, initially insisted upon congressional acceptance of the Administration's plans and defended the President's power to assign troops abroad without the consent of Congress. But in ensuing weeks, the Administration's supporters modified their earlier views to the point of accepting a congressional resolution ratifying the defense plans previously announced by the White House.

Alarmed by the damage to American prestige occasioned by this increasingly belligerent controversy, a group of moderates within each party sought late in January to effect a compromise that would satisfy the major demands of both groups and would restore at least some semblance of bipartisanship to American foreign relations. Senator H. Alexander Smith (Republican of New Jersey) felt that the President "needs Congress and public opinion behind him and the way to get it is to have Congress share in the decision" (10, Jan. 14, 1951). For the Democrats, Senator Connally attempted, in a major foreign policy address on January 11, to show that compromise was possible on the troops-to-Europe issue. "The debate is not on the ends of our foreign policy but on the means to the end." Under persistent and not altogether friendly questioning by Senator Wherry, Connally conceded that "before any considerable number of troops are sent to Europe the Congress will be advised about it" (4, p. 143).

This evident willingness by Administration spokesmen to meet Republican demands at least halfway evoked concessions from Taft and Wherry. Senator Wherry said that senators who voted for his resolution "in no way commit themselves for or against the sending of American boys to Western Europe . . ." (4, p. 320). Taft, on January 19, told the press that he would "leave the legal question" of the President's authority in foreign affairs "in abeyance," provided the Administration showed a conciliatory spirit toward the Wherry resolution (6, Jan. 19, 1951).

In the weeks that followed, two events brought the Great Debate to a denouement: the testimony offered by General Eisenhower, and the Senate Foreign Relations Committee hearings on this issue. On February 1 General Eisenhower addressed a joint session of Congress. The gist of his report was that while Europe was making progress in its own defense effort, the United States must continue to furnish military equipment and troops "in direct ratio to what Europe is doing so that we know that we are all going forward together . . ." (4, p. 875). Later in the day General Eisenhower argued (in secret session) for a flexible American commitment, unhampered by a congressionally imposed ceiling or ratio of American to European troops (6, Feb. 2, 1951).

In ensuing Foreign Relations Committee–Armed Services Committee hearings, information not yet made public but essential to any resolution of this problem was finally revealed: the precise number of American troops that the Administration contemplated assigning to NATO. Defense Secretary Marshall told these committees on February 15 that four additional American divisions (roughly 60,000 men) were scheduled for duty in Europe. This revelation was considerably below the estimates entertained earlier by the Administration's critics;[5] and after this information became known, the Great Debate lost much of its earlier bitterness and moved, however leisurely, to a settlement acceptable to both groups.

On April 4 a resolution proposed by Senator John L. McClellan (Democrat of Arkansas) passed the Senate by a vote of 69 to 21. The McClellan resolution embodied the Administration's plan to defend Europe with American troops, but it also incorporated Republican demands that Congress be permitted to join in making this decision and in approving the assignment of additional military units abroad. In addition, this resolution approved the selection of General Eisenhower as Supreme Commander of NATO, reaffirmed the concept that the major contribution to the armed forces of NATO must come from Europe, and advised the President to report to Congress at six-month intervals on the status of European defense (4, pp. 3254–82). With the passage of this resolution, no serious doubt re-

[5] Senator Knowland (Republican of California) had originally estimated the number of troops to be sent to Europe at ten divisions (or roughly 150,000 men). And Senator Russell (Democrat of Georgia), chairman of the Armed Services Committee, had anticipated that six divisions would participate in NATO (4, p. 158; 6, Feb. 16, 1951).

mained that substantial majorities in each party endorsed the principle of American military co-operation with NATO and that both had rejected the neo-isolationist proposals made in earlier weeks by Hoover and Taft.

The two case histories in the evolution of American defense policy presented in this chapter afford us the opportunity to evaluate several important questions that arise in the attempt to approach foreign affairs on a bipartisan basis. We may note at the outset that no other instance in the postwar era illustrates so well the value, even at times the indispensability, of bipartisanship in foreign affairs. There is no question but that the Great Debate had resulted in substantial damage to American prestige in the eyes if its cold-war allies. Hamlet-like, the United States appeared to be vacillating, uncertain whether to defend Europe from attack as she had pledged to do by the North Atlantic Treaty and by the Mutual Defense Assistance Program, or to abandon Europe as indefensible and merely to "liberate" her after an attack had occurred. Despite some vagueness and inconsistency in the views of Hoover and Taft, the last alternative had been strongly implicit in their proposals. Had the United States followed this course, doubts would have arisen the world over about the stability and reliability of American foreign policy.

Perhaps, as the Hoover-Taft school of defense argued, the Truman administration should not have pledged the United States to join the NATO defense system without the consent of Congress—which meant, in effect, the consent of GOP congressional leaders. There is considerable merit to this argument. Ever since the Senate debate on the North Atlantic Treaty, it had been evident that many members of Congress were deeply disturbed about the prospect of garrisoning American ground troops in Europe. This had been a major theme with the opponents of the treaty. Repeatedly, spokesmen for the Administration had declared that there was no plan or intention for sending American troops abroad; and before it ratified the treaty, the Senate had eliminated any provision from that document which, even by implication, obligated the United States to furnish troops to Europe except with the consent of Congress. When Congress later debated the Mutual Defense Assistance Program, the same issue arose again; and once more Senator Vandenberg himself refused to accept MDAP until it had been redrafted so that the President could furnish substantial arms and troops to Europe only with congressional approval.

Yet when the Administration decided after the outbreak of the Korean War to furnish American military units to NATO and to recommend that General Eisenhower be made Supreme Commander, no significant effort was made to communicate this fact to Republicans until after a decision had been reached by the executive branch and until after the NATO countries themselves had been so informed. Once more Congress had been presented with a *fait accompli* in foreign affairs; but in contrast with the Greek crisis in 1947, unilateral executive action on this occasion could not be justified by reference to the urgency of the crisis confronting the nation. Only one explanation was possible: the procedures and techniques designed to promote two-party co-operation in foreign affairs had fallen into almost complete disuse, and neither the Administration nor Republican leaders showed any evident desire to restore them.

More detailed consideration of why bipartisanship all but disappeared from American foreign policy in this period will be reserved for Chapter 5. Here we shall observe that among the major contributing factors were the retirement of Senator Vandenberg; the protracted disagreement between both parties over the course of events in Asia since World

War II, climaxed by the collapse of Nationalist China late in 1949 and the Korean War in the spring of 1950; growing doubts within the Republican party (derived from recent experience with the Mutual Defense Assistance Program) that the Truman administration sincerely desired biparti- sanship in foreign affairs; an unending cycle of congres- sional "investigations" of the executive branch, undertaken with the evident purpose of proving that widespread in- competence and disloyalty had pervaded the Roosevelt and Truman administrations; and an increasing awareness within each party that bipartisanship could entail rather serious political liabilities. These factors combined to destroy the atmosphere of mutual respect that had been vital to earlier two-party co-operation in the foreign policy field. It was left for the Eisenhower administration to close the breach by actively seeking the collaboration of leading Dem- ocrats in the initial stages of policy formulation.

References

1. "The Congress and U. S. Foreign Relations," *Congressional Digest,* **30** (February, 1951), 35–39. Pages 35 and 64 contain a useful background treatment of the Great Debate.
2. *Congressional Quarterly,* 1949, Vol. 5. Pages 343–50, *passim,* review the arguments by opponents to the North Atlantic Pact. A convenient summary of legislative action on MDAP is given on pages 351–60.
3. *Congressional Record,* Vol. 95.
4. *Congressional Record,* Vol. 97.
5. *Department of State Bulletin,* **24** (February 21, 1951), 323–30.
6. *New York Times.*
7. Senate Foreign Relations Committee, *Hearings on European Recovery Program,* 80th Congress, 2nd Session, January 8–15, 1948.

8. ——, *Hearings on North Atlantic Treaty,* 81st Congress, 1st Session, April 27–May 3, 1949.

9. Vandenberg, Arthur H., Jr. (ed.), *The Private Papers of Senator Vandenberg.* Boston: Houghton Mifflin Company, 1952.

10. *Washington Evening Star.*

FIVE

Nationalist China:
"A Maze of Imponderables"[1]

Thus far, our study of bipartisanship in foreign affairs has been centered on preparation for the establishment of the United Nations and the major developments in American foreign policy toward Western Europe. Now we turn our attention to the Far East, and more particularly to relations between Nationalist China and the United States from the Second World War to 1949. This latter date is chosen because it marks both the military collapse of Nationalist China and the year in which bipartisanship disappeared from the realm of American Far Eastern policy.

China receives primary emphasis in this chapter because the foremost problem confronting American policy makers in this period was preserving the independence of Nationalist China in the face of increasingly ominous Communist attacks. And consideration of this problem serves to illuminate a new difficulty in approaching foreign policy issues on a bipartisan basis, a difficulty that did not arise toward European affairs in the postwar era: the extent to which cooperation between both parties can be expected to collapse

[1] This phrase is Senator Vandenberg's (9, p. 525).

after a major diplomatic defeat has been sustained. The factors responsible for the defeat do not concern us here. We merely accept two incontrovertible facts: the United States failed to preserve the independence of Nationalist China by its early wartime and immediate postwar policy of "coalition government" as a means of preventing a full-scale civil war; and, when a resumption of the war could not be averted, it was equally unsuccessful in preventing a Communist victory on the Chinese mainland. It may be that one or both of these objectives were unrealistic and outside the effective control of the United States, but this in no way mitigates the seriousness of the loss of China to the free world. An event of such far-reaching magnitude—easily among the most serious defeats in American diplomatic history—inevitably had a profound impact upon American domestic politics. The consequence most pertinent to our study was that after 1949 neither party showed any notable desire to continue the bipartisan approach to foreign affairs. So fundamental was this disagreement over Asian problems —a disagreement that, as the previous chapter indicated, soon extended into the area of European affairs—that the national election of 1952 turned to a remarkable extent on foreign policy issues.

1. Sino-American Relations during World War II

During World War II the one goal paramount in the Far Eastern diplomacy of the United States was to bring about the unconditional surrender of Japan. Historically, and with few exceptions, the United States had maintained friendly relations with the Republic of China. President Roosevelt and Secretary Hull had been determined to preserve harmonious relations during the war and to continue their support of the Nationalist government under Chiang Kai-shek as the legitimate government of China. Since the 1920's, however, China had been torn internally by intermittent civil war between Chiang's supporters and a powerful Communist faction, which by the Second World War had occupied substantial territories in Manchuria and north China. Although the Japanese attack on China evoked pledges from both groups that they would co-operate to defeat the common enemy, these pledges were continually violated by both sides. Periodic resumption of the civil war after 1941 threatened in time to hamper the Allied war effort in the Pacific, with the result that the Roosevelt administration made several attempts to effect a political truce in the country (6, Chap. 3).

Before 1944, these efforts had been only spasmodically successful, and in August, President Roosevelt dispatched General Patrick J. Hurley as his personal representative to China in a new attempt to effect a truce. Hurley's objective was to terminate the civil war without jeopardizing the claim of Nationalist China as the legitimate government of the country. Although the Hurley mission also failed to produce a lasting truce, the General left China in September, 1945, confident that in time differences separating the two factions would be settled and that peace would eventually be restored (6, pp. 105–12).

This and earlier wartime efforts by the Roosevelt administration to bring about a cease-fire in the Chinese civil war are important to us not because they were in any sense bipartisan undertakings, but because they laid the groundwork for the policies followed by the United States toward China as late as 1946. There is no record of consultation between leading Democrats and Republicans concerning the advisability of American wartime intervention in Chinese affairs. Neither is there any evidence that such steps were disapproved by spokesmen for either party. During the war, the principle of bipartisanship in foreign policy had been applied almost exclusively to the problem of creating a post-war international security organization, so that there was no substantial complaint from the Republican opposition that the bipartisan principle had been ignored in Chinese affairs.

2. The Marshall Mission

The surrender of Japan in September, 1945, opened the way for a resumption of the Chinese civil war on an unprecedented scale by removing the only issue upon which both Nationalists and Communists could unite—their mutual hostility to the Japanese. By the end of 1945 the conflict in China posed a serious threat to political stability in the Pacific area and to the peace of the world generally. Consequently, President Truman requested General George C. Marshall to undertake a final effort at compromise between the two contending groups. Except for a brief return to the United States in March, Marshall remained in China throughout 1946. But his mediation failed, as had earlier efforts before him. He left China early in 1947 after blaming both sides for violating the cease-fire agreement in the hope of gaining a temporary military advantage from his mediation.

With the possible exception of the Yalta Conference in 1945, perhaps no event in recent American diplomatic history has evoked such prolonged disagreement between the two parties as the Marshall mission. Critics of the Roosevelt and Truman administrations have condemned the mission as a glaring example of Democratic incompetence in foreign affairs and as a tragic illustration of the blindness exhibited by Democratic policy makers to the true aims of world communism. Responsibility for this undertaking is frequently placed upon alleged pro-Communist elements within the Department of State. Accordingly, the Republican party, joined by a scattering of isolationist-inclined Democrats, has divorced itself from any responsibility for Marshall's effort to restore peace in China by bringing both factions together into a coalition government. The Marshall mission is cited as irrefutable proof, in the words of Senator Vandenberg, that "there was no . . . [bipartisan] liaison in respect to China policy" (9, p. 532).[2]

This argument has considerable validity. There is no evidence to indicate that the decision to send General Marshall to China was a product of the kind of prior consultation in foreign affairs that had resulted in such landmarks in American diplomacy as the United Nations Charter or the North Atlantic Pact. If it is true, however, that the decision to send Marshall to China was made by the Truman administration without consulting the opposition party, we must beware of jumping too hastily to the conclusion that the Republican party either opposed the Marshall mission or that it sought opportunities to express its dissent and was denied them. Widespread complaints that the mission did not have the support of Republicans and right-wing Democrats were not heard in Congress until well after the General's return from China.[3] Thus Senator Vandenberg, who

[2] Other Republicans throughout the postwar period have expressed this view even more forcefully. For example, Senator Ives of New York, who was usually inclined to support the Truman administration's foreign policy proposals, held that "Partisan politics—rank, shameless, unforgivable partisan politics—have resulted in an American foreign policy with respect to Asia which has been blighted by weakness, indecision, vacillation and—most reprehensible of all—appeasement" (2, July 6, 1950, p. 9864).

[3] A search of the *Congressional Record* for the period of the Marshall mission confirms this claim. Few statements were made in either house regarding China; those which were made tended overwhelmingly to favor Marshall's attempt to effectuate a truce. For instance, Representative Judd (Republican of Minnesota), who in time became one of the Truman administration's most outspoken critics on Asian affairs, inserted several articles into the *Congressional Record* that supported the principle of mediation in China. On one occasion Judd commended a writer's "good understanding and balanced judgment" and called his article a "penetrating and, I think, accurate evaluation" of the need in China. The writer

insisted until his death that bipartisanship had never applied to Far Eastern problems, stated on the floor of the Senate on June 11, 1948:

. . . I certainly have no complaint that [I] was not consulted with respect to . . . China, under the mission of General Marshall. I think it is a fantastic unreality to think there can be cooperation either between the legislative branch and the executive branch or between the two major parties in any such specific detail in respect to the conduct of foreign affairs [5, p. 7800].

Vandenberg freely admitted that the Marshall mission was an undertaking coming purely under the jurisdiction of the executive branch. Moreover, he regarded this case as a clear illustration of a potential danger inherent in a bipartisan approach to foreign affairs. Prior consultations held between Democrats and Republicans in this instance, he argued, would have had the effect of making Republicans responsible for a decision over whose implementation they could have had no effective control (5, p. 7801).

The major concern of those few Republicans who expressed themselves publicly regarding the policies of the United States toward China in this period was that the claim of Chiang Kai-shek to sovereignty throughout China must not be jeopardized by American efforts to promote a coalition government. This objective was also shared by the Truman administration and was reiterated in the President's instructions to General Marshall (6, pp. 605–9). On two occasions—in March, 1946, and in February, 1947—General Marshall reported to committees of Congress on the difficulties encountered in carrying out his assignment. These meetings were lengthy, and the opportunity was ac-

---

(Barnet Nover of the *Washington Post*) said of the Marshall mission: "No task needs doing more than the one with which he [Marshall] has been entrusted. . . . The peace of the world may depend on the success or failure of his mission" (3, pp. A-5648–49).

corded legislators of both parties to interrogate him fully. And on January 7, 1947, when the Senate confirmed his appointment as Secretary of State by unanimous vote, Senator Vandenberg said of General Marshall:

[He will] bring to his assignment a stout heart, a shining integrity, a rich experience, and a lifetime of dedication to his country. *He has always had the total confidence of Congress,* as well as that of his military and civilian colleagues at home and abroad [4, p. 159; italics inserted].

Marshall's appointment, Vandenberg continued, would contribute to the maintenance of an "effective bipartisan foreign policy."

Our purpose is not to try to settle the partisan controversy that has raged since 1946 over the question of which party was "responsible" for the Marshall mission or other American attempts to end the Chinese civil war through mediation. Instead, this case highlights a fundamental weakness of the bipartisan approach to foreign affairs as it was applied throughout the entire postwar period. The weakness is a failure on the part of both parties to agree precisely upon what bipartisanship in foreign affairs implies and upon the procedures required to attain it. Judgments as to whether the Marshall mission was or was not a bipartisan undertaking must, therefore, vary widely according to the way in which bipartisanship is itself defined. If it means a set of mutually agreed-upon procedures by which the two parties consult in arriving at important foreign policy decisions, then this case clearly was not a bipartisan venture. On the other hand, if it means essentially that bipartisan decisions are those which have the support of members in both parties, even though little formal liaison is used to generate that support, then the Marshall mission must be viewed as coming within the terms of the definition.

3. The China Aid Program

After General Marshall's return to the United States early in 1947, the Truman administration abandoned its goal of effecting a truce in the Chinese civil war and began to formulate a foreign aid program for Nationalist China. The State Department had completed a draft program by October, and on November 10 and 11, Secretary of State Marshall outlined its purpose and scope before a joint session of the House Foreign Affairs–Senate Foreign Relations committees. Here Marshall frankly confessed that American economic assistance to China entailed a calculated risk. The State Department could not guarantee that with such aid Nationalist China would win the civil war; rather the program must be viewed as a "stay of execution" to permit Chiang Kai-shek to institute certain urgently needed economic and political reforms and to strengthen his military position against steadily increasing Communist pressure.

Again in February, 1948, Secretary Marshall appeared before these same committees; by this time the military position of Nationalist China had deteriorated appreciably as a result of determined Communist attacks. Once again he stressed that American assistance to China might prove an indecisive factor in the civil war. Marshall emphasized that "An attempt to underwrite the Chinese economy and the Chinese Government's military effort represents a burden on the U.S. economy and a military responsibility which I cannot recommend as a course of action for this Government" (6, p. 382).

President Truman on February 18 asked Congress (now controlled by the GOP) to appropriate 570 million dollars to implement the China aid program. When the House Foreign Affairs Committee reported this bill favorably in March, Chairman Eaton told the House that the China aid program was the product of two months of "exhaustive and unbiased" study by the executive and legislative branches. Eaton commended the State Department for its co-operation, and he urged the House to take prompt and favorable action (5, p. 3322). But in debate that followed, there appeared formidable opposition to the China aid program, led by right-wing Republicans and Democrats. A year earlier Congress had passed the Greek-Turkish aid program. It was currently debating the Marshall Plan. A minority in the House, therefore, felt that additional foreign spending imposed an unjustifiable burden on an already swollen peacetime federal budget. In the face of this opposition, members of the GOP House leadership made impassioned appeals to their colleagues to support a program that had received the closest scrutiny from the Foreign Affairs Committee, working in collaboration with the executive branch. The House, argued Majority Leader Charles A. Halleck of Indiana, should consider this measure "without regard to narrow partisan politics" in order to enact a program which represented "the very best judgment of the Congress of the United States as a whole" (5, pp. 3366–67). The GOP leadership reminded dissident Democrats (many of whom supported economic, but not military, aid for Chiang Kai-shek) that this bill was the product of a long series of conferences between the Truman administration and spokesmen for the GOP, and was necessary to advance the nation's interests in foreign affairs. The prevailing view in the House was that the only hope of saving China from Communist domination was to approve the China aid bill promptly. Such, for example, was the view of Representative Judd, who said that the China aid program should enable Chiang Kai-shek to preserve his government's independence (5, p. 3872).

In contrast with other major foreign policy developments

during the tenure of the Eightieth Congress, the China aid program apparently involved little initial collaboration between the State Department and the Senate Foreign Relations Committee. Nevertheless, Senator Vandenberg and the committee supported the program, but only with the understanding that its adoption did not constitute a precedent for additional economic assistance to China or imply eventual American military involvement in the civil war. In its report to the Senate, the Foreign Relations Committee had endorsed the program by stating that "this bill should appreciably strengthen the position of the Nationalist Government without, at the same time, involving the United States in any additional commitments of a military nature" (9, pp. 524–25). Senate debate on the bill authorizing the China aid program was perfunctory. Six Republicans and one Democrat actively opposed the measure chiefly on the grounds of economy. But with the backing of a unanimous Foreign Relations Committee, the China aid bill passed the Senate by voice vote on March 30. By April 2, both houses had agreed to a conference report which provided 448 million dollars in economic assistance and 125 million dollars in military aid to Nationalist China (5, p. 4027).

The China aid program of 1948 stands as an exception to the rule that there was no bipartisan liaison toward Far Eastern questions in the postwar period. And it is an important exception. This program reflected a fundamental reorientation in American Far Eastern foreign policy, away from the goal of ending the civil war in China through coalition government or other peaceful means, and toward adoption of a policy of limited, but unequivocal, American support for the Nationalist regime.

The Truman administration's attempt to apply the doctrine of containment to China occurred in the eleventh hour of the civil war. Within a few months after Congress had approved the aid program, Nationalist China's military position became virtually hopeless. "The impending collapse of [Nationalist] China," writes Fifield, "was clearly apparent after the battle of Suchow in the late fall of 1948" (7, p. 201). Thereafter, eventual Communist victory was only a matter of time. Nationalist morale, both civilian and military, deteriorated; inflation undermined free China's economy; and Communist troops proved well-nigh invincible in their steady advance southward. By September, 1949, Red troops stood only one hundred miles from Canton, and by the end of the year Chiang Kai-shek's government had been driven into exile on the island of Formosa.

The disappearance of bipartisanship from American foreign policy toward the Far East can be correlated with fair accuracy with the collapse of Nationalist China. At the time of the passage of the China aid program, Chiang Kai-shek's forces still controlled sizable territories and, in spite of steadily mounting inflation and declining morale, both parties within the United States believed the program would postpone Chiang's defeat long enough for the tide of battle eventually to turn in his favor. Not until late 1948 and early 1949, by which time events in China had passed beyond any hope of American help, was there any significant demand in Congress that additional American assistance be granted Nationalist China. Led by Republican Senators Knowland, Wherry, and Bridges, Democratic Senator McCarran, and Representative Judd, an increasing circle of legislators began to call for a vastly expanded program of aid to China. By November, 1949, their demands had culminated in a proposal sponsored by Senator McCarran and supported by fifty senators that Congress grant 1.5 billion dollars in additional aid for China. Although this plan encountered strong White House disapproval, the major spokesman for this group, Senator Knowland, contended that this fact ought not to deter Congress from acting independently, since "Congress has the highest obligation to speak and to make its voice heard" (8, Nov. 3, 1949).

The Administration's view was that this and similar belated proposals to save Nationalist China could not affect the outcome of the civil war, and that American equipment sent to China would eventually fall into Communist hands. This view received its official expression in August, when the State Department published the so-called "China White Paper," detailing the history of Sino-American relations since the nineteenth century, but with particular emphasis upon the postwar period. "The unfortunate but inescapable fact," wrote Secretary of State Acheson in this document, "is that the ominous result of the civil war in China was beyond the control of the government of the United States" (6, p. xvi). This view strongly implied that the Truman administration had abandoned further hope of preventing a Communist victory through American economic or military assistance to Chiang Kai-shek, and this policy was made explicit by the President on January 5, when he publicly stated that "the United States Government will not provide military aid or advice to the Chinese forces on Formosa" (8, Jan. 6, 1950).

Publication of the China White Paper marks the end of an era in American postwar diplomacy toward the Far East. Thereafter, until the outbreak of the Korean War in June, 1950, the United States pursued a policy of nonintervention in Chinese affairs. But the China White Paper may also be taken as a convenient terminal point for the study of bipartisanship in American postwar Asian policy. Although one cannot precisely date the rupture in relations between the two parties over Far Eastern questions, by the late months of 1949 their positions toward such questions had begun to diverge sharply. The partisan storm ultimately generated by American postwar diplomacy in Asia, wrote John C. Campbell, was "no ordinary disagreement which democracy could take in its stride. Too deep for compromise, it was potentially capable of undermining the effectiveness of American foreign policy the world over" (1, p. 66).

After 1949 all the symptoms evidenced an American body politic rent internally by intense partisan animosities. Frequent and caustic Republican-led attacks on Secretary of State Dean Acheson (climaxed by an unprecedented House move in the summer of 1951 to terminate his salary), the numerous congressional investigations into Far Eastern policy (the most exhaustive of which occurred after President Truman dismissed General MacArthur in the spring of 1951), the increasing frequency with which foreign policy issues appeared in political campaigns (with the election of General Eisenhower in 1952 being widely interpreted as a mandate to Republicans to reorient American foreign policy in the direction of firmer resistance to Communist expansion)—all these illustrated the existence of fundamental disagreement between both parties toward Asian problems.

The reasons for the gradual disappearance of unity within the government toward the problem of Nationalist China are not difficult to discover. Indeed, one reason stands out above all others: the collapse of Nationalist China ranks as one of the most decisive and far-reaching diplomatic defeats experienced by the United States throughout its entire diplomatic history. It would be hopelessly utopian to suppose that unity between the two political parties could survive a defeat of this magnitude, except perhaps during time of war when there exists an evident and grave challenge to national security, in which case the need for continued unity might still be paramount.

The fact that the partisan storm engendered by the Communist victory in China carried over into the national elections of 1950 and 1952 naturally served to aggravate outstanding differences between the two parties. Having been the minority party for twenty years, Republicans were seeking issues that would help them gain control of the government. One such issue—perhaps the main campaign issue in 1952—was the Truman administration's diplomatic record in the Far East. Republican candidates used this issue to maximum advantage. Little is to be gained, however, from viewing this phenomenon as reflecting a calloused indifference to the national interest on the part of the Republican party. Partisan controversies are a democracy's substitute for force and violence as a means of changing policies and public officials. Neither in the circumstances described here nor in similar circumstances during the years that followed could an opposition party be expected to support a policy whose inadequacy had been amply proved by events.

As this chapter has shown, Republicans did participate in making certain important decisions with regard to American foreign policy toward Nationalist China. Yet this fact alone could not preserve bipartisan co-operation after Nationalist China's collapse. Because future chapters will develop this point in considerable detail, it is unnecessary here to enter into a consideration of the role of an opposition party within a democratic system of government. It is enough to point out that even if the opposition party collaborates with the party that controls the executive branch in pursuit of certain foreign policy objectives, such bipartisan collaboration is still not likely to survive a diplomatic defeat. To expect continued bipartisan co-operation under these circumstances is to ask the opposition to accept any policies that are formulated, on the ground that unity must be preserved at all costs. This, in turn, would be tantamount to saying that the chief duty of both political parties is to preserve unity, no matter what the cost to national security.

But other factors besides a major diplomatic defeat contributed to the decline of bipartisanship in foreign affairs after 1949. Chief among these was the prolonged illness of the man most responsible for maintaining intimate party co-operation in the postwar period, Senator Arthur Vandenberg. By the end of 1949, illness prevented Vandenberg from continuing his duties in the Senate. His retirement, at a time when increasingly serious differences appeared between the two parties over Far Eastern questions, compounded the problem of re-establishing effective bipartisan liaison. While a fuller consideration of the difficulties inherent in locating a "successor" to Vandenberg must await treatment in Chapters 7 and 8, we may observe that the Truman administration was unable to find another Republican capable of assuming the key role Vandenberg had played in the bipartisan process.

In our earlier discussions we have called attention to some of the difficulties inherent in attempting to conduct foreign affairs on a bipartisan basis. Later chapters explore the difficulties more comprehensively. In this case study we may note one such difficulty which proved particularly acute after 1948: the lack of any established procedures *for reviewing the nation's foreign policy on a bipartisan basis in the light of changing circumstances.* It will be recalled that a procedure for periodic review was established by Congress when it approved the first Marshall Plan appropriation, a fact which contributed heavily to the continued support both parties gave the Marshall Plan after 1948.

Down to the period of the China aid program both parties were in substantial agreement over the fundamentals of American foreign policy toward China; and both were fully cognizant of the fact that the China aid program was a calculated risk. Events soon proved the program inadequate to avert a Communist victory. Yet after the passage of this program neither Republicans nor Democrats demanded additional bipartisan consultations to review events in China and to re-examine existing American policy in the light of these events. Not until *after* Chiang Kai-shek's military position had become virtually hopeless was any attempt made by Republicans to "investigate" the Truman administration's diplomacy in Asia. By that time, the only matter left to investigate was why China had collapsed. Earlier investigations and consultations, on the other hand, might conceivably have produced a more realistic American policy. For its part, the Truman administration in late 1948 and throughout 1949 did little to inform Republicans of the growing crisis in China or to elicit their suggestions for drafting a more effective policy.

The evidence presented here offers some ground for believing that bipartisanship as it has been practiced since World War II does not lend itself well to dealing with problems of crisis diplomacy. Certainly the minimum condition for the success of a bipartisan approach to external events in a state of rapid flux is some agreed-upon machinery for holding frequent re-examinations of policy in order to assure that decisions originally adopted on a bipartisan basis are not outmoded by rapidly changing circumstances. Assuming that the United States might have prevented the collapse of Nationalist China—an optimistic assumption at best —a policy to attain this goal would have called for numerous consultations between Democrats and Republicans in the government. No such consultations were held, or even suggested, by leading figures in either party.

This suggests that the minimum prerequisite for bipartisan co-operation in foreign affairs is a reasonably successful foreign policy. The desired unity is not likely to be attained so long as the party that controls the executive branch is unable to formulate policies capable of advancing the nation's diplomatic objectives. Even if we grant the Truman administration's claim that events in China were beyond the control of the United States, it seems evident that such a claim will be accepted by the opposition party only after it is convinced that all feasible alternatives have been considered and that no solution to the problem in question exists within the nation's resources. The Republican party did not accept this claim in large part because no appreciable bipartisan effort was made after 1948 to study alternatives and to formulate a more realistic and up-to-date policy. Perhaps disunity would have prevailed even if such efforts had been made. But it seems certain that all efforts to maintain unity within the United States in the face of adverse developments in the Far East were not exhausted. Under these circumstances, it was probably inevitable that each party would assess the national interest differently and that acute partisan conflicts would develop over Sino-American relations in the postwar period.

References

1. Campbell, John C., *The United States in World Affairs, 1949*. New York: Harper and Brothers, 1950.
2. *Congressional Record* (daily edition).
3. *Congressional Record*, Vol. 91.
4. *Congressional Record*, Vol. 93.
5. *Congressional Record*, Vol. 94. Typical attacks by right-wing Republicans and Democrats are discussed on pages 3627–3856, *passim*.
6. Department of State, *United States Relations With China*. (Publication No. 3573, "Far Eastern Series," No. 30.) Washington, D.C.: Office of Public Affairs, 1949. Pages 26–37 give a detailed treatment of America's wartime diplomacy in

China. Chapter 5 contains a full account of the Marshall mission in China. The military and economic collapse of Nationalist China is fully discussed on pages 311–23 and 360–71.

7. Fifield, Russell H., "American Foreign Policy in the Far East, 1945–1950," *World Affairs,* 5 (April, 1951), 200–210.

8. *Herald Tribune* (New York).

9. Vandenberg, Arthur H., Jr. (ed.), *The Private Papers of Senator Vandenberg.* Boston: Houghton Mifflin Company, 1952.

Ferment in the Middle East

Continuing the pattern set in earlier case studies, in this chapter we turn to a detailed consideration of the final problem in American foreign policy to be dealt with in this study: the postwar diplomacy of the United States toward the Middle East.[1] Two aspects of that diplomacy—the Israeli-Arab conflict in Palestine and American relations with Egypt—will be emphasized. Our purpose here, as in previous chapters, is not so much to present a detailed history of American policy or to assess its effectiveness as it is to discover what implications this problem reveals in respect to the difficulties of conducting foreign policy on a bipartisan basis.

UNITED STATES POLICY IN THE MIDDLE EAST BEFORE WORLD WAR II

The United States, writes Lenczowski, "displayed no steady political interest" in the Middle East before World War II (**20**, pp. 422–23). Contacts between the United States

[1] Confusion often arises between the terms "Near East" and "Middle East." Most of the area dealt with in this chapter has traditionally been regarded as lying in the Near East. Contemporary American usage, however, tends to favor Middle East. We shall, therefore, use it throughout this chapter to include Egypt, Iraq, Jordan, French North Africa, Lebanon, Syria, Saudi Arabia (and the Arabian sheikdoms), Iran, Israel, and Cyprus. Turkey is geographically a part of this region but in recent times has tended to be thought of as a European power.

government and the Middle East countries had been limited and sporadic. Private groups within the United States, however, had manifested sustained interest in Middle Eastern affairs as early as the middle of the nineteenth century. These groups consisted chiefly of missionaries, educators, and charitable and philanthropic agencies. Their activities had created a reservoir of good will for the United States which lasted until it was exhausted by waves of anti-American sentiment that swept through the Arab world following the partition of Palestine in 1947.

In the 1920's and 1930's, American oil companies gradually acquired a direct and substantial economic stake in the Middle East. During the 1920's they sought a share in the development of the oil fields of Turkey and Persia. From this beginning, American companies moved on during the 1930's to acquire substantial oil holdings in their own right, particularly in Saudi Arabia.

During the Second World War the United States began to appreciate the strategic importance of the Middle East in world affairs. Iran served as an indispensable Allied base for sending supplies into southern Russia. Egypt and Palestine provided bases for troops and aircraft engaged in North Africa. Allied shipping utilized ports throughout the Middle East. The region's oil supplies provided a vital ingredient in the Allied war machine. One of the decisive campaigns of the Second World War was fought on the deserts of North Africa. Spokesmen for the United States government visited the Middle East in this period, and their visits were an indication of the extent to which their government had taken an active interest in Middle Eastern affairs.

United States Policy from World War II to Partition

Despite the emergence of a more realistic conception of the strategic importance of the area, no clear American foreign policy toward the Middle East emanated from World War II. By 1947 the United States still possessed no definite policy except for a vague desire to remain on good terms with all the countries in the area.

Very soon after the Second World War, the United States began to view the Middle East within the context of the cold war. Early in 1946 Iran called upon the United Nations to deal with Soviet intervention in the affairs of her northern provinces. The United States championed the cause of Iran before the United Nations, and by late spring of 1946 the USSR had agreed to withdraw its troops from Iranian territory. America's role in the Iranian case added to its stock of good will throughout the Arab world. In the same year, its evident support for Syria and Lebanon in their complaints before the United Nations against French colonialism also created friendship for the United States in the Middle East (**13**, pp. 279–92). This period, hindsight reveals, marked the zenith of Arab-American friendship. Within a few brief years the United States had dissipated its accumulated good will and had displaced Britain and France as the object of Arab enmity. The reason, of course, was American foreign policy toward Palestine, and it is to that problem that we now turn for a more detailed analysis.

1. The United States and Palestine

Evolution of American Policy

During the First World War Britain issued the Balfour Declaration promising the Jews a national home in Palestine. The declaration was endorsed by the American government, although no concrete steps were taken to effectuate it. In the period between the two world wars, the center of Zionist [2] agitation was located in Britain. It was to Britain

[2] Zionism was a movement that sought to establish a Jewish national state in Palestine. Thus it was essentially a political, rather than a religious, movement. In the words of one authoritative study, Zionism had not sought "national inde-

as the mandate power in Palestine that Zionists addressed their demands. With her very existence dependent upon ocean life lines and Middle East oil, Britain had by the late 1930's become progressively less receptive to the Zionist program, especially to the insistent demand that large numbers of Jewish immigrants be admitted into Palestine. In 1939 the British government issued a white paper on Palestine severely limiting immigration and announcing opposition to the creation of a Jewish national state there, on the ground that such a course would violate assurances already given to the Arabs and that it would constitute an injustice to the Arab majority inhabiting the country.

The British white paper of 1939 marked a turning point in American foreign policy toward Palestine. Imperceptibly but steadily, sentiment began to grow within the United States in behalf of Zionist aspirations. By the early years of World War II it had become apparent that leading Zionist spokesmen had adopted pressure upon the United States government as the most promising means for achieving their goals. Throughout the war and early postwar period, heavy pressure was exerted on all branches of the government and on American public opinion by groups espousing the Zionist cause, creating what James Reston described as "one of the most powerful lobbies ever organized in Washington" (22, Oct. 7, 1946).

During the war and the years immediately thereafter, decisions affecting the Middle East came more and more to be made in the White House instead of in the War, Navy, or State departments. The viewpoint of officers in these departments differed little from that of the British government

---

pendence for Jews in the European lands where they were . . . but their emigration to and settlement in the land of Palestine, the traditional home of their religion" (26, p. 21). It must be emphasized that all Jews are not Zionists (some are strongly anti-Zionist), just as all Zionists are not Jews. Similarly, since World War I Arab spokesmen have drawn a distinction between being anti-Zionist (which they are) and anti-Jewish (which they say they are not).

toward Palestine. Impressed by the strategic role of the Middle East in the war, and especially by the necessity to preserve Allied access to the oil supplies of the region, military and State Department spokesmen tended to emphasize the necessity of preserving friendly relations with the Arab world. Friendship with the Arabs was also a principle endorsed by the White House, as indicated by President Roosevelt's pledge to Arab leaders during World War II that the United States would support no program for Palestine that did not have their concurrence (15, pp. 129–32).

PRE-PARTITION POLICY

By the end of the war two considerations combined to swing American foreign policy behind Zionist demands. First, military arguments against upsetting the political equilibrium of the Middle East no longer applied. The Axis powers had been defeated; it was much too soon to foresee the important role the Middle East was to assume later in the cold war. Second, there was the plight of thousands of European Jews who had suffered indescribable persecutions from the Nazis. Sympathy for these Jews ran high in the United States and was unquestionably one of the leading factors inducing President Truman to support the partition of Palestine (32, pp. 137–42).

President Truman, on August 31, 1945, called upon the British government to admit one hundred thousand Jews into Palestine. Having long resisted such demands from Zionist circles, Prime Minister Attlee countered this proposal by suggesting that an Anglo-American committee of inquiry be established to examine the question fully. In effect, Attlee was asking the United States to share in the responsibility for carrying out the President's recommendation. The committee was established and by April 20, 1946, it had submitted a unanimous report. The report endorsed President Truman's proposal concerning immigration, but it opposed the long-standing Zionist demand that a separate Jewish state be created in Palestine, recommending instead that the country be continued as a British mandate until such a time as it might become a trusteeship of the United Nations. The report was favorably received in Washington, but Britain made no commitment other than to study the recommendations in detail.

The next stage in the development of American policy toward Palestine, which perhaps irrevocably launched the United States along the path of support for partition, came during the congressional elections of 1946. On October 4, President Truman reiterated his demand that Britain permit one hundred thousand Jews to enter Palestine. At the same time he supported a "fair" solution to the problem of a Jewish national home—a solution widely interpreted as an endorsement of Zionist demands for a separate Jewish state. The context of Truman's statement permits little doubt that it was heavily motivated by political events within the United States. In the first place, it was issued on the most important Jewish holiday, Yom Kippur. Then, the statement was made just a month before the election, after many Zionist groups had indicated extreme dissatisfaction with the Truman administration's policies to date on Palestine. Finally, there was clearly a connection between the timing of the statement and developments within the pivotal state of New York. There, the gubernatorial campaign appeared to be going heavily in favor of Republican Governor Dewey. Democratic party chieftains were convinced that Dewey planned to issue a statement endorsing Zionist demands, and they urged the President to beat him to the punch or risk heavy losses in New York City where approximately 40 per cent of the Jews in the United States reside. Truman's statement was therefore widely viewed as an obvious and skillful bid for Jewish votes. Partisan considerations, however, did not motivate Democrats alone. By October 6, Governor Dewey called upon Britain to admit "several hundreds of thousands" of Jews into Palestine (22, Oct. 7, 1946). In Britain, Truman's statement was, in the words of one correspondent, dismissed as a "vote-getting device" that was "destined for home consumption" (22, Oct. 5, 1946).

THE UNITED NATIONS ADOPTS PARTITION

By early 1947, Britain, as we noted in Chapter 3, had begun to liquidate many of her overseas commitments. Moreover, British authorities within Palestine proved increasingly incapable of dealing with Jewish extremists and terrorist groups within the country. These considerations led her to convey the problem of Palestine to the United Nations. On April 2, 1947, Britain requested the General Assembly to find a solution to the Palestinian problem that would be acceptable to Jews and Arabs alike. A special committee on Palestine considered the question from April 28 to May 15, at the end of which time a majority on the committee recommended that Palestine be partitioned into separate Jewish and Arab states, while the minority supported a federation which would give Jewish and Arab elements considerable local autonomy under the hegemony of a central government. After months of debate, on November 29 the General Assembly voted in favor of the majority report, with the United States, France, and the Soviet Union voting for it, Britain abstaining, and the Arab-Asian nations voting almost unanimously against it.

It is not pertinent to our inquiry here to examine the conflicting Jewish and Arab claims to Palestine. The merits of the controversy do not concern us. What does concern us is the effect produced throughout the Middle East by American advocacy of partition. The full impact of this effect was not felt for years to come, but time revealed that the consequences for American foreign policy were little less than disastrous. Arab spokesmen regarded the United States as chiefly responsible for the decision of the UN to partition Palestine (24). As the years passed, the onus for this decision was placed almost entirely upon Washington, with the Arab countries choosing to forget that the Soviet Union too had voted for partition and had verbally supported the Zionist cause before the United Nations.

Judgments concerning the wisdom of American support for partition may vary widely. What is less debatable is the fact that the Truman administration was reacting to strong internal pressures directed against it by vocal citizens' groups and leaders in both political parties. Furthermore, it is clear that the American decision on partition was based primarily upon humanitarian-emotional grounds. The effect upon America's long-range strategic and political interests in the Middle East was given little weight. No evidence exists that the Truman administration consulted with the Republicans (and by 1947 the GOP had a majority in Congress) in its decision to support partition (32, pp. 132–69). The decision cannot therefore be called a bipartisan undertaking as the term is defined throughout this study. But it could be argued that no consultation was necessary. The views of leading Republicans were well known. Many of them had berated the Administration in earlier months for its failure to move fast enough in supporting Zionist demands. This decision, then, was comparable to those made in the same period toward Nationalist China: it carried out a policy that enjoyed almost unanimous consent of spokesmen for both political parties.

ISRAELI-ARAB CONFLICT AFTER PARTITION

The events that followed in the Middle East are well known and need not be described in great detail. Throughout late 1947 and early 1948, Jews resident in Palestine exerted unremitting pressure upon Britain to relax immigration restrictions, a policy which Britain continued to oppose. Violence flared repeatedly between British and Jewish forces. Thousands of Jewish immigrants entered the country illegally. Meantime, the Arab nations prepared to resist partition by force. Mounting tensions in the Middle East at length persuaded the Truman administration to reappraise its position. The result was that in March, 1948, the American delegation in the UN proposed that Palestine become a trusteeship of the United Nations. This decision, too, was made without consultation between Democratic and Republican leaders. The Zionist reaction to it was so adverse, however, that the American-sponsored proposal was never adopted.

Soon American foreign policy swung back again to a more pro-Zionist course. When the British mandate expired on May 14, 1948, the Jewish National Council at Tel Aviv immediately proclaimed the existence of the State of Israel, and within a matter of hours President Truman had extended American recognition to Israel. Immediately upon the withdrawal of British troops, Arab armies crossed the borders of Palestine; and the hostilities that were to inflame the Middle East for years to come had begun. Efforts by the UN to effect an armistice finally bore fruit in the autumn of 1949. The truce was based upon the existing territorial *status quo,* leaving nearly three-quarters of Palestine in Jewish hands and resulting in the displacement of almost one million Palestinian Arab refugees from their homes.

Attempts since 1949 to convert this armistice into a permanent peace have broken against the rock of the refugee issue. Whose responsibility are they? Israel has consistently refused responsibility on the twofold ground that the problem is a direct outgrowth of the unprovoked Arab attack against her and that the refugees left their homes voluntarily. Similarly, the Arab states disclaim responsibility, arguing that the refugees are natives of Palestine, that Israel has expropriated their property, and that consequently any peace settlement must be based upon Israel's willingness to re-habilitate them and to compensate them for the suffering they have endured. Responsibility for caring for these refugees in the years that followed devolved mainly upon the United Nations and the United States.

Actually, the refugee issue may be little more than a pretext invoked by each side to cover up more fundamental difficulties in the path of a permanent peace. Deep and powerful currents of antagonism surge beneath the surface on both sides. Israel, victorious over the first Arab armies thrown against her and proud of her internal accomplishments against great odds, has been in no mood to tolerate continuous Arab provocations and is determined to preserve her security against all threats. Meanwhile, talk of a second round against Israel has echoed around the Arab world. Led by Premier Abdel Nasser of Egypt, Arab leaders have so inflamed the masses against Israel that they dare not talk of peace in Palestine. It may be that the Arab leaders need the Palestinian issue to justify the absence of political and social reforms within their own countries. In any event, the Arab countries have been steadily at work since 1949 building up their armies with weapons supplied by the West and, more recently, by the Communist bloc.

Since the armistice was signed, raids and retaliatory raids, border incidents, guerrilla fighting, and economic warfare have characterized relations between Israel and the Arab world. Deeply resentful and suspicious of each other, each side is determined to achieve its minimum demands. For Israel, the minimum demand is self-preservation. For the Arab countries, it is the extermination of Israel.

THE EISENHOWER ADMINISTRATION'S POLICY
TOWARD PALESTINE

Efforts by the United States to formulate a policy capable of dealing with the Arab-Israeli conflict continued after 1949. Officially, Washington was committed to a policy of neutrality toward both sides. The professed aim was a durable peace settlement acceptable to Israel and the Arab states. Yet after the Eisenhower administration took office, the policies of the United States toward a host of closely related issues—Middle East oil, the British-Egyptian dispute over Suez, the problem of regional defense, and the provision of American military, economic, and technical assistance—came to have a distinctly pro-Arab cast.

The United States cannot fairly be accused of having abandoned Israel after 1949. Israel continued to be the beneficiary of economic and technical assistance from the American government, as well as the recipient of millions of dollars in private donations from American Jews and other citizens supporting the Zionist cause. Moreover, the United States periodically affirmed its support for the Tripartite Declaration of 1950 by which, along with Britain and France, it agreed to guarantee whatever frontiers might eventually be established between Israel and the Arab world (7, pp. 831–35). Recognizing the imminent threat of war in Palestine, the Eisenhower administration repeatedly pledged that the United States, working through the United Nations, would support any country that was the victim of aggression in the Middle East, and that if the differences between Israel and the Arab states were settled it would join in guaranteeing established boundaries (9, pp. 12–21).

Yet none of these considerations changed the fact that the long-range direction of American foreign policy was more favorable to the Arab than to the Israeli cause. Royalties from American oil companies undergirded the economies of several important Arab countries; American economic, military, and technical assistance contributed to stability within the Arab nations and, indirectly at least, helped them to create an effective military machine; American pressures were exerted on Britain to evacuate Suez, as we shall see more fully later in this chapter, and on France to liquidate her colonial claims in North Africa. These factors tipped the balance in favor of the Arabs. In American relations with Israel, on the other hand, neutrality resulted in a steady decline in American economic, technical, and—most crucial of all—military aid in the face of growing Arab power; in an attempt to slight Israel by deliberately excluding her from the Middle East defense system, culminating in the Baghdad Pact of 1955; in a growing disposition on the part of the United States to hold Israel solely responsible for border clashes; and in several instances involving American foreign policy in the Middle East, and especially toward Egypt, which gave the appearance of surrender by the West before truculent Arab demands. Observing as early as 1951 that "this country lacks a long-range policy" for the area, Wallach characterized American diplomacy by saying:

Up to now, our policy has been muddled and self-contradictory, and our actions have been ill-timed and halting. Because our intentions have been ambiguous, our official acts have been ultimately self-defeating. As a result, the Near East sees the United States as a friendly but giddy giant, dissipating his energy in efforts to go in all directions at the same time [33, p. 508].

To advance its self-interest, the United States sought a workable balance among three conflicting objectives in the Middle East: preserving the security of Israel, winning and holding Arab allegiance in the anti-Communist alliance, and maintaining a course of neutrality in the Arab-Israeli conflict. Political controversy within the United States over Palestine did not become significant until after the Eisenhower administration took office in 1953. Thereafter it began to grow in intensity, and by 1956 it had become a leading issue in the presidential and congressional elections. A closer examination of the reasons why American foreign policy became a leading election issue will illumine many problems that arise in an attempt to conduct foreign relations upon a bipartisan basis.

Hardly had the Republican administration taken office in 1953 when the newly appointed Secretary of State, John Foster Dulles, along with the director of the Mutual Security Program, Harold Stassen, embarked upon a tour of the troubled Middle East. Their trip, the first ever made there by an American Secretary of State, symbolized the urgency with which the Administration viewed conditions in the area. After his return Secretary Dulles reported to the nation at length upon his tour. His report made it clear that the Eisenhower administration planned to give significantly greater weight to security considerations in formulating policy toward the Middle East. Dulles tried to put the Arab-Israeli conflict within the total framework of prevailing regional problems. Any settlement in Palestine consequently had to be closely tied up with the settlement of other issues that tended to foment tension: the Arab refugee problem, the Suez and the Sudan, the widespread need for American economic and technical assistance to raise living standards, the development of the waters of the Jordan Valley for irrigation and electric power, and, perhaps above all else, progress in creating some kind of regional defense system (8). In short, the Palestinian problem did not exist, and could not be settled, *in vacuo*. The Eisenhower administration therefore proposed to deal with it through a broad-gauged program designed in the short run to maintain peace and in the long run to eliminate the underlying causes of instability throughout the Middle East (29, pp. 287-303).

One prong of the Administration's attack upon Middle Eastern problems was directed at securing an agreement between the Jews and Arabs over the development of water resources of the Jordan Valley. Writing in 1955, one commentator called this project "the kingpin of current American foreign policy in the Arab-Israeli conflict . . ." (23, p. 397). American support for this undertaking, a kind of Middle Eastern TVA, initially stemmed from the visit made in 1953 by Eric Johnston, who had been sent there by the President to find means of relieving the mounting tension. Johnston returned convinced that the Jordan Valley plan was the key to the Palestinian conflict. If agreement could be secured upon development of these waters for irrigation and electric power, thousands of people in the area, particularly the unemployed Arab refugees, could be put to work. The project would raise living standards and would so integrate the economies of Israel and the adjacent Arab countries that the possibility of another war between them would be materially reduced. Furthermore, this scheme would provide a way for constructive American economic assistance to be furnished impartially to both sides.

Numerous technical difficulties had to be worked out before the plan could be launched, and it soon became clear that both the Jews and the Arabs viewed the Jordan Valley project within the context of the prevailing politico-military conflict. Each side advanced exaggerated claims to the water supplies that were to be made available for irrigation and to the electric power that would be produced. The location of the storage reservoirs and the extent to which tributaries of the Jordan River were to be utilized were questions with important implications for military security. Despite the fact that by 1955 Johnston had considerably narrowed the area of disagreement, neither Israel nor the Arab states affected were ready to accept a final plan. The chief stumbling block was the insistent Arab view that agreement upon the Jordan Valley project would be tantamount to a recognition of the State of Israel. The hope that agreement could be secured on this issue was further darkened after 1955 by Western, and especially American, efforts to foster a regional security system in the Middle East and by the policies of Britain and the United States toward the Suez Canal controversy. The result in both instances, as we shall see more fully below, was a serious blow to the unified support that Johnston had attempted to create within the Middle East for the Jordan Valley scheme.

This project engendered little direct conflict between the Eisenhower administration and the Democratic opposition (which in 1954 had won control of both Senate and House). Democrats as well as Republicans supported the plan to develop the Jordan Valley. Scattered criticism was directed at the Administration's failure to move rapidly enough in getting the project under way. From time to time, Democrats, especially those from New York State and other states with heavy Jewish constituencies, importuned the Administration to exert pressure upon the Arabs for agreement. Some critics even favored unilateral development of the valley by Israel in the hope that such a move would eventually compel Arab co-operation (3, Mar. 24, 1955, pp. 2991–92, 3666).

A second prong in the Administration's attack upon Middle Eastern problems consisted of efforts to deal with the thorny refugee issue. As we have already observed, Washington hoped that the Jordan Valley plan would aid in solving the refugee problem. In the meantime there appeared to be no alternative but to continue the policy begun under the Truman administration of providing funds for refugee relief, both directly by the United States and through the United Nations. By 1954–56, leading Democrats had begun to express the opinion that continued American relief to the Arab refugees merely encouraged Arab obduracy toward Israel by permitting the Arab nations to evade their rightful responsibility for the refugees. Increasingly, Democrats expressed the belief that refugee relief amounted in fact to an American endorsement of the Arab position that Israel must take back roughly nine hundred thousand displaced Arabs before peace could be assured. The Democrats supported the Jordan Valley plan and a program of long-range economic assistance to the Arab nations that would permit resettlement of the refugees throughout the Middle East.[3]

MIDDLE EASTERN DEFENSE AND UNITED STATES ARMS AID

Partisan disagreements over the Jordan Valley plan and the problem of the Arab refugees, however, were insignificant compared to the discord engendered by the Eisenhower administration's efforts to create a Middle Eastern defense system comparable to NATO in Western Europe. It was in connection with these efforts that Democrats accused the Administration of having reversed earlier American policy toward Palestine, virtually abandoning Israel to the untender mercies of the Arab world and opening the door for a Communist foothold in the Middle East.

By 1952 the nucleus of a regional defense system existed in the adherence of Greece and Turkey to NATO. If other Middle Eastern countries could be brought in, security

[3] See speeches, extensions of remarks, and insertions on the Middle East by various Democratic legislators in the *Congressional Record* (daily edition) for 1956, pp. 2991–92, 5150–54, 5171–73, A-2902–4, and A-5472–76.

The Democratic Platform for 1956 pledged: "We will assist in carrying out large-scale projects for their [refugee] resettlement in countries where there is room and opportunity for them" (6, p. 12).

would be promoted in two ways: by creating a northern tier of anti-Communist states along the Middle Eastern borders of the Soviet Union, and by reducing the prospect of armed conflict among the countries in the area. Abortive attempts had been made under the Truman administration to launch a Middle Eastern defense command, but no progress had been possible while Britain was quarreling with Egypt over Suez and with Iran over the nationalization of British oil holdings. By 1953, however, it appeared (in the case of Egypt, erroneously) that both of these disputes were well on the way to satisfactory resolution. Furthermore, the impetus for a new attempt at creating a security system was provided by the British desire to revise her treaty relationship with Iraq. A new treaty between these two countries was followed in 1955 by an Iraqi-Turkish pact. In September, Pakistan was admitted to this chain; and in October, Iran also joined it.

The defense cordon established by the Baghdad Pact now extended along the southern border of the USSR from Turkey to Pakistan. A connecting link with Western Europe was afforded by Turkish membership in both NATO and the Baghdad Pact; and the membership of Pakistan in the Southeast Asian Treaty Organization extended the defense chain to the Pacific area. Although the United States initiated the Baghdad Pact, it did not join the Middle Eastern security system, a fact that doubtless detracted significantly from its usefulness as a deterrent to aggression by countries both inside and outside the immediate area. The American observer at the Baghdad Pact conference is reported to have explained his country's reluctance to join it on two grounds: fear that such a step might alienate Egypt and other Arab countries not included in the agreement, and apprehension that it would evoke a proposal by Israel for a mutual defense treaty with the United States to protect her borders. If the latter proposal were adopted, relations between the United States and the Arab world would be further strained (22, Nov. 25, 1955, dispatch by Kenneth Love). An additional explanation may be that the two principal sponsors—Britain and the United States—in time held different conceptions of its underlying purpose. The *Christian Science Monitor* correspondent, Neal Stanford, reported that "London sees the pact as a peace-keeper for the Middle East. Washington sees it as a link to contain the Soviet Union" (2, Mar. 23, 1956). These were not necessarily contradictory interpretations, but they did point to a fundamental difference in emphasis between the two countries. By late 1955 the United States had come to realize more fully how intricately related the problems of the Middle East were, and how efforts to bring stability toward one problem might easily bring instability toward another.

The Baghdad Pact set off a wave of violent anti-Western, and especially anti-American, sentiment, which swept the Middle East from Egypt to India. To most of the Arab states the only immediate threat to their existence was Israel, and the Baghdad Pact was viewed as an attempt to force the Arab states to abandon their hostility toward Israel. The response of the Arab countries not included in the pact was to form their own alliance system built around the Damascus Pact, initially signed between Egypt and Syria, but later joined by Saudi Arabia. Jordan, Lebanon, and Yemen were also invited to join, but to date they have refused to join either the Baghdad or Damascus defense system.

As a natural consequence of efforts by the Eisenhower administration to promote Middle Eastern defense and the defense of the non-Communist world generally, the United States began after 1953 to provide military aid to the Arab countries as part of the Mutual Security Program. The issue of arms aid to the Arabs was one of the principal sources of partisan controversy toward Middle Eastern questions after 1953. To many Democrats, particularly those from states with large Jewish populations, the policy of arms aid constituted convincing proof of the pro-Arab sympathies of the Eisenhower administration. How, Democrats asked, could the Administration simultaneously invoke the policy of neutrality toward the Arab-Israeli conflict, arm the Arab states, refuse to arm Israel, and continue to exclude Israel from the Baghdad defense system? How could there be any security, not to mention permanent peace, in the Middle East, when the military balance of power was being swung against Israel by the steady accretion of Arab military might? To these questions the Administration replied that the Tripartite Declaration of 1950 had committed the United States to consider requests for arms on the twofold basis of the security needs of a country and its part in promoting regional security. According to these standards, arms aid to Israel did not seem warranted. In addition, the United States was furnishing arms only to those countries in the Middle East (and elsewhere) that had pledged not to use them for aggressive purposes. Finally, the Baghdad Pact, along with repeated American pledges of assistance to any country that became the victim of aggression, constituted a sufficient guarantee that Arab countries would not use their American-supplied arms to destroy Israel (10, pp. 388–89; 4, pp. 5172–73).

Democrats—who more and more accused the Administration, and particularly Secretary Dulles, of unjustifiable optimism—were not impressed by such assurances. By 1956 the question of American arms shipments to the Arab world had become a leading campaign issue. Democratic spokesmen accused the Administration of capitulating to truculent Arab demands for military equipment, thereby vastly magnifying the danger of war and the threat to the existence of Israel. They accused the Administration of being too much concerned with the Soviet threat to the area and of ignoring serious problems within the region. They charged that American arms were being used by Arab dictators to strengthen their own positions while deferring long overdue domestic reforms. Even more alarming, because of the USSR's offer of arms to Egypt, the United States had been maneuvered into a position of having to continue to supply arms throughout the Arab community regardless of the consequences. American arms, moreover, were being utilized by fanatical Arabs to undermine the positions of Britain and France in the area—and hence of the whole free-world alliance. In short, leading Democrats charged that the policy of arms aid was a bankrupt policy: it had gained little or no good will among the Arabs for the United States because they continued to hold the United States largely responsible for the creation of Israel, and it had come close to alienating one of the few dependable allies that the United States possessed in the Middle East—Israel. To these specific charges, Democrats added the more general indictment that the Administration had not even been consistent in its attempt to furnish military assistance to the Arabs. State Department vacillation over the delivery of eighteen tanks to Saudi Arabia in February, 1956, for example, had largely nullified any gain that might have accrued to the nation from sending these tanks in the first place.

During 1955 and 1956, heated debates were heard in Congress over the question of Middle Eastern defense and arms aid for the Arab countries. A penetrating indictment of existing policy was given by Senator Mike Mansfield (Democrat of Montana), a member of the Foreign Relations Committee. Outlining concrete proposals to remedy the defects in American policy, Mansfield began by suggesting a number of "don'ts" for American policy makers. American policy must *not:* (1) aim at pleasing everybody, because it will then please nobody; (2) abandon Israel or let Israel expand at the expense of the Arab states; (3) be exclusively, or even primarily, guided by concern for the security of oil holdings in the Middle East; (4) attempt to "buy good will" throughout the Arab world; or (5) concentrate unduly upon military problems at the expense of nonmilitary problems in the Middle East.

What, then, ought to be the ingredients of a new American policy? Mansfield proposed the following elements: a firm United States commitment to guarantee the present borders of Israel (rather than the agreed-upon borders that the Tripartite Declaration of 1950 had called for); a Big Four conference at which the United States should take the lead in seeking agreement among the Great Powers to work out a basis for a permanent peace in Palestine; a concerted effort to find alternative oil supplies for Western Europe, so that it would not be so dependent upon the whim of oil-rich Arab rulers; a reappraisal of the need for American military bases throughout the Arab world; a further reappraisal of American foreign assistance programs, so that aid would be given only to countries intent upon keeping the peace; an American acceptance of British dominion over Cyprus, so that the presence of Great Britain in the Middle East would provide some kind of stabilizing influence in this troubled region (3, Apr. 18, 1956, pp. 5819–29).

From the frequent interruptions of Mansfield's speech by approving Democratic senators, it was clear that he was voicing the opinion of a substantial number of Democratic congressmen. And when the Democratic party chieftains gathered in Chicago in August, 1956, their discontent with the Eisenhower administration's policies in the Middle East found ample and pointed reflection in the party platform. "In the Middle East," the platform stated,

the Eisenhower Administration has dawdled and drifted. The results have been disastrous, and worse threatens. Only the good offices of the United Nations in maintaining peace between Israel and her neighbors conceal the diplomatic incapacities of the Republican Administration.

As is characteristic of platforms, the Democratic position was somewhat hazy on precisely what steps would be taken to remedy this situation. Among those listed, however, was the promise to "redress the dangerous imbalance of arms in the area resulting from the shipment of Communist arms to Egypt," and a pledge to furnish "defensive weapons to Israel" and to promote such "security guarantees as may be required to deter aggression and war in the area" (6, pp. 6–12).

Making allowance for the exaggeration that is customary during national elections, it is clear that the question of American arms to the Arab world had become a volatile campaign issue in 1956. A remarkable parallel existed with the situation during the election of 1948. Then the Republicans had denounced the Truman administration for drifting in its policies toward Nationalist China. Now Democrats hurled the same charge at the Republicans, and they promised that if they were elected the dangerous imbalance of military strength in the Middle East would be promptly rectified.

2. The United States and Egypt

The United States had few contacts with Egypt or other Middle Eastern countries before World War II. Trade relations between the two countries were established early in the eighteenth century when Egypt was still part of the Ottoman Empire. By and large, however, the United States accepted the primacy of British influence in Egypt for almost a century thereafter. Reference has already been made to the crucial role of the Suez Canal and other Middle Eastern bases during World War II. Throughout the war the United States assisted Egypt in training her armed forces and also provided her with materials of war. After defeat of the Axis, the United States became the second largest exporter of goods to Egypt, and American shipping formed an important part of the traffic using the Suez Canal. But the first American was not named to the canal's board of directors until 1948.

As we noted early in this chapter, American prestige throughout the Middle East was high in the immediate postwar period—higher than at any time before the war or in the years that followed. This era of good feelings between the United States and the Arab world ended with American espousal of the Zionist position on Palestine. After the Arab states began to look upon the United States as the major force within the UN behind the partition plan, and after Egypt began to rise to a position of leadership within the Arab community, suspicion and discord, giving way finally to violent anti-American sentiment on the part of Egypt, began to characterize relations between the two countries. In time, Egypt regarded the West, and particularly the United States as the leader of the Western coalition, as the source of most of her internal and external problems. None of the policies followed by the Truman or Eisenhower administrations was capable of halting the deterioration in American-Egyptian relations. As hostility between the two nations increased, so did political conflict within the United States over American diplomacy in the Middle East. This was the pattern in broad outline. In order to appraise the problem in light of bipartisan considerations, it is necessary to examine American-Egyptian relations in somewhat greater detail.

AMERICAN POLICY TOWARD THE SUEZ CANAL CONTROVERSY

Early in the postwar period, Egypt began to press Britain to evacuate the Suez Canal. The attitude of the United States toward this dispute was compounded of idealistic sentiments and considerations of *Realpolitik*. Often it was difficult to decide which of these elements predominated. The United States had traditionally been sympathetic to colonial peoples in their efforts to obtain independence from foreign rule. Yet the United States was also mindful of the strategic importance of Suez, especially after 1947 when the American position on most international questions was heavily influenced by the ever-present threat of Soviet expansionism. Until 1953–54, the Anglo-American position on Suez was that Egypt could not be entrusted unilaterally to defend the canal, all the more so in the light of Egypt's poor performance in the Arab-Israeli war.

By July, 1952, Egyptian demands for British evacuation of Suez stiffened, as King Farouk was overthrown by a military junta headed by General Mohammed Naguib. Although Naguib had been swept into office by nationalist elements, especially by the officer corps, he was looked upon by the West as being more reasonable on the Suez issue than many other figures in Egyptian public life. Contemporaneously with these events within Egypt, the United States had begun to press its plans for a Middle East defense command. In the American view, establishment of such a command might satisfy the demands of both the British and the Egyptians. If a regional defense system could be set up, the British could evacuate Suez with the assurance that the security of the canal, and the Middle East generally, would be safeguarded. The American policy, however, was defeated by a vicious circle: Britain would not withdraw from Suez until after an adequate system of regional defense had been established, and Egypt would not discuss such a system until after Britain had left the Suez Canal.

Events late in 1952 and early in 1953 gradually brought the issue to a climax. After his trip to the Middle East, Secretary of State Dulles proposed that negotiations be undertaken between Egypt on the one side and the United States and Britain on the other. Egypt promptly rejected this suggestion, being unwilling to regard the United States as a party to the Suez Canal dispute. Nevertheless, negotiations between Britain and Egypt were resumed in April. As the talks progressed, the United States simultaneously urged both sides to join a Middle Eastern defense system and held out to Cairo the prospect of American economic and technical assistance as an inducement for agreement on a solution of the Suez problem. Finally, after weary months of seemingly fruitless negotiation, Britain and Egypt agreed upon a plan calling for the withdrawal of all British forces from Suez. By this agreement both sides reaffirmed their support for the Convention of 1888 that specified the conditions under which the canal was to be used. The crux of this agreement was that the Suez Canal was an international waterway open to the traffic of all nations in war and peace. Theoretically, the terms of the convention were to be enforced by an international commission; actually, they had been enforced by Great Britain since 1888.

The settlement of 1954 appeared to be satisfactory to both countries, and for a period of more than a year it seemed that the Suez problem had receded as an issue disturbing the political equilibrium of the Middle East. In November the regime of General Naguib was overthrown by the militant nationalist Colonel Abdel Nasser. Events revealed that Nasser would be content with nothing less than Egyptian nationalization of the Suez Canal, even if such a step meant risking military conflict throughout the Middle East and perhaps throughout the world.

EGYPTIAN ACQUISITION OF ARMS FROM THE COMMUNIST BLOC

From the beginning of the cold war, the United States had viewed the Middle East as a fertile field for possible Communist penetration. American policy makers tried to relate policy there to the larger objective of containing the Communist bloc within its existing orbit. Therefore, as part of the global policy of containment, both the Truman and Eisenhower administrations provided American technical, economic, and military assistance to Arab and Asian countries, while attempting at the same time to unite these countries into a regional defense system. Within the Middle East, Greece and Turkey (and, after the Baghdad Pact in 1955, the northern tier countries) received American arms aid under the Mutual Security Program. The total amount of American aid of all types to Middle Eastern countries was never more than a small fraction of American postwar assistance to foreign governments. Yet the technical and economic aid furnished these countries constituted at least a beginning toward a long-range improvement in living standards and a start toward industrialization.

The quantity of military aid given by the United States to these nations was not, however, as important as the circumstances under which it was given and the ramifications of such aid for American Middle Eastern diplomacy generally. From the beginning of the Mutual Security Program in 1951, the principal Eastern beneficiaries were Greece and Turkey—nations that consistently remained friendly to the United States. Among the other countries in the area, Iraq was the only one to receive substantial arms shipments. The underlying American objective of building a regional defense belt against the Communist bloc no doubt justified the provision of arms to the northern tier countries of the Middle East. But when this aid was viewed in another dimension—when it was seen within the context of the Arab-Israeli conflict—the American policy had profound repercussions. There had been a steady build-up of Arab military power after the armistice in the Palestinian war. Arab leaders talked incessantly of a second round against Israel.

When viewed against this background, the American policy of providing arms aid to Arab countries strongly suggested that the United States was indifferent to the fact that the balance of power in the Middle East was becoming highly inimical to Israel. Repeated requests from Tel Aviv for American arms resulted only in assurances from the State Department that the question was under consideration. Assurances from the United States and the Arab world that American arms would never be used against Israel pacified neither Israel nor its supporters within the United States. Increasingly, Secretary of State Dulles had difficulty explaining to his critics—and on this issue they were mainly Democrats—why the announced American policy of aiding any nation that was threatened with aggression did not apply to Israel. Still, until the autumn of 1956, the Eisenhower administration stood by its policy of refusing arms aid to Israel, although (unofficially at least) it did consent to the acquisition of arms by Israel from other members of the Western alliance, notably from Canada and France.

The imbalance in military power between Israel and her Arab neighbors became especially serious after the summer of 1955, when the Communist bloc offered to supply arms to

Egypt. On September 27 Premier Nasser announced that Egypt and Czechoslovakia had consummated an arms agreement. This announcement confirmed the worst fears of the critics of the Eisenhower administration's diplomacy in the Middle East. It meant that Russia was on the verge of achieving one of her historic diplomatic objectives, an objective that had been thwarted for well over a century: penetration of the Middle East. The arms agreement further signified that the Western powers had lost effective control over the actions of the Arab states and that the security of Israel was in graver jeopardy than at any time since 1949.

The Czech-Egyptian arms deal widened the cleavage that had already appeared between the Administration and leading Democrats (joined by a handful of Republicans) over issues in the Middle East. Month after month, the Administration reiterated its refusal to grant arms to Israel because, said Secretary Dulles, it wanted "to avoid participating in what might become an arms race . . ." (9, p. 18). Spokesmen for the Administration maintained that genuine peace could come to the area only by a settlement of outstanding differences and not by increasing the danger of military conflict. As tension increased between Israel and the Arab states, President Eisenhower offered an American guarantee of any settlement that the two sides might make, and he warned both sides against the consequences of renewed hostilities (9, p. 19).

The Administration's critics, however, were not satisfied. The question, they believed, was not whether there would be an arms race—one had already begun—but whether Israel would soon be so outstripped militarily that her very existence would be endangered. Daily the relative position of Israel was growing more precarious. Nationalist ferment in North Africa, Cyprus, Jordan, and elsewhere was steadily undermining Western influence throughout the Arab-Asian world. As early as March, 1955, Senator Herbert Lehman (Democrat from New York) urged the Administration to move "with full force and vigor to rescue Israel from the isolation which now engulfs her in the Middle East" (3, Mar. 24, 1955, p. 3665). Throughout ensuing months other influential members of Congress supported Lehman's demand. Senator Warren Magnuson (Democrat from Washington), for example, warned the Administration that if it did not speedily revise its policy, it would risk formidable opposition from Democrats toward the entire foreign aid program (3, June 2, 1955, pp. 7478–79). In time, even occasional Republicans endorsed these demands. Senator George Bender (Republican from Ohio) stated that he "objects strenuously" to the shipment of arms to Arab countries without the provision of arms for Israel; he was convinced that "our policies are playing directly into the hands of Russia" in the Middle East (3, June 4, 1956, pp. 8480–82). Such pleas, however, were unavailing. And to Democratic party leaders the Administration's refusal to provide arms for Israel constituted additional evidence that its diplomacy toward the entire Middle Eastern area was inadequate. Their only recourse appeared to be to take the issue to the electorate in the national election of 1956.

THE ASWAN HIGH DAM

Egyptian leaders had long talked of constructing a dam on the upper reaches of the life-giving Nile River to provide for flood control, irrigation, and the generation of electric power. The proposed dam, one of the largest undertakings of its kind ever envisioned, was to require many years for construction; estimates of its ultimate cost ran over a billion dollars. Foreign assistance would of course be necessary for its construction, meaning primarily American assistance. By 1955 the United States had undertaken studies of the dam's feasibility, and in December the State Department announced that the United States would join with Britain and the World Bank to provide the necessary financial assistance. No doubt it was hoped that this offer would help to reverse the decline in Western prestige throughout the Middle East in preceding months. More specifically, its immediate aim was to offset in some degree the increased influence of the Communist bloc occasioned by the recently consummated Czech-Egyptian arms agreement. Studies undertaken by the World Bank called attention to numerous unsolved engineering and financial problems in the path of the dam's completion. In the light of these problems and of Egypt's acquisition of Communist arms, it seems clear that, in the words of Cooke, the Eisenhower administration's decision to finance the dam was "motivated far more by political than by economic considerations" (5, p. 9).

The American offer of assistance had little or no effect in diverting Nasser from his efforts to cultivate closer ties with the Iron Curtain countries. Instead, in the months that followed, Nasser expanded the original arms agreement with Czechoslovakia, negotiated trade agreements with other Communist nations, dramatically extended Egyptian recognition to Red China, actively helped rebel forces in North Africa who were fighting against French authority, increased the tempo of his anti-Western propaganda, and repeatedly expressed friendship with the Communist world. Finally, as though flinging a gauntlet at the feet of the free world, he strongly suggested that Soviet Russia was prepared to finance the Aswan High Dam on more favorable terms than had been proposed by the West. All these moves were taken within a context of increasingly militant Arab nationalism, at the center of which movement stood Nasser, who seemed to fancy himself some kind of Arab Moses, destined to lead his country, and the Moslem world generally, out of bondage to supposed Western colonialism.

These events evidently induced the Eisenhower administration to re-examine its position on the Aswan High Dam. On July 19, 1956, Secretary Dulles declared that the project did not seem "feasible in present circumstances," mentioning numerous technical difficulties that remained unsolved. Since these difficulties had existed all the time, it was clear that they were not the underlying reason for the change in American policy. Instead, it could be attributed to a growing disenchantment with Nasser throughout the Western world and a heightened apprehension that Egypt might not be counted upon to remain a member of the free-world coalition (5, pp. 6–11).

WAR IN THE MIDDLE EAST

The withdrawal of the American offer to assist with financing the Aswan High Dam evoked prompt and decisive action on the part of Nasser. On July 26 he proclaimed the nationalization of the Suez Canal. Nationalization apparently was designed to serve the twofold purpose of demonstrating graphically Egypt's disdain for Western opinion and of furnishing her with a source of revenue with which she might proceed alone to finance construction of the dam. Whatever the reasons for Nasser's action, it had far-reaching repercussions. England and France were ready to intervene with troops at once to enforce the Suez Agreement of 1954. Throughout succeeding weeks, however, they were deterred by the overriding desire of the Eisenhower administration to resolve the Suez issue peaceably. It is not relevant to our purpose to trace the events of those tense weeks. Suffice it to say that no effective plan was found to reconcile the Egyptian and Western positions in respect to the canal. Nasser's victory added fuel to the partisan controversy al-

ready taking place within the United States over the Eisenhower administration's diplomacy. Critics of the Administration viewed the event as the climax of a long and increasingly grave series of blunders by Republican policy makers in handling the problems of the Arab world.

In the autumn of 1956 crisis piled upon crisis. On October 29 Israel, after years of Arab provocations and after repeated rebuffs in her attempt to secure Western arms to protect her borders, took matters into her own hands by invading the Sinai peninsula in force. Within hours, Britain and France (probably by prearrangement with Israel) also attacked Egypt on the pretext of protecting the canal.

Faced with a breakdown in the Western alliance and with the prospect that the war might involve the entire Middle East and might eventually spread throughout the world, the United States took the lead within the United Nations in trying to arrange a cease-fire. After that had been accomplished, the Eisenhower administration contended, the issues that had precipitated the war could be settled by negotiation. Although Britain and France reluctantly agreed to a cease-fire early in November, Israel refused to evacuate Egyptian territory until she had received pledges that would permit her to use the Suez Canal and the Gulf of Aqaba and that would also assure the safety of her borders against further Egyptian commando raids. Months were required before Israel finally accepted American assurances that her legitimate grievances would be satisfied after she had evacuated Egyptian soil. By the spring of 1957, a shaky truce prevailed in the Middle East. United Nations troops patrolled the borders between Egypt and Israel. Contemporaneously, negotiations were being carried on among the parties to the dispute. But as time passed, Israel and her supporters within the United States became increasingly skeptical concerning the Eisenhower administration's diplomacy toward the Suez crisis. The Administration had persuaded the Western allies and Israel to relinquish the gains they had won on the field of battle by repeatedly assuring them that the outstanding issues could be settled without resort to force. But as the summer drew near, it appeared that Nasser was in effective control of events. After the evacuation of foreign troops from his soil, he appeared more adamant than ever in refusing Israel use of the canal and access to the Gulf of Aqaba. Moreover, it was clear that he expected all nations to use the canal on Egypt's terms. Only the future would determine whether the Eisenhower administration's diplomacy had been a master stroke in averting a possible third world war or whether, on the contrary, it had seriously undermined the strength of the free-world alliance and had, in effect, left Nasser the victor in the Middle East conflict.

BIPARTISANSHIP AND AMERICAN DIPLOMACY IN THE MIDDLE EAST

By the closing weeks of the presidential election of 1956, the injection of Middle Eastern affairs into American domestic politics forcefully demonstrated that bipartisan liaison between the two major parties had all but collapsed with respect to this issue. Not since the intensely partisan attacks by the Republicans against the Truman administration's policies toward Nationalist China in the period 1948–50 was there such bitter and unrestrained criticism of one party by the other. Democratic party leaders attempted to turn the Middle Eastern crisis into a leading campaign issue. Thus over a coast-to-coast television hookup on November 1, the party's presidential candidate, Adlai E. Stevenson, presented an appraisal of the Administration's foreign policies. Acknowledging that any consideration of foreign policy ought to be "above politics," Stevenson nevertheless was convinced that "our Middle Eastern policy is at absolute dead end." The "bankruptcy of our policy," he believed, had permitted Soviet Russia to achieve two great diplomatic victories: penetration of the Middle East and disruption of the Western coalition. After reviewing events that had precipitated the recent crisis, Stevenson summarized the Administration's diplomacy in these words:

Here we stand today. We have alienated our chief European allies. We have alienated Israel. We have alienated Egypt and the Arab countries. And in the U.N. our main associate in Middle Eastern matters now appears to be Communist Russia—in the very week when the Red Army has been shooting down the brave people of Hungary and Poland. We have lost every point in the game. I doubt if ever before in our diplomatic history has any policy been such an abysmal, such a complete and such a catastrophic failure [11, Nov. 2, 1956].

On the next day, six Democratic members of the Senate Foreign Relations Committee described the Middle Eastern crisis as the "worst diplomatic disaster in memory" and agreed that the Administration's policies had ended in bankruptcy. These senators were unanimous in believing that "four years of indecision, tactlessness, timidity, and bluster have reaped their reward" (11, Nov. 3, 1956). Making allowance for the partisan charges to be expected during an election year, these sentiments seemed to indicate convincingly that if any bipartisan co-operation had ever prevailed in American postwar foreign policy toward the Middle East, it had now completely disappeared.

Several important lessons emerge from an analysis of the Middle Eastern diplomacy of the United States as a case study in conducting foreign relations upon a bipartisan basis. Since they can be dealt with more profitably within the chapters that follow, we shall do no more here than briefly identify these lessons. First, there is the difficulty—perhaps even the impossibility—of preserving bipartisan co-operation after a major diplomatic defeat has been incurred, or after the opposition party believes such defeat has been incurred. Many of the reasons why bipartisan co-operation cannot be carried on under these circumstances have been set forth in an earlier chapter dealing with United States policy toward Nationalist China. One major difference, however, should be noticed between the problems of the Middle East and Nationalist China. In the latter instance the inadequacies of American foreign policy were so clearly apparent to both the opposition party and the public at large that the earlier bipartisan co-operation could not survive in the face of widespread public dissatisfaction with the Truman administration's Far Eastern diplomacy. In the case of the Middle East, the opposite conditions prevailed. There had been little or no bipartisan collaboration in formulating policy for the Middle East, and yet Democrats made little headway in trying to make political capital out of the Eisenhower administration's Middle Eastern policies during the election of 1956. Leading Democrats pointed to major inadequacies in American foreign policy toward the Middle East, but the electorate remained unconvinced. No disaster comparable to the collapse of Nationalist China had occurred in that area. The vast majority of the American people apparently accepted the claims of President Eisenhower and his supporters that his foreign policy in the Middle East had been successful.

Once again, we are led to the conclusion that the question of whether a foreign policy will receive widespread public support will be determined not so much by the fact that bipartisan procedures are used to formulate it, as by the fact that the policy is successful, or at least is believed to be successful, by large segments of public opinion. When and if it has been proved unsuccessful, then disunity is likely to ensue, regardless of whether or not it had bipartisan support in its inception.

Second, this case study emphasizes the important influence

that constituent pressure plays in shaping the attitudes of members of Congress on foreign policy issues. Most of the causes of tension in the Middle East derived from the partition of Palestine in 1947; and the influence of the Jewish vote within the United States was unquestionably of primary importance in shaping American policy on that issue. American advocacy of partition and speedy recognition of Israel were probably the root causes of a majority of the problems that the United States encountered later in its attempt to influence events in the Middle East. And there can be no doubt but that the viewpoints of both political parties on this question were substantially determined by considerations of American domestic politics.

Third, this key decision was a policy that initially enjoyed wide bipartisan support, although, as we have noted, there was in fact little actual consultation between the parties in formulating this policy. Bipartisan support for partition, of course, vastly strengthened the hand of the government in seeking support for the policy in the United Nations and elsewhere. Yet this fact raises a fundamental question about the advisability of bipartisan foreign policy. Was partition in retrospect a wise policy for the American government to advocate? If so, then bipartisan support for it would appear to be amply justified. If not, then such support may have created a kind of irresistible pressure with which those persons within the government who urged caution could not cope. This is but to suggest a point that must be elaborated in later pages: the value of bipartisan foreign policy is likely in the long run to be determined not so much by whether unity was attained in foreign affairs but by *whether unity was attained in behalf of sound policies.* In short, unity may or may not be a virtue, depending upon whether in any given situation it in fact advances the nation's interests in world affairs.

Finally, we may reiterate a point made in earlier chapters,

and especially in our treatment of American relations with Nationalist China. Certain kinds of foreign policy situations do not lend themselves well to a bipartisan approach. Among these problems none is perhaps more fundamental than a foreign policy crisis or a series of crises. Effective diplomacy toward an international crisis usually demands prompt and decisive action—action that is not likely to be forthcoming when bipartisan consultations have to be carried out. In this situation an incumbent administration may be forced to make what it regards as an unpleasant choice between ignoring bipartisan procedures or delaying decisions necessary in the foreign policy field until after the right time has passed. Which choice it will make depends of course upon many circumstances, not the least of which will be how vital it regards the achievement of unity in foreign affairs. If the administration chooses to ignore bipartisan procedures, it risks alienating the opposition party. If it chooses to postpone an important decision in favor of seeking unity, it risks possible diplomatic defeat. The dilemma is cruel, but it must be faced. If American experience in foreign affairs since World War II furnishes a reliable guide, when an administration is confronted by this dilemma, it has customarily and wisely preferred to take whatever action was necessary to deal with pressing external problems, without permitting a rigid concern for unity to interfere with the action demanded.

References

1. Atyeo, Henry C., "Arab Politics and Pacts," *Current History,* 30 (June, 1956), 339–46. A detailed treatment of the Baghdad Pact.
2. *Christian Science Monitor.*
3. *Congressional Record* (daily edition).

4. *Congressional Record,* Vol. 101.

5. Cooke, Morris Llewellyn, *Nasser's High Aswan Dam.* Washington, D.C.: Public Affairs Institute, 1956. A thorough treatment of the American policy in respect to the financing of the Aswan High Dam.

6. Democratic National Committee, *The Democratic Platform for 1956.* Washington, D.C., 1956.

7. *Department of State Bulletin,* 28 (June 15, 1953), 831–35. Contains a statement by Dulles issued when he returned from a Middle Eastern trip in 1953, in respect to guaranteeing Israel-Arab frontiers.

8. Department of State, *Report on the Near East.* (Publication No. 5088, "Near and Middle Eastern Series," No. 12.) Washington, D.C., 1953.

9. ———, *U. S. Policy in the Near East, South Asia, and Africa —1955.* (Publication No. 6330.) Washington, D.C., 1956.

10. Donovan, Robert J., *Eisenhower: The Inside Story.* New York: Harper and Brothers, 1956.

11. *Herald Tribune* (New York).

12. Hollingworth, Clare, *The Arabs and the West.* London: Methuen and Company, 1952. Pages 193–213 describe the growth of American oil interests in the Middle East. Further background on American relations with Egypt before World War II is given on pages 34–61.

13. Howard, Harry N., "The Arab-Asian States in the United Nations," *Middle East Journal,* 7 (Summer, 1953), 279–92.

14. ———, *The Development of the United States Policy in the Near East, South Asia, and Africa.* Washington, D.C.: Government Printing Office. This annual series written for the Department of State discusses, in the 1951–52, 1953, 1954, and 1955 editions, the scope and nature of American assistance of all kinds in the Middle East, and its relation to the total pattern of foreign aid. For an over-all survey of the period 1945–51, see the articles by the same author in the *Department*

of State Bulletin, November 19 and 26, 1951, pp. 809 ff. and 839 ff., respectively.

15. Hurewitz, J. C., *Middle East Dilemmas.* New York: Harper and Brothers, 1953. Pages 7–50 contain further background on American relations with Egypt before World War II.

16. Lawrence, E. V., *Egypt and the West.* New York: American Institute of International Information, 1956. A useful treatment of the course of negotiations over the Suez Canal.

17. Lehrman, Harold, "American Policy and Arab-Israeli Peace," *Commentary,* **17** (June, 1954), 546–56. A detailed treatment of the Arab refugee issue.

18. ——, "Two Middle East Conferences in Washington," *Commentary,* **19** (April, 1955), 335–45. Details the Arab "case" against the United States in respect to the decision in the United Nations concerning the partition of Palestine.

19. ——, "What Price Israel's Defense?" *Commentary,* **22** (September, 1956), 199–210. Discusses the effects of American policy in the Middle East during 1955 and 1956.

20. Lenczowski, George, *The Middle East in World Affairs.* Ithaca, N.Y.: Cornell University Press, 1952. This is among the best studies of the Middle East currently available. It is especially valuable for providing historical perspective on postwar American foreign policy.

21. Leonard, L. Larry, "The United Nations and Palestine," *International Conciliation,* **454** (October, 1949), 607–786. A convenient summary of the Zionist and Arab positions as presented to the United Nations and of subsequent UN action.

22. *New York Times.*

23. Peretz, Don, "Development of the Jordan Valley Waters," *Middle East Journal,* **9** (Autumn, 1955), 397–412.

24. Polk, William R., *What the Arabs Think.* ("Headline Book," No. 96.) New York: Foreign Policy Association, 1952.

25. Roosevelt, Kermit, "The Partition of Palestine," *Middle East Journal,* **2** (January, 1948), 1–16. This article, though written

from a strong pro-Arab viewpoint, is a valuable study of the evolution of United States policy toward Palestine.

26. Royal Institute of International Affairs, *The Middle East*. London, 1954.

27. Spain, James W., "Middle East Defense: A New Approach," *Middle East Journal,* 8 (Summer, 1954), 251–67. A detailed treatment of the Baghdad Pact.

28. Speiser, E. A., *The United States and the Near East*. Cambridge, Mass.: Harvard University Press, 1950. Pages 1–87 contain a detailed treatment of the activities of private American groups in the Middle East.

29. Stebbins, Richard P., *The United States in World Affairs, 1953*. New York: Harper and Brothers, 1955.

30. Stevens, Georgiana G., "Arab Refugees: 1948–1952," *Middle East Journal,* 6 (Summer, 1952), 281–97. A detailed analysis of the Arab refugee issue.

31. ———, "The Jordan River Valley," *International Conciliation,* 506 (January, 1956), 225–83. Gives full particulars concerning the difficulties in securing agreement on the Jordan Valley Plan.

32. Truman, Harry S., *Memoirs,* Vol. 2, *Years of Trial and Hope*. Garden City, N.Y.: Doubleday and Company, 1956. Pages 156–62 discuss the views of former President Truman on the intensity of Zionist pressures upon the White House. Differences within the government over the Palestinian issue are discussed in Chapters 10–12, *passim.*

33. Wallach, Sidney, "Decision in the Near East," *Yale Review,* Vol. 40, No. 3 (March, 1951), pp. 504–17.

34. Zander, Walter, "Arab Nationalism and Israel," *Commentary,* 22 (July, 1956), 13–19. Gives background on the effects of American policy in the Middle East during 1955 and 1956.

SEVEN

Determinants of
Bipartisanship (I)

"Politics stops at the water's edge!" So goes the familiar maxim which in the decade following the Second World War has almost become an article of faith among supporters of bipartisanship in foreign affairs. All too frequently this and other slogans associated with bipartisanship—"The national interest ahead of partisan advantage," or "Politics is adjourned"—evoke an automatic and uncritical acceptance on the part of the public. The feeling is that the true patriot *must* believe in bipartisanship. Anyone who questions its basic assumptions risks the charge that he is indifferent to national security in a period of international tension and danger.

In short, the principle of bipartisanship has virtually become a sacred cow. Politicians may depart from its spirit. By their actions they may effectively prevent the achievement of genuine co-operation between the parties in the sphere of foreign relations. Nevertheless they are expected to support the idea of bipartisanship even while they are frustrating its attainment. This phenomenon represents something more than a failure on the part of political and governmental leaders to practice their own preachments. Experience with the bipartisan principle indicates rather clearly that each major party has come more and more to see the imperfections and liabilities of the principle. Dissatisfaction is seldom expressed overtly and almost never by a direct attack upon the principle itself. There is still a marked reluctance on the part of public officials and political leaders to examine bipartisanship openly, even though doubts concerning its universal utility may have multiplied. Subsequent pages will illustrate some of the ways these dissatisfactions and subsurface criticisms have been expressed.

In the final chapters of this study it is our purpose to examine the concept of bipartisan foreign policy critically and in detail. As we observed in Chapter 1, there were isolated attempts to follow this principle before the Second World War. But not until the postwar period was there a sustained effort to apply it often and to a wide range of foreign policy problems. Some of these problems have lent themselves admirably to solution through a bipartisan approach. Toward other problems only a limited degree of bipartisan co-operation has been achieved. And toward still other problems no significant progress has been made in finding bipartisan solutions. Moreover, evidence presented in earlier chapters clearly reveals some of the consequences of pursuing a bipartisan approach to foreign relations. Some of these consequences have unquestionably been beneficial; others—and these to date have received too little attention from public officials or students of government—have been detrimental. Still other consequences cannot as yet be evaluated with any degree of finality, since it will perhaps require years to reveal their full influence.

Surely, however, there is now a need for some kind of evaluation of the bipartisan principle. After reflecting upon the implications and consequences of this principle, the reader may decide that it has proved its worth as a useful tool of American foreign relations. If so, such an evaluation ought to give him a more rational basis for supporting his belief. If, on the other hand, there are valid grounds for questioning the utility of the principle, wisdom demands that these grounds be examined. Two broad questions will provide the frame of reference for our inquiry in the second half of this study. These questions are: What are the factors that facilitate or hinder the realization of bipartisan co-operation in foreign affairs? and What are the consequences, both beneficial and detrimental, of adhering to the bipartisan principle? This chapter and the one that follows deal with the first of these questions. The second question is treated in Chapter 9.

We turn then to an examination of the factors—designated here "determinants of bipartisanship"—that contribute positively or negatively to party co-operation in the foreign policy field. These may be conveniently grouped as follows: the factors inherent in the ambiguity of the term "bipartisanship," those deriving from the nature of the foreign policy problem toward which a bipartisan approach is being followed, those associated with the President's position of leadership in foreign relations, those attributable to the organization and operation of Congress, those having to do with the nature and function of the American party system, and those related to the personal and psychological atmosphere within which bipartisan procedures are employed.

1. Bipartisanship As an Ambiguous Symbol

A major barrier to two-party co-operation in foreign affairs is the ambiguity inherent in the term "bipartisanship." It does not have a clearly defined or universally accepted content; it has been used in a number of senses, most frequently as a vague plea for all citizens to place the good of the nation as a whole above their own or their party's interest. When used in this sense, bipartisanship is equated with unity, but beyond a faint implication that party members should exercise self-restraint, nothing is told concerning *the means by which the desired unity is to be achieved.*

As was pointed out in the Introduction, the term "bipartisanship" may be used in basically two senses. It may be viewed as an end to be attained—unity in foreign relations. In this sense, the goal is clearly foreign policies supported by both major parties and the public at large. Or, second, the term may be used to suggest certain procedures to attain the end. A bipartisan approach to foreign relations implies that certain steps must be taken when important foreign policy problems arise.

Vagueness and misunderstanding hinder efforts to reach agreement between the two parties when bipartisanship is thought of primarily as procedures, techniques, and machinery designed to create unity. It is one thing for participants in the foreign policy process to agree upon the need for unity. It is quite a different matter for them to agree upon the means to accomplish unity. Even after a decade's experience with the principle, there is no agreement concerning which means are fundamental to the bipartisan process. Nevertheless, one lesson that emerges from postwar efforts to achieve unity is that unity is not likely to appear spontaneously, except when the nation is in manifest danger from an external threat. Numerous examples from American postwar diplomacy could be cited to indicate that bipartisanship must be cultivated by means acceptable to both parties.

But *which* means? In the absence of an answer which would be acceptable to the two parties, an incumbent administration has frequently had to improvise and to "play by ear." Furthermore, obscurity surrounding the meaning of bipartisanship has bred bickering between the two major parties over which foreign policy undertakings were, and which were not, included within the area of bipartisan agreement. Several techniques have been utilized from time to time in the postwar period (some of them having been used before World War II) to promote harmonious inter-party relations toward foreign affairs. Before we examine these techniques in detail, it might be well first to point out that vagueness implicit in the term may under certain circumstances actually be an advantage to those working for party collaboration in foreign affairs.

It is evident from our earlier treatment of case studies involving application of the bipartisan principle that a high degree of flexibility is required if the principle is to be applied to a variety of foreign policy problems. Procedures useful for approaching one kind of problem (e.g., the negotiation of international agreements such as the United Nations Charter or the North Atlantic Pact) will not necessarily be well suited for essentially different types of problems (such as that confronting the United States during the Chinese civil war). Nothing is to be gained from trying to pour the concept of bipartisanship into a rigid procedural mold. Experimentation and adaptation are clearly required if the United States is to cope effectively with changing external circumstances. To the extent that vagueness contributes to this flexibility it can be regarded as a factor that promotes rather than hinders harmonious interparty relations toward foreign affairs.

But admitting that a rigid definition is both undesirable and unattainable, it is still true that a clarification of the concept is needed. The minimum requirement is agreement between the parties that a bipartisan approach to foreign affairs *normally* involves certain fairly well defined practices and that these will be utilized to encourage interparty cooperation whenever circumstances permit. Experience with bipartisanship since World War II suggests that four such practices have been regarded by participants in the foreign policy process as of fundamental importance.

NATIONAL INTEREST ABOVE PARTISAN ADVANTAGE

A theme recurrent in the arguments of those advocating bipartisan foreign policy is that partisan advantage must be subordinated to the nation's diplomatic interests. While concrete expressions of this requirement also suffer from acute vagueness, often reducing themselves to little more than a pious hope that both parties will be conscious of the need for unity, it is nevertheless possible to indicate several specific ways in which this concept may be applied. The objective toward which each party should strive, said Senator Vandenberg in 1947, is "an unpartisan American foreign policy— not Republican, not Democratic, but American—which substantially unites our people at the water's edge in behalf of peace . . ." (6, Nov. 4, 1947). This same conception of bipartisanship was reflected in the Republican party platform of 1948, which pledged the GOP to "cooperate with the minority party . . . in order to prevent political considerations from interfering with the development of a consistent American foreign policy" (6, June 20, 1948). Bipartisanship is thus regarded as a kind of higher loyalty, obligating party members to place the national interest above partisan advantage in their consideration of foreign policy issues. But if bipartisanship is to involve something more than a pious and nebulous declaration of intention, the specific practices needed to translate these ideals into actuality must be defined with some precision. Among these practices, two stand out as especially significant.

When criticism of existing policies is necessary, it should be constructive and not destructive criticism. In his State of the Union message on January 8, 1951, for example, President Truman declared:

> I ask Congress for unity in these crucial days. . . . I do not ask for unanimity. I do not ask for an end to debate. . . . Let us debate the issues, but let every man among us weigh his words and deeds. There is a sharp difference between harmful criticism and constructive criticism [2, p. 101].

The line between constructive and destructive criticism may be difficult to draw; but the supposition is that an attempt to draw it shall be made by those sincerely desirous of following the principle of bipartisanship.

Moreover, when bipartisanship is defined as devotion to the national interest rather than party interest, a major expectation is that no party or candidate should attempt to make political capital out of either successes or failures in the foreign policy field. Emphasis upon bipartisanship in recent years has been held (erroneously) to have had its origin in the election of 1944, when President Roosevelt and Governor Dewey agreed to exclude foreign policy questions from the presidential campaign.[1] Progressively since 1944, each party has departed from this principle, so that in 1950, 1952, and especially 1956, foreign policy questions became central issues in national elections. Each party, nevertheless, has periodically condemned the other for ignoring this requirement. Typical of Republican accusations was a minority report issued by the House Foreign Affairs Committee on March 25, 1949. This report charged:

> We have seen the [Truman] administration attempt to take sole credit for achievements in which our party deserved at least

[1] See, for example, Governor Dewey's claim that he initiated bipartisanship during the election of 1944 (6, Oct. 13, 1948). But see Chapter 1 of this study for bipartisan practices before 1944.

equal credit. For politics to stop at the water's edge, there must be
. . . bipartisan sharing of credit for success of such policies.

The opposite complaint came from Democratic spokesmen,
who accused the GOP of seeking to evade responsibility for
failures in the foreign policy field. Republicans, said Senator
Sparkman of Alabama in 1951,

too frequently . . . seek to find official scapegoats for conditions
which they themselves helped to create. They, and all of us,
should realize that to assume public responsibility in these days is
to accept the heavy burden of dealing with inevitable problems,
fears, and failures . . . [6, Feb. 7, 1951].

Despite not infrequent departures from the requirement
by each party, the attempt to capitalize upon foreign policy
issues for partisan gain has been widely regarded by advocates of the bipartisan principle as highly inimical to its
attainment.

Prior Consultation over Foreign Affairs

A second procedure often thought indispensable for bipartisanship is consultation between spokesmen for both
major parties before foreign policy decisions are adopted.
Normally, this may be regarded as the *sine qua non* of
genuine two-party co-operation in foreign affairs. Its absence
has been frequently cited by both parties as the chief barrier
to unity in the foreign policy field.[2] The foremost examples
of productive bipartisan collaboration in the postwar era—
the United Nations Charter, the Marshall Plan, and the

[2] Typical of the emphasis upon the necessity for consultation *before* decisions
are adopted was the attitude of Senator Taft toward the British loan in 1946. At
the Senate hearings, Taft told representatives of the State Department: ". . . no
man in Congress was consulted about this thing in any respect until after the
whole contract was completed. They [members of Congress] were never consulted as to possible alternatives or as to what might be approved, neither any
Republican or [*sic*] any Democrat. . . . Now you come around and tell us that
we must either take it or leave it: it is a yes or no proposition; there is no
alternative" (8, p. 335).

North Atlantic Pact—involved thorough and prolonged preliminary study by representatives of both parties before major decisions were made. By contrast, the foreign policy issues that precipitated heated partisan differences—the British loan in 1946, tariff and reciprocal trade questions, American diplomacy toward Nationalist China after 1948, the conduct of the Korean War and the negotiations of a cease-fire agreement, American military assistance to Europe, American diplomacy in the Middle East—were preceded by little significant consultation between the majority and minority parties in the stage of policy formulation.

To be productive of lasting agreement between the parties, consultations must meet both quantitative and qualitative criteria. Quantitative standards refer to the duration and number of such consultations and to the range of individuals included in them. Qualitative standards relate to such questions as whether or not consultations were representative in the sense of according an opportunity to all important factions within both parties to express their views; whether the consultations permitted a full and frank exchange of opinions *before* decisions were reached or, by contrast, whether the opposition party was merely afforded an occasion to be informed of impending decisions; and whether the atmosphere prevailing during such consultations was such as to encourage a sincere effort by both parties to arrive at acceptable solutions.

On the basis of experience with bipartisanship since the Second World War, it is possible to construct a model consultation substantially fulfilling these criteria. Such a model is offered with the awareness that circumstances will often, if not always, prevent its complete attainment. Ideal consultations would begin far enough before the time a decision must be made so that there would be time for a full exchange of viewpoints; they would be repeated until a consensus had been reached regarding the proper course to be followed; they would encourage the opposition party to express its views frankly; they would be entered into by all participants in an attitude of good faith and mutual sacrifice to advance a common end; they would result in the widest possible area of agreement compatible with national security; and, after initial decisions had been reached, consultations would be repeated as often as necessary to modify existing policy in the light of new circumstances and evident inadequacies.

ACCEPTABLE LIAISON CHANNELS AND PROCEDURES

If bipartisanship contemplates placing the national interest ahead of partisan advantage and requires that consultations be held between the two parties as major foreign policy issues arise, a third requirement relates to the liaison channels that ought to be utilized to provide the communication needed. What groups or individuals should serve as liaison channels between the parties? No clear-cut understanding on this issue has emerged from attempts to follow the bipartisan principle.

The executive branch has most frequently consulted the members of the Senate Foreign Relations and House Foreign Affairs committees. Whenever policies have required legislative action, one or both of these committees has usually worked in close conjunction with the State Department in drafting the required legislation and in generating support for it in Congress. In general, these two committees constitute the most logical, and often the most valuable, channel of communication between the two major parties when foreign policy decisions are required. During the period of the Eightieth Congress, for example, bipartisanship was largely a matter of harmonious and frequent contacts between the State Department and the Senate Foreign Relations Committee, whose chairman was Senator Vandenberg. However, there are important limitations upon the degree to which these key committees can provide the communication needed, the most important of which is that they are by no means the only committees in Congress whose province is foreign affairs.

A second group instrumental in providing liaison has been the leaders of each party, both inside and outside the government. Throughout preliminary studies of the United Nations Charter, the Roosevelt administration sought the advice of recognized Republican leaders in Congress and from the nation as a whole. This practice was virtually abandoned by the Truman administration, but it was revived by the Eisenhower administration after 1952, when leading Democrats were invited to the White House at periodic intervals to discuss foreign, as well as domestic, policy (6, Nov. 24 and Dec. 19, 1954). The Truman administration tended to rely much more heavily upon selected individuals —most notably, of course, Senator Vandenberg. After Vandenberg's retirement the Administration utilized John Foster Dulles and John Sherman Cooper (former Republican senator from Kentucky) as Republican "advisers" to the State Department.

Basically, then, three groups may be utilized singly or in combination to provide the needed liaison: members of congressional committees, political leaders inside and outside the government, and selected individuals who are peculiarly well qualified to bring about agreement in the foreign policy field. By far the greatest reliance throughout the postwar era, at least until 1952, has been placed upon the first of these groups. In the next chapter we shall discuss more fully how executive-congressional relations affect the problem of party co-operation in the area of foreign affairs. It is enough here to observe that when important questions of foreign policy arise it is both natural and in some cases indispensable that there be an exchange of information between the committees of Congress that deal with external affairs and the executive branch.

Political leaders inside and outside the government, particularly those in Congress, have provided valuable liaison toward certain foreign policy problems. The Truman administration, however, did not make consistent use of this channel for communicating with the opposition party. During the tenure of the Truman administration several major obstacles existed to utilizing political leaders to provide an exchange of views, not the least of which was the recrimination and personal animosity surrounding any consideration of the Administration's Far Eastern policies. Given an attitude in Washington of extreme partisan discord and mutual distrust, little was to be gained from trying to arrive at common ground by meetings between party leaders. We may note here that the effectiveness of any liaison channel depends in considerable part on the spirit manifested by the individuals using the channel. After the collapse of Nationalist China, little constructive purpose could have been served by periodic conferences between high-ranking Democratic and Republican party spokesmen.

Rather than seeking to arrive at bipartisan agreements by meetings between party leaders, the Truman administration relied much more heavily upon other individuals whose task was to further two-party co-operation in the foreign policy field. Earlier we called attention to the roles of John Foster Dulles and John Sherman Cooper; these gentlemen sought to achieve bipartisan collaboration toward certain foreign policy problems arising during the Truman administration. Dulles took over almost complete responsibility for drafting a Japanese peace treaty acceptable to both Democrats and Republicans. Despite Dulles' success in creating bipartisan support for this treaty, as a general rule little success has been achieved in using such individuals as

Dulles and Cooper to provide the desired liaison between the political parties. Leading members of the GOP publicly criticized the Truman administration's reliance upon these individuals on the ground that the Administration ought to work through existing liaison channels, principally through congressional committees and the recognized leadership of the minority party. Typical of the comments from leading Republicans were those by Senator Watkins, who said, "Naming an appointee who has no direct contact with and who doesn't know the wishes of Republicans in the Senate doesn't make real bipartisan foreign policy" (13, Apr. 7, 1950). Similarly, in the early weeks of the Eisenhower administration Democrats gave a cool reception to the suggestion by Secretary of State Dulles that a high-ranking Democrat be appointed as an "adviser" to the State Department for the purpose of promoting two-party co-operation in foreign affairs. The suggestion was dropped when the Democrats failed to endorse it. The opposition party preferred to utilize existing legislative and political channels whenever an exchange of viewpoints became desirable (6, Nov. 24, 1954, dispatch by William S. White).

Each of the avenues of communication between the two parties alluded to here—legislative committees, political leaders, and selected individuals—has certain advantages and disadvantages which we shall later discuss more fully.

Party Spokesmen As Negotiators and Observers

A fourth practice associated with bipartisanship in American foreign relations is the use of congressmen as negotiators and observers at international conferences.[3] The Roosevelt administration followed this custom during the Second

[3] Data made available to the author by the Department of State indicate that in the period 1944–50 congressmen participated in a total of thirty-four international conferences. In addition, they attended numerous foreign ministers meetings and sessions of the United Nations as observers and participants.

World War when it sent congressmen to a number of international conferences, the most important being the 1945 San Francisco Conference on International Organization. After the war, Senators Connally and Vandenberg devoted months to negotiating the Axis satellite peace treaties. Having participated in the wearisome negotiations of these treaties, the two senators were in a position to support the Administration's claim that unsatisfactory as these documents were, they were the best obtainable under the circumstances (11, Chap. 16).

The case for utilizing congressmen as negotiators and observers at international conferences has been summarized by Fleming:

> When powerful Senate leaders act as negotiators of a treaty they acquire a paternal interest in the document and are likely to defend it vigorously. . . . Other Senators, too, are likely to look upon the treaty as made by capable, friendly hands and therefore to be attacked with much more restraint [5, p. 27].

Clearly such a practice is inconsistent with the American doctrine of checks and balances. Senator Vandenberg, for example, admitted that when he became a delegate to international conferences he was "not a free agent" after he returned to the Senate "to function in my Congressional capacity." But in spite of this fact, Vandenberg felt that such participation had been "indispensable in the initial stages" of the search for peace in the postwar era (11, pp. 330–31).

Among the practices associated with a bipartisan approach to foreign relations, the custom of sending representatives of the opposition party to international conferences has the greatest weight of tradition behind it. Furthermore, no practice is perhaps so suitable for creating the impression abroad of solidarity within the government. The practice has the twofold virtue of demonstrating to foreign governments that both parties are united in support of decisions reached and of virtually guaranteeing that agreements reached at such conferences will in fact be supported by rank-and-file party members at home. The principal limitation upon the use of this procedure, however, lies in the fact that comparatively few foreign policy problems are settled by international conferences. Outstanding success was achieved in attaining unified governmental policy toward such problems as the UN Charter, the North Atlantic Treaty, the Japanese treaty, and other treaties of mutual defense in the postwar period. But this technique was not adaptable to such problems as the Greek-Turkish aid program, the Chinese civil war, the Mutual Defense Assistance Program, the Middle Eastern crisis, and the issue of high tariffs versus reciprocal trade. To a lesser extent it is also limited by the realization that such a technique is substantially at variance with the principle of separation of powers and that it may impinge upon the President's leadership in the foreign policy field.

THE PRICE OF AMBIGUITY

Beyond the belief shared by most party members that unity should prevail in the sphere of foreign relations, there is little agreement upon the exact meaning of the term "bipartisanship." Among its several important and reasonably distinct meanings—placing the national interest ahead of party advantage, consultation in the stage of policy formulation, liaison channels acceptable to both parties, and the use of party spokesmen in negotiations—little attention has been devoted to the question of which of these requirements are indispensable to the achievement of bipartisanship and which are ancillary. The problem was succinctly outlined by Senator Ferguson (Republican of Michigan) when he observed on the floor of the Senate:

Many men in this body are thoroughly dissatisfied with the way bipartisan foreign policy operates.

. . . The very concept of bipartisan policy seems to have been left purposely vague. . . . There have been no simple rules or understandings by which bipartisan action is to be guided. Bipartisan foreign policy calls on both parties to unify their actions on matters of foreign policy. Yet there are no rules and no machinery to determine how this unity is to be achieved and operated.

. . . Men in the parties must know what is expected of them. When action is taken, they must feel confident that it is according to rules and agreements which they recognize to be a fair basis for bipartisan relations.

. . . So long as the rules are non-existent or vague, there will be loopholes and excuses to tempt men in both parties to make partisan capital out of American foreign policy [1, May 5, 1950, p. 6499].

The absence of accepted rules and procedures for implementing the principle of bipartisanship has produced several detrimental consequences in the search for unity in foreign affairs. Differences of opinion have arisen among party members over which foreign policy decisions were, and which were not, bipartisan—a condition well illustrated by the recurrent controversy over the degree of bipartisanship that characterized the Truman administration's Far Eastern policies. In the absence of a clear understanding, each party has naturally arrogated to itself the right to determine which policies were subject to public criticism. As long as the term "bipartisanship" remains nebulous, this condition will continue to pose a formidable barrier to unity in foreign affairs.

Moreover, ambiguity has bred endless bickering between

the two parties over the degree to which existing machinery and procedures were adequate to realize two-party co-operation in the foreign policy field. During the tenure of the Truman administration, Republicans complained repeatedly that the Republican congressional leadership was not being kept informed concerning important foreign policy developments, a criticism echoed later by the Democrats when they accused the Eisenhower administration of taking steps before adequate consultation was had with Democratic leaders. Lacking a basic consensus over what is implied by the concept of bipartisanship, it has been difficult for the party in power to avoid improvising procedures to achieve unity that may or may not actually contribute to closer two-party co-operation in foreign affairs.

We conclude, then, that one major determinant of bipartisanship in foreign affairs is the extent to which both parties are agreed upon the practices required to achieve the unity desired. Clearly there must be sufficient flexibility to permit experimentation and adaptation as new circumstances arise at home and abroad. Still it would appear highly desirable to have agreement upon certain practices as normal, to be followed whenever circumstances favor their use. Until there is such agreement, efforts to follow the bipartisan principle are likely to remain erratic and, at times, highly ineffectual.

2. *The Nature of the Foreign Policy Problem*

A second important determinant of two-party agreement in foreign affairs concerns the nature of the foreign policy problem toward which a bipartisan approach is being followed. In earlier pages we have suggested that some foreign policy problems are more amenable to bipartisan approach than others. Let us now identify and explore these foreign policy questions.

As we consider which problems have been conducive to a bipartisan solution and which have not, three specific desiderata stand out. These are: whether the external problem has been of a crisis or noncrisis nature, whether it has had substantial implications for domestic policy, and whether it has raised constitutional questions, especially the issue of executive versus congressional control over the military establishment.

In the light of case studies presented in earlier chapters, it seems hardly necessary to prove that foreign policy crises are not ideally suited for solution upon a bipartisan basis. The key element lacking during a crisis is time for the usual procedures associated with bipartisan foreign policy to operate. Thus with the Greek-Turkish aid program and the Chinese civil war, there may have been a degree of unity but there was little bipartisanship. The distinction here is fundamental. Unity may prevail during a crisis largely because both parties are aware of the urgency and delicacy of the diplomatic situation and of the consequences of creating disunity when an external threat exists. Crises —war being the best example—promote the widespread feeling that all parties and factions should close ranks behind the President's leadership. Pressure for agreement comes from external events and not from bipartisan machinery. When such agreement emerges, it is often not regarded as a bipartisan agreement so much as acquiescence.

To state this distinction differently, as our definition of bipartisanship set forth in Chapter 1 and followed throughout this study implies, two interrelated but relatively distinct ideas are suggested by the term. It envisions an end—unity —along with certain (usually unspecified) means to reach the end. Unity in the face of crises meets the first of these definitions but not the second. Such unity is negative rather than positive. It is not the product of a joint collaborative effort, but of a political truce inspired by the hour of danger. It is a unity that has little to sustain it beyond the fear of the consequences of disunity. Genuinely bipartisan agreements, on the other hand, may be expected to endure even after the danger that might have prompted them is over, because they are rooted in a rational discussion of the issues and in a belief that a given course of action accords with the national interest.

The second element in the foreign policy problem that may determine whether or not bipartisan co-operation results is whether the problem has ramifications into the area of domestic affairs. In the mid-twentieth century all foreign policy issues touch domestic matters to some extent, so that the distinction here must obviously be one of degree. Nevertheless, when an issue in the foreign policy area has an evident and substantial bearing upon domestic policy—as with the issue of tariff versus reciprocal trade, foreign aid spending, and the size and composition of the armed forces —then the difficulty of arriving at bipartisan understandings is greatly increased. Not only is the difficulty increased, but the desirability of bipartisan co-operation may be greatly reduced, if not altogether eliminated. In evaluating the extent to which bipartisanship in foreign affairs is possible, it must be remembered that the case for two-party co-operation rests in large measure upon a myth. Myths of course are not always false; and in many cases they must be preserved irrespective of whether they are true or false. The myth alluded to here is that the problems confronting the nation may be clearly divided into foreign and domestic questions, and that while the former must be approached on a bipartisan basis, the latter are properly left to the interplay of partisan influences. Since later pages, especially in Chapter 8, will deal with the relation between foreign and domestic issues in greater detail, we shall not consider it further here.

The third characteristic of the foreign policy problem that influences efforts to apply the bipartisan principle is whether the problem raises troublesome constitutional issues. Throughout the postwar period the chief issue of this kind has been executive versus congressional control over the military establishment. On three significant occasions since World War II, much time and energy has been consumed debating this question before the government could arrive at bipartisan agreements. Such debates occurred when President Truman committed American troops to resist aggression in Korea, when Truman dismissed General Mac-Arthur from his command, and when the Great Debate raged in Congress over American defense policy. The precise boundary between executive and congressional control over the armed forces remains today, as in the past, highly indistinct. No doubt the situation allows adaptability and experimentation as new problems arise requiring the use of the armed services (7).

Nevertheless, the absence of a clearly defined boundary between executive and legislative authority in the foreign policy field affords a standing invitation for each branch to attempt to expand its powers at the expense of the other. Institutional competition becomes almost unavoidable as specific foreign policy problems arise that require at least an *ad hoc* decision on the proper sphere of each branch. Moreover, a debate on fundamental constitutional issues can create an atmosphere of suspicion and recrimination within the government that is well-nigh fatal to the realization of two-party co-operation toward external affairs. Little doubt exists, for example, that two such disputes in the first half of 1950—the controversy over the dismissal of General Mac-Arthur and over American defense strategy—did much to eliminate all remaining vestiges of bipartisanship from the diplomacy of the Truman administration.

3. The President's Role in Foreign Affairs

We turn now to consider the importance of a third determinant of bipartisanship in American foreign relations—the dominant position of the President. Attempts to follow the bipartisan principle must take place within a context of executive leadership in the foreign policy field. The Constitution, as now interpreted through evolving usage and tradition, places responsibility in the hands of the President for the security of the nation. Always his first consideration must be the preservation of the nation; all other goals, bipartisanship included, are secondary. Sometimes he may try to preserve national security by seeking maximum unity in foreign affairs. But the President is necessarily and inevitably the final judge of when bipartisanship or any other technique of foreign policy accords with the national interest. He must evaluate all the means at his disposal in the light of the ultimate goal.

This suggests that one of the implications sometimes conveyed by the idea of bipartisan foreign policy—that decisions in foreign affairs can be reached through a kind of meeting of the minds among the major participants—may have little foundation either in American constitutional tradition or in reality. Certainly an incumbent administration can be offered advice and guidance by the opposition party; and consultations between the parties can bring to light valuable suggestions for policy. But in the last analysis the President must decide whether or not to follow a bipartisan approach. The question of who should take the initiative for securing bipartisan co-operation has arisen from time to time in the postwar period, and it cannot be said that there is a clear consensus on this point. The predominant view, however, is that the President should "invite" the opposition party to collaborate. Frequently circumstances will dictate that he choose the course most conducive to unity within the government and the nation as a whole. Yet he cannot permit a concern for unity to interfere with his superior and ultimate constitutional responsibility.

What are the circumstances that may persuade a President to ignore, or to use only sparingly, the bipartisan approach to foreign relations?

WHEN A FOREIGN POLICY CRISIS IMPENDS

Earlier we have referred to the difficulty of approaching external crises upon a bipartisan basis. Since bipartisanship usually demands that consultations between the parties be held prior to the adoption of policy, on several occasions since World War II the President has been forced to chose between adherence to the bipartisan principle and taking prompt and vigorous action to deal with an external crisis. Examples include the Greek crisis in 1947, the Berlin blockade, the Communist attack against South Korea, and the British-French-Israeli invasion of Egypt in 1956. Confronted with this painful choice, the President has acted after little or no consultation with spokesmen for the opposition party. Unilateral executive action is at variance with the prevailing conception of bipartisanship, but on occasion it is unavoidable unless the security of the nation is to be jeopardized.

WHEN A CONSTITUTIONAL IMPASSE IS THREATENED

Preceding chapters have cited several instances in which constitutional conflict between the President and Congress has seriously interfered with efforts to follow the bipartisan principle. Although the President cannot and should not prevent Congress from debating issues in the foreign policy field, he cannot permit a controversy between himself and legislature to undermine his leadership in foreign relations. A constitutional impasse is no substitute for policy. The consequences of permitting it to become so are well illustrated by the quandary facing President James Buchanan late in 1860 and early in 1861. Buchanan was torn between conflicting views of his constitutional powers. On the one hand, he believed that the states could not legally secede from the Union; on the other hand, he was convinced that the national government could do nothing about it if they did. The result was that the Union disintegrated while he attempted to resolve this constitutional conundrum.

This example from domestic affairs has clear application to foreign affairs. In the light of the Constitution and historical precedent, the President is charged with preserving national security. Congress, it is true, possesses certain fairly well defined powers in foreign affairs; in addition, there still exists a kind of constitutional no man's land in which the exact scope of executive and legislative authority remains undefined. The latter condition is well illustrated by the recurrent controversies that have taken place within the government throughout the postwar period over the use of the armed forces to carry out diplomatic objectives. Thus, as we observed in Chapter 4, spokesmen for the Truman administration emphasized throughout the Great Debate on American defense strategy that the President did not "need" a congressional resolution authorizing him to commit American troops to the European defense system, but that such a resolution would be welcomed "in the interest of unity." The Truman administration, that is to say, was not prepared to abandon a commitment deemed vital to the nation's interests in foreign affairs merely because of possible legislative disapproval. Charged with the responsibility of protecting the vital interests of the country, the President felt compelled to adopt certain policies and to leave Congress with the alternative of either accepting them or of repudiating them at the risk of impairing the prestige and leadership of the United States before the entire world.

WHEN SECRECY AND DELICACY IN NEGOTIATIONS ARE REQUIRED

"The President," said John Marshall as early as 1800, "is the sole organ of the nation in its external relations, and its sole representative with foreign nations" (10). This view was affirmed over a century later in the classic case, *United States* v. *Curtiss-Wright Export Corporation* (1936), when the Supreme Court stated that in foreign affairs "the President alone has the power to speak or listen as a representative of the nation." Congress, said the Court, "must often accord to the President a degree of discretion and freedom from statutory restriction which would not be admissible were domestic affairs alone involved" (10). As the sole medium through which the United States communicates with foreign countries, the President has the power to decide when, where, and how to conduct negotiations with other countries. Negotiations often involve delicate matters of state and must frequently be conducted in secret. During World War II opposition party members were not included in the major wartime conferences held among the Allies, such as those held at Yalta and Potsdam in 1945. Similarly, during the Korean War the Truman administration made no notable effort to include Republicans in discussions within the government leading to a cease-fire. Again, the Truman administration refused for an extended period of time to disclose publicly the number of American divisions scheduled for assignment to NATO, in spite of the fact that Republicans regarded such information as necessary for a bipartisan consideration of the issue of national defense.

The same limitation hampered efforts to achieve harmony between the two parties toward Far Eastern problems. Leading Republicans repeatedly accused the Truman administration of withholding information regarding American foreign policy toward Nationalist China, a charge with considerable foundation in fact, though distorted for partisan ends. Yet even Senator Vandenberg, who stated on several occasions that bipartisanship had not been followed toward Far Eastern problems, nevertheless recognized the President's dilemma. A public disclosure of Nationalist China's conditions, he wrote, would have "precipitated and underscored a discussion of Chiang's weaknesses and would have nullified any remnant of his prestige" (11, p. 527).

In considering the feasibility of bipartisan co-operation in foreign affairs, it must always be remembered that the State Department, alone among executive departments, has the clear legal duty to withhold information from Congress when the public interest requires it. At the time of its establishment the State Department was charged with conducting foreign affairs "in such manner as the President of the United States shall, from time to time order and instruct" (9, p. 14). When release of such information is deemed by the President to be injurious to national security, or when it can be given only to a limited number of participants in the foreign policy process, this fact will necessarily hinder maximum co-operation between the parties in the realm of foreign affairs.

When Congress Bears No Responsibility for Contemplated Action

Another obstacle to bipartisan foreign policy derives from the fact that under the Constitution, Congress bears little or no responsibility for certain kinds of action in the area of external affairs. Since we discussed congressional powers in the foreign policy field in Chapter 1, we shall merely summarize them here. The Senate must of course ratify treaties and confirm diplomatic appointments. Congress as a whole must declare war, furnish money for conducting foreign affairs, determine the size and composition of the military establishment, and generally oversee the conduct of the government in all spheres through its investigative powers. But toward numerous foreign policy problems, Congress bears no *direct* responsibility and has little or no power to determine courses of action. Well-known examples in the postwar period include the Marshall mission to China; military missions that have visited Greece, the Near East, Formosa, and other trouble spots; and the responsibility of recognizing foreign governments, particularly Red China.

Experience in the postwar period indicates that when the bipartisan principle is followed toward problems such as these, one of two consequences may be expected: either Congress will approve, expressly or tacitly, the President's action, without at the same time assuming any responsibility for the success or failure of such action; or it will approve the action and as a price for doing so demand that it be permitted to intrude into an area traditionally regarded as within the jurisdiction of the executive branch. The Marshall mission may be regarded as an example of the former alternative. As we noted in Chapter 5, there is no evidence that Republicans opposed American mediation in the Chinese civil war; at least no concerted opposition to that policy was voiced until it had become apparent that the mission was a failure. Yet Republicans as a whole have adopted the view of Senator Taft that the GOP bore no responsibility for the "wild-goose chase for a Communist-Nationalist coalition in China" (6, Feb. 13, 1948).

The second alternative is illustrated by the problem involved in the recognition of Red China by the United States. Recognition is constitutionally an executive function. By the latter part of 1950, leading Republicans were demanding that the Truman administration pledge itself not to recognize Red China and to oppose her admission into the United Nations. Such a pledge, said Senator Styles Bridges (Republican of New Hampshire) was "the absolute minimum for compromise." He was convinced that there could be no "bipartisan unity on any policy short of that" (12, Dec. 10, 1950). The Truman administration had to choose between accepting these Republican demands as a price for bipartisanship or of rejecting them at the risk of precipitating disunity at home. In this instance it followed the former course. The implications of such a choice for American foreign relations will be discussed more fully in the next chapter.

References

1. *Congressional Record* (daily edition).
2. *Congressional Record,* Vol. 97.
3. Corwin, Edward S., *The President's Control of Foreign Relations.* Princeton, N.J.: Princeton University Press, 1917. A lengthy and scholarly treatment of the President's role in foreign relations.
4. Dulles, John Foster, *A Peace Treaty in the Making.* San Francisco: Japanese Peace Conference, September 4–8, 1951. A brief but useful treatment of the Japanese peace treaty (especially pages 42–45).
5. Fleming, D. F., *Treaty Veto of the American Senate.* New York: G. P. Putnam's Sons, 1930.
6. *New York Times.*
7. Richards, James P., "The House of Representatives in Foreign Affairs," *Annals of the American Academy of Political and Social Science,* 289 (September, 1953), 66–72.

8. Senate Banking and Currency Committee, *Hearings on Anglo-American Financial Agreement,* 79th Congress, 2nd Session, March 5–20, 1946.
9. Stuart, Graham H., *The Department of State.* New York: The Macmillan Company, 1949. Chapter 2 discusses the establishment of the Department of State.
10. *United States* v. *Curtiss-Wright Export Corporation,* 299 U.S. 304 (1936).
11. Vandenberg, Arthur H., Jr. (ed.), *The Private Papers of Senator Vandenberg.* Boston: Houghton Mifflin Company, 1952.
12. *Washington Post.*
13. *Watertown Democrat-Times* (New York).

EIGHT

Determinants of Bipartisanship (II)

In this chapter we continue our analysis of the factors that affect bipartisan co-operation in foreign affairs. Let us now examine three additional categories of such factors: those relating to the organization and operation of Congress, those implicit in the nature and function of the American party system, and those associated with the personal and psychological environment within which the bipartisan principle is being applied.

4. Congressional Organization and Procedure

The Constitution divides responsibility for the control of foreign relations between the President and Congress. As we have seen earlier, this is not an equal division of responsibility. Tradition and precedent in American diplomatic history have established the President in the pre-eminent position vis-à-vis Congress. Still, the Senate retains its right to ratify treaties and confirm appointments, and Congress must obviously co-operate in any foreign policy undertaking that requires appropriations or changes the military establishment. Congressional committees may investigate particular foreign policy problems; members may make speeches that can have international repercussions; resolutions can express the opinion of Congress on vital issues, even though they have no binding force upon the President. As the Truman administration discovered, congressional opinion makers are often able to muster powerful followings both inside and outside the government to support their views.

Throughout American history, resourceful presidents have discovered means of evading legislative checks upon their power. Executive agreements may be used by a president to by-pass the treaty-ratifying power of the Senate. A president may utilize his power as Commander in Chief to nullify the power of Congress to declare war. A strategically timed foreign policy speech may commit the nation to a given policy and leave Congress little option but to approve it or risk serious damage to the nation's prestige.

Public officials and students of American government have come to recognize, however, that effective diplomacy, especially in an era of international tension, requires cooperation and harmony between the two branches of the government instead of conflict. Opposition party members usually recognize as fully as the incumbent administration the necessity for collaboration in pursuit of common goals if governmental paralysis in the face of a totalitarian threat is to be avoided. In the postwar period this realization has led to the creation of new channels of liaison between both branches and to more frequent use of these and existing channels. Both the House Foreign Affairs and Senate Foreign Relations committees, for example, have established subcommittees to facilitate the exchange of information between themselves and the State Department. Congressman James P. Richards, chairman of the former committee in 1955–56, wrote as follows in 1953:

These subcommittees approximate the major divisions of the Department of State. Four of them are geographic and five functional subcommittees. One of the most helpful signs in collaboration between the executive and legislative branches has been a greater use of the subcommittees. Today the Assistant Secretaries [of State] invariably seek out Members of the appropriate subcommittee and arrange a meeting to impart the latest developments in their particular fields of responsibility. This approach has provided a tremendous sense of participation even though Congressmen may be listeners. It builds up a mutual confidence on the part of both branches [19, p. 71].

The postwar emphasis within Congress itself upon providing more effective liaison procedures between the two branches has had its counterpart in certain actions taken by the executive branch. Recognizing the increasingly important role that Congress has assumed in foreign affairs since World War II, the State Department has established an Office of Congressional Relations whose purpose is to promote co-operation between the executive and legislative branches. Such an office had been proposed by the Hoover Commission in 1949 when it recommended "a coordinated program of Congressional liaison under the supervision of an Assistant Secretary with no other duties." The Office of Congressional Relations has worked closely with Congress, most particularly with the Senate Foreign Relations and House Foreign Affairs committees, to arrive at mutually satisfactory policy decisions. Both formal and informal techniques of liaison are utilized. The former include such practices as dealing with vast quantities of congressional mail that raise questions about foreign policy, appearing before both public and secret congressional hearings, and rendering assistance to congressmen and committees planning travel abroad. Informal techniques include meeting with small groups of legislators and briefing them on global problems, holding discussions with members of Congress who are interested in particular foreign policy problems, and supplying information to committees and individuals within Congress.

Another practice of the executive branch is to hold periodic conferences at the White House at which the President discusses world problems with legislative and party leaders. President Eisenhower has frequently utilized such conferences to create widespread support for his policies, domestic as well as foreign. The conferences are no doubt also valuable for permitting an exchange of viewpoints on fundamental issues.

White House conferences, however, also have limitations as means of achieving bipartisan co-operation in foreign affairs. Some are political limitations, which we shall examine more fully in Chapter 9. Let us note here that such conferences in most instances have been concerned with immediate, day-to-day problems in foreign affairs rather than with long-range, basic objectives. Although White House conferences on Nationalist China or the Middle East or Soviet Russia's acquisition of the atomic bomb contribute to bipartisan co-operation, they do not get around to considering the over-all direction in which American foreign policy is moving or to raising questions about its basic assumptions.[1] As a result, these conferences have done little to overcome one of the main criticisms leveled against American foreign policy in the postwar period both by informed foreigners and by commentators at home—namely, too often foreign policy has been made piecemeal as specific problems have arisen in world affairs. While seemingly satisfactory decisions may be made to meet such challenges, the general direction of policy in the long run may drift, at times even running contrary to the national interest. In

[1] Examples of such conferences include those held by the Truman administration during the Greek crisis of 1947 and in the early days of the Korean War, and those held by the Eisenhower administration in 1955 and 1956, in regard to the Geneva Conference and the Middle Eastern crisis, respectively.

brief, foreign policy in the United States has been living a hand-to-mouth existence, approaching concrete problems largely upon a basis of expediency. That this charge has considerable merit can hardly be denied. The reasons for it are complex, and it would not be directly relevant to this study to treat them at length. Suffice it to say that bipartisan techniques utilized within both the executive and legislative branches have often done little to surmount this tendency.

Much, therefore, remains to be done if more effective liaison between the White House and Capitol Hill is to be achieved. Formidable difficulties remain to be overcome. Among them the following continue to be troublesome.

Congressional Committees and Foreign Affairs

We have already observed that as a rule, legislative proposals concerned with foreign policy questions fall within the province of the House Foreign Affairs and Senate Foreign Relations committees, which in 1957 consisted of thirty-two and fifteen members, respectively. During the last decade these have been extremely popular committee assignments. Members of these committees normally possess greater seniority than is required for membership on less important committees; and while it is true that seniority is not always equivalent to political influence, individuals on these committees probably also possess greater influence in their party councils than the average member of Congress. Within recent years politically influential members of Congress have sometimes deliberately requested assignment to these committees concerned with vital foreign policy issues.

Nevertheless, there still sometimes exists a considerable gulf between the members of these committees and the party organizations in Congress. This gulf is well illustrated by the change in the composition of the Senate Foreign Relations Committee occasioned by the retirement of Senator

Walter F. George (Democrat of Georgia) in 1956. Senator George had been the ranking Democrat on this committee, and his voice also carried great weight in the deliberations of the Democratic party organization within Congress. Upon his retirement, the octogenarian Senator Theodore F. Green (Democrat of Rhode Island) became the new chairman. Senator Green's seniority was one of the highest in the history of Congress. Yet a number of senators many years younger than he exercised vastly more influence in the deliberations of the Democratic party. This fact confronted the Eisenhower administration with a problem that has hindered efforts to follow the bipartisan principle ever since the Second World War. When the executive branch consults with members of the foreign affairs committees in each house, it has no guarantee that it is consulting with either the best informed or politically most influential groups within Congress. Whatever decisions emerge as a result of such consultations therefore may or may not receive the support of the opposition party leadership and rank-and-file party members. And if the President consults the acknowledged party leaders within Congress, he risks making the bipartisan process cumbersome and time-consuming, thereby magnifying the danger that the nation will be slow to meet challenges abroad and that confidential information will be made public. A further obstacle to broadening consultations beyond the two foreign affairs committees is the problem of seeming to by-pass these committees in order to work more closely with individuals whose political influence is deemed to be greater.[2]

So long as Senator Vandenberg remained active in behalf of bipartisanship, no significant difficulty was encountered

---

[2] This latter point was stressed by State Department officials with whom the writer discussed the problem of bipartisan foreign policy during the summer of 1951.

in bridging the gap between the two committees and the opposition party's political leadership. Vandenberg's unique contribution to bipartisanship was his effectiveness as the connecting link between these groups. He was the ranking Republican and, during the Eightieth Congress, the chairman of the Senate Foreign Relations Committee. As his party's acknowledged elder statesman in foreign affairs, he possessed sufficient political influence virtually to guarantee that agreements worked out between his committee and executive officials would be supported by a decisive majority within the Republican party. After Vandenberg's retirement, there was no other Republican to play his crucial role. Senator Taft was undoubtedly the outstanding GOP leader in Congress, but he lacked Senator Vandenberg's knowledge and perceptive judgment about foreign policy issues. The other members of the Foreign Relations Committee did not carry notable weight in Republican party councils. Not until after the Eisenhower administration took office in 1952 did there emerge an individual whose legislative duties were in foreign affairs and who was at the same time capable of rallying leaders of his own party behind decisions reached. That man was Senator Walter F. George, Democrat of Georgia (24).

The two foreign relations committees of Congress continue to be the usual channel through which the executive and legislative branches communicate. But because of the increasing complexity of world affairs, the trend since World War II has been for a larger and larger number of congressional committees to be concerned with foreign policy issues. One authority reports that during the Eighty-second Congress, "At least fifty public laws enacted in that session in the field of foreign relations were reported out of a committee other than Foreign Relations and Foreign Affairs." He observes that three-quarters of the total membership of Congress served on these other committees, or "over 300 members of the House and about 75 members of the Senate who were not on their respective foreign relations committees" (4, p. 85). Here we can do no more than suggest the almost infinite variety of problems with which such committees are concerned.

Within recent years the United States has sought to encourage economic contacts among nations. When legislative measures contemplate changes in tariff regulations, the Finance Committee in the Senate and the Ways and Means Committee in the House are concerned with adjusting tariff rates to carry out the desired end. Similarly, efforts to amend the treaty-making process (as envisioned, for example, by the "Bricker amendment") are referred to the Senate Judiciary Committee. The two Agriculture committees have to consider any plan having a bearing upon domestic agriculture, such as sending American surplus commodities into foreign markets or contributing foodstuffs to areas where famine exists. Almost every major foreign policy undertaking in the postwar period has come at least indirectly within the province of the Armed Services committees in the Senate and House, particularly those projects such as NATO that envision long-range and fairly substantial troop commitments. Loans to foreign governments are within the province of the Banking and Currency committees of each house. Proposals affecting the American merchant marine come within the compass of the Committee on Interstate and Foreign Commerce in the Senate and the Committee on Merchant Marine and Fisheries in the House.

These are some of the substantive fields that are covered by congressional committees other than the Foreign Relations and Foreign Affairs committees. In respect to unified governmental policy, three important congressional committees must be consulted. They are the Appropriations committees in each chamber and the Rules Committee in the House. In Chapter 3, dealing with the Marshall Plan, the key role of the Appropriations committees was discussed. Theoretically, these committees do not determine policy; they merely decide upon the appropriation necessary to implement policy. Such a conception of the role of these committees, however, can be very misleading. Time and time again in the postwar period the Appropriations committees have substantially altered policy previously determined by congressional action. These committees can substantially change the objectives of a program by reducing prior legislative authorizations, not to mention original executive budget requests, considerably below the level deemed necessary to carry out the program. Until there is some attempt to draw these two powerful committees more closely into the bipartisan process before they are presented with an agreed-upon program that they had no voice in formulating, there will always remain the risk that proposals worked out by the Executive in conjunction with other committees will be modified, if not emasculated, by the Appropriations committees.

Another group within Congress that has played little part in the bipartisan process since World War II is the Rules Committee of the House. This is considered to be the most important committee on Capitol Hill. Its members tend to be among the most experienced and politically influential legislators in Congress. Yet throughout the postwar period the Rules Committee has seldom been consulted in the formative stage of policy making. The consequences of this neglect were clearly demonstrated in 1951 when the Truman administration sought legislative authorization to send American surplus wheat to India, a move designed to gain the good will of India and of neutralist areas generally. Opposition to this proposal by the Rules Committee delayed passage of the requested legislation for over six weeks, with the result that Soviet Russia offered wheat before the program was approved by Congress (6, pp. 233–37).

Clearly, then, the existence of a number of committees in Congress with jurisdiction extending into foreign affairs constitutes a serious difficulty for bipartisan procedures. This problem may be partially overcome by the use of joint hearings, such as those held from time to time by the Senate Foreign Relations and Armed Services committees. But joint hearings are not a complete answer to this problem, chiefly because the committees are themselves far from enthusiastic about joint hearings. Most committees prefer to follow their own schedule and to go about their legislative business in their own way. The widening jurisdiction of congressional committees is a product of the variety and complexity of problems confronting the United States in the twentieth century both at home and abroad.

LEGISLATIVE DELAY AND FOREIGN AFFAIRS

It has been emphasized repeatedly throughout this study that a bipartisan approach to foreign relations must operate within a constitutional framework of executive leadership and initiative in the foreign policy field. Certain kinds of undertakings in foreign affairs necessitate congressional approval. Outstanding examples in the postwar period include the Marshall Plan, programs of arms aid to foreign countries, the Point Four Program, and reciprocal trade and tariff legislation. In these instances the executive branch has had no alternative but to work closely with Congress to translate executive proposals into policies.

There have been other instances, however, in which extended co-operation between the President and Congress has not been mandatory but optional. The President has requested congressional concurrence in a proposed undertaking in foreign affairs in order to achieve maximum unity within the government. When unity is desired, collaboration between the branches of the government doubtless contributes to that unity. Yet there is a limit to such optional collaboration, beyond which it may jeopardize national security. External crises may pose the familiar dilemma to an incumbent administration of either seeking close collaboration with Congress in a desire to generate wide bipartisan support for the policy contemplated, or neglecting such collaboration at the risk of disunity because external events require prompt and decisive action by the Chief Executive. The danger always exists that undue delay by Congress in considering executive proposals may detract from the effectiveness of the nation's diplomacy. The leisurely pace by which Congress acted on the Marshall Plan in 1947-48, for example, gave the impression abroad (however erroneously) that it was indifferent to Europe's increasingly acute economic distress. Similarly, the protracted debate in Congress that accompanied President Truman's proposal to send surplus wheat to India virtually negated any benefit that the United States hoped to gain by cultivating Indian good will.

Perhaps the most forceful illustration of the point being made here concerns the criticisms directed by Republicans against the Truman administration's decision to commit American troops in Korea without a declaration of war by Congress. President Truman did not ask Congress for a declaration of war, even though such a request, had it come in the first week or two of the conflict, would doubtless have bound Democrats and Republicans much more closely together in a joint foreign policy venture. That the Administration was concerned with the need for unity in this instance was indicated by the revival of consultations between leaders of both parties before the President publicly announced American intervention (7, June 27, 1950, p. 9365). Subsequent debate in Congress clearly indicated that the President's action had overwhelming support in both parties. The prevailing sentiment in Congress (even with those Republicans and a few Democrats who blamed the Truman administration for the Korean War) was voiced by Senator Knowland (Republican of California) when he said that the President "should have the overwhelming support of all Americans, regardless of party affiliation" (7, June 27, 1950, pp. 9363–64). This was a clear case in which the advantages to be gained from bipartisan procedures were outweighed by the necessity for prompt and decisive executive action. In the President's view, and he alone could make the decision, the likelihood of a protracted debate in Congress was plainly a barrier to utilizing the bipartisan principle.

In concluding this section on the difficulties for bipartisanship posed by congressional organization and procedure, we may agree with one authority on Congress that, "It is only recently that the co-ordinate and even affirmative role of Congress has been recognized in this tremendously important field [foreign affairs]." Merely recognizing Congress' role, however, will not solve the difficult problems alluded to in this chapter. Nor does it help materially to suggest, as this same authority does, that "ways and means must often be found whereby the responsibility for policy formulation may itself be shared with the legislative branch" (11, p. 11). Ideally, foreign policy decisions ought to represent more of a collaborative effort between the branches than has sometimes occurred in the past. But liaison between the President and Congress, especially when not required by the Constitution, is acceptable only when it meets one standard, and that standard is whether co-ordination contributes to the national security. If a procedure does not, it must yield before the obligation of the Executive to manage foreign affairs in whatever way will best promote the national interest.

5. Limiting Factors in the Party System

No group of factors likely to contribute toward unity or disunity in foreign affairs is perhaps more important than those associated with the American political system. As we shall see more fully below, the weight of these factors is generally against bipartisan co-operation in the foreign policy field. This does not mean that unity cannot emerge during periods of crisis and that it cannot be maintained for short periods of time; nor does it mean that bipartisanship cannot survive toward certain particular types of foreign policy problems for many months or even years. The influences present in the nature and operation of the American party system that predispose against bipartisanship tend to be long range and largely subsurface in nature. Consequently, they relate in most instances more to the problem of maintaining unity than to generating it when specific problems arise in the diplomatic field.

Before we examine these negative influences in detail, however, let us first note certain characteristics of the party system which contribute favorably to two-party agreement in foreign affairs. At the outset, we may refer to the role of ideology in American politics. Few great issues divide the two major parties of the United States. Compared with other democracies throughout the world, party battles in this country are not fought over creeds, philosophies, or ideologies. National elections are much more concerned with concrete problems confronting the nation at home and abroad, the record of the incumbent administration, and the personalities of the candidates. However much party orators may point with pride to the party's "distinctive principles," the fact is that the party platforms are more alike than dissimilar. When differences can be discovered, they tend to be differences of emphasis and degree rather than of principle. There is a substantial amount of bipartisanship at all times in American politics. Lacking a tradition of sharp cleavage over public issues, the parties accommodate themselves to agreement on most matters of fundamental policy. The postwar emphasis on bipartisan foreign policy, then, is consonant with the general similarity in the positions taken by the major parties on domestic policy questions.

Moreover, the absence of strict party discipline is a factor that aids in securing unity between the parties toward foreign affairs (although, as we shall see below, it may also constitute a barrier to unity). On the national level, and especially in Congress, party members seldom adhere rigidly to a party line when they vote on issues of policy. Members of Congress are normally much more responsive to the desires of their constituents than they are to the views expressed in their party platform. Numerous pressures can be applied in Congress by the party leadership to influence the vote of members. And whenever possible, a legislator will prefer to work harmoniously with his party leaders. But in the last analysis, members of Congress possess freedom—as much freedom as is found in any other legislative body in the world—to evaluate policy questions on their merits and to vote as judgment dictates. A striking illustration of the operation of this factor was furnished during the Eisenhower administration's first two years of office by the Republican party's floor leader in the Senate, Senator William Knowland of California, who sought on several occasions to force the Administration to pursue a more vigorous anti-Communist policy in the Far East, especially toward Red China. Yet even as floor leader, Knowland was unable to muster support for his position in the Senate and in Congress as a whole.

The two important factors that normally may be expected to favor the achievement of bipartisan co-operation in foreign affairs are the nonideological nature of American parties and the absence of strict party discipline in Congress. These positive factors, however, are offset by certain other features of the political system that militate against two-party agreement in the foreign policy sphere. These negative features are numerous and, on occasion, extremely difficult to overcome. As a group they present probably the most troublesome obstacles in the path of bipartisan co-operation. Yet to date many of them have been virtually ignored by officials seeking to achieve such co-operation and by students of American foreign policy. Because these factors are serious and have received little attention, we shall examine them in considerable detail.

Partisanship or Bipartisanship—The Theoretical Dilemma

Like Hamlet, proponents of a bipartisan foreign policy are beset by the dilemma of whether "To be, or not to be. . . ." They cannot decide whether a vigorous party system is or is not vital to the preservation of American democracy and to the American role of leadership in the free-world coalition. In theory, they reject the idea of sharp and penetrating controversy between the parties on questions of foreign policy, because it is inimical to the national interest, at least during times of global crisis. Yet, while advancing this theory, they concurrently affirm their belief in an alert and informed opposition party as fundamental to a healthy party system. The more serious the international situation, the more earnestly the advocates of bipartisanship seek the best of both worlds—the worlds of partisanship and of bipartisanship. If it is imperative that the welfare of the nation be placed above the welfare of party, it is equally necessary that the facts concerning the international situation be set forth, that mistakes be pointed out and corrected, that the record be kept straight, and that the pertinent issues be debated.

A recurrent symptom of the dichotomy here described may be seen in a curious phenomenon that has taken place within the United States since World War II. Two rather contradictory trends have been visible in the area of politico-governmental affairs. On the one hand, political scientists, joined by numerous outstanding public officials and journalists, have shown an increasing concern over the lack of responsibility and discipline characteristic of the American party system. Platforms are customarily vague, platitudinous, and ambiguous; party lines in Congress are crossed with impunity when votes are taken on serious public issues; personalities often tend to be much more important in campaigns than policy questions; frequently there is little correlation between promise and fulfillment by a victorious political party. As one means of remedying these and other defects, a committee of the American Political Science Association has proposed a sweeping set of recommendations designed to make the system a more effective instrument of representative government (1). While it would not be relevant to our study to enter into a detailed discussion of this report, we may observe simply that its over-all purpose is to strengthen the party system by moving in the direction of the British model, where a victorious party receives a mandate to carry out certain policies and where a high degree of party discipline in Parliament normally makes this task possible.

A contemporaneous development within the United States has been the unprecedented emphasis upon the principle of bipartisanship in foreign affairs. Here the stated goal is to remove foreign policy questions from the political arena. In the former movement, the basic supposition is that a dynamic political system is an integral feature of democratic government. In the latter case, the underlying assumption is that partisan controversy over one of the most vital areas of public policy is detrimental to the national interest and must therefore be eliminated. Senator Vandenberg was one of the few advocates of bipartisanship in the postwar period who recognized that this paradox existed; and he was virtually the only one who appeared to have given serious thought to the question of whether it could be resolved. In the weeks just before his death, he wrote: "I am trying to figure out whether the equally important and equally indispensable maintenance of a two-party political system does not inevitably collide with [the principle of bipartisanship in foreign affairs]" (21, p. 548).

Vandenberg left no evidence to indicate that he had resolved it, perhaps because in the final analysis it cannot be resolved; it can only be evaded. How, after all, does one reconcile the idea of a vigorous and well-disciplined party system patterned somewhat after the British model with the idea that this system must be suspended in the critically important area of foreign affairs? How is it possible to have a dynamic party system when paramount questions are to be exempted from politics?

This question has been squarely faced by very few advocates of bipartisan foreign policy. Attempts to resolve it have been made on occasion by resort to language that obscures more than it illuminates the problem. Thus the perennial phrase "politics stops at the water's edge" represents the kind of meaningless generality that disguises the difficulties in the path of bipartisan foreign policy and suggests that bipartisanship involves little more than an act of will power on the part of politicians. Frequently the phrase is used in the sense of a kind of magic formula by which it is hoped that partisanship will disappear. The phrase ignores the fact that parties are indispensable to the survival of democratic government; it in no way indicates how partisan conflict can be eliminated from the area of foreign affairs without inflicting serious damage upon the American system of government.

More than a decade's experience with the bipartisan principle clearly indicates that many political leaders do not believe in bipartisanship at all, as the term has been defined in this study. What they do believe in is an understanding whereby their party is left free to co-operate or not with the other party, so long as such co-operation advances what they conceive to be the interests of the nation. The point is (and we must leave a fuller development of it for the final chapter) that each party reserves a right under the bipartisan approach—a right it has always exercised toward both foreign and domestic affairs—to agree with its opponent over some policy issues and to disagree over others, depending upon how it interprets the national interest. The dilemma is not resolved by admonishing parties to place the national interest ahead of partisan advantage. It is an elementary axiom of politics that each party in fact *identifies its position with the national interest.* Could Republicans in the postwar period possibly admit that their strong opposition to the recognition of Red China, or their widespread support for General MacArthur's strategy during the Korean War, or their demand for the dismissal of Secretary of State Acheson was opposed to the national interest? Similarly, under the Eisenhower administration, Democrats saw no conflict between the national interest and their forceful attacks upon Republican policies toward the Middle East, the Soviet satellite empire, or southeast Asia. On the contrary, Democrats believed that such attacks were in fact necessitated by their belief that the national interest would suffer if these policies were not changed.

One answer to the dilemma may be to pretend on occasion that a dilemma does not exist, that is, to seek unity in the foreign policy field *at whatever cost* to the American democracy. Such an answer may at times be the only possible one. When external crises arise it may be the only conceivable alternative to follow. But an evasion of the problem is no answer to it. For it is clear from the history of American foreign relations since World War II that there will be many occasions when the parties will decide that bipartisanship is not worth the price its successful realization would exact from them and from the political system as a whole. What are the considerations that may influence party leaders in coming to such a conclusion?

THE *Raison d'Etre* OF AMERICAN PARTIES

The hallmark of the two major parties within the United States is their nonideological nature and their concern with practical and immediate goals. For both parties the foremost goal is identical—to gain and hold public office, and especially to capture the presidency. Party platforms and issues are means to this end. Through them the party seeks to convince the electorate of its concern with existing domestic and foreign problems and with its capacity to solve these problems in the public interest. And the foremost issues in American politics at any given time are the immediate problems confronting the nation at home and abroad.

Yet bipartisanship in foreign affairs is a call for the parties to eliminate foreign policy questions from their catalogue of political issues. Indeed, the more crucial the foreign policy problem, the greater apparently is the need for putting politics aside for the sake of unity at home. War, of course, furnishes the clearest example of when unity on the home front is almost universally held to be indispensable to the achievement of victory. The anology of wartime experience is applied by proponents of bipartisanship to periods of peace or cold war, when (at least in the latter case) the need for unity may be only slightly less compelling. Now there can be no doubt that the analogy has merit; but, as with all analogies, it can be deceptive. The difficulty of securing unified governmental policy at home under ideal circumstances, combined with a totalitarian threat abroad, furnishes an almost irresistible temptation to argue that the bipartisan principle should be followed, at least as long as the world is divided into hostile power blocs.

There is, however, a fundamental weakness in such reasoning, and this weakness goes far toward explaining why bipartisanship in foreign affairs under certain circumstances is an impractical goal. The national interest is at times clearly discernible. There was no substantial doubt, for example, what course the United States had to follow after the Japanese attack on Pearl Harbor in 1941. The more normal situation, however, is that public opinion is divided over the correct course to pursue in foreign affairs. It is profitable to recall that during every major war in American history sharp differences of opinion have prevailed over political issues arising out of the war. This pattern prevailed after World War II, when public opinion was split over the host of foreign policy issues that emerged from that conflict. Who can say even now what course of action the national interest dictated toward such intricate diplomatic problems as the Chinese civil war, the Jewish-Arab conflict in Palestine, the spread of communism throughout southeast Asia, Red Chinese belligerence toward Formosa and the off-shore islands, global disarmament, control of atomic and hydrogen bombs, and numerous other problems that American policy makers have been called upon to grapple with since World War II? We may accept the view that the national interest should become the star by which the nation charts its course in world affairs. But how is the national interest to be discerned toward specific foreign policy problems? What individuals or groups inside, or outside, the government shall make this determination? Whose interpretation is to become binding upon the government?

This is the crux of the difficulty of attempting to approach foreign affairs on a bipartisan basis. For the essence of democratic government would seem to be that in the long run the people determine the national interest by the kind of public officials they select. The most useful (though by no means exclusive) device for translating the people's wishes into policy is the party system. Crude as it may be for registering public opinion, the American party system remains the principal agency for shaping the character of governmental policy in all fields. Parties, in turn, operate upon the premise that the national interest and the programs advocated by the party are identical. To do otherwise would be tantamount to admitting that the party was pledged to govern with no necessary concern for the public interest!

Excessive campaign oratory, unbridled partisan harangues, and personal irresponsibility on the part of candidates widen the divisions within American society over foreign policy issues. But it is more true that disunity prevails because of the difficulty and complexity of problems confronting the nation and because the proper course in foreign affairs is by no means self-evident. "Issues" normally arise between the two parties as there is in fact *an issue* before the country—whether it is some domestic question or whether its theme is high tariff versus reciprocal trade, foreign policy in the Far East, defense policy, or foreign aid programs. Even Senator Vandenberg conceded as early as

1947 that foreign policy was "a legitimate subject of partisan conflict if there is a deep division" among the people (**17**, Nov. 4, 1947).

The parallel between war and peace—that because unity is necessary in war it ought also to prevail in periods of peace or cold war—is thus faulty in one important particular. It ignores the fact that in war the national interest is usually plainly discernible, whereas in peace the national interest is hard to discover. And when this occurs, it is the party system that fosters discussion of the alternatives and permits one interpretation to be chosen over another. Partisan conflicts over foreign policy questions are thus rooted in the nature of democratic government. They cannot be permanently avoided without denying the possibility of the democratic method as it relates to foreign affairs.

The Inseparable Connection between Domestic and Foreign Issues

Arguments advanced in behalf of the bipartisan principle in foreign affairs almost invariably rest upon a tacit assumption that domestic and external problems have no necessary connection with each other. Partisanship is permissible toward the former category of problems but impermissible toward the latter.

If a clear line of demarcation could ever have been drawn between the internal and foreign policies of a nation, that line, for the United States since World War II, would have become quite indistinct. It is necessary only to remember that foreign assistance programs and a huge peacetime military establishment have constituted the major weapons by which the United States has sought to prevent Communist expansionism throughout the postwar period. Each of these diplomatic weapons has an intimate relationship with domestic problems, since each involves such questions as the level of taxation, federal spending, the national debt, conscription and military reserve laws, the composition of the armed forces, and so on. The inescapable relationship between internal and external policies, and the difficulty this poses for implementing the bipartisan principle, was succinctly put by William S. White in 1955:

The state of the world has got the politicians by the throat. How, in the last analysis, does one separate the question of how many infantry officers should be trained at Fort Benning, Ga.— a "domestic" budgetary question—from the question of what the Administration should say to Moscow about a Four-Power Meeting? [17, Jan. 9, 1955.]

The Marshall Plan perhaps illustrates better than any major foreign policy undertaking in the postwar period the point being discussed here. Before June, 1950, an economy bloc in Congress, consisting of Republican and Democratic conservatives, sought to cut the annual Plan appropriation as a first step in reducing the over-all level of federal taxing and spending. The group was instrumental in delaying legislative approval of Marshall Plan funds throughout 1947. Frequent attempts were made by this same group to reduce funds in subsequent years, a move justified by Senator George (Democrat of Georgia, and one of the leaders of the economy bloc) on the ground that "nobody can expect members of Congress to cut down on our domestic programs unless we first make a reduction in foreign spending. If we are going to pare down anywhere, we must start there" (9, p. 2).

The interaction between domestic forces and American foreign policy can also be discerned in the approach of many members of Congress to major international issues affecting their local constituencies. Reference has already been made to the fact that party lines in Congress are not rigid and that members can and do vote against their party's national platform or legislative program with little hesitation. No other single factor is as important in explaining this phenomenon as local constituent pressure upon legislators. Unlike Great Britain, where individual members of Parliament are looked upon as representing the nation as a whole, members of Congress are chosen to represent the views of their constituents. Members of the House are elected by small groups of voters organized into congressional districts. Senators, of course, represent the voters in their states. And while it may be theoretically true that members are supposed to think of the interest of the whole country when they deal with major questions of public policy, in fact they are heavily swayed by the attitude of the voters at home on domestic and foreign issues. The voters throughout the country as a whole will not re-elect or defeat them; the voters in their constituencies will!

This means that in their approach to foreign affairs, members of Congress are influenced more by constituency pressure than by the program of their party or by efforts to achieve bipartisan agreement. If the absence of ideological cleavage between the major parties in the United States may be regarded as a factor that predisposes in favor of bipartisan collaboration, the importance of constituency pressure upon legislators must be seen as the opposite side of the coin, often predisposing against bipartisan co-operation in foreign affairs.

Illustrations of the significance of constituency pressure abound in the record of American postwar foreign relations. As we observed in Chapter 6, it was of great importance in shaping the viewpoints of spokesmen for both parties (but chiefly for the Democratic party) toward the partition of Palestine. Moreover, since World War II the presence of large national minorities in certain key states has doubtless been responsible for shaping the attitudes of members of Congress from those states on foreign policy issues. Thus Senator Robert Taft was probably influenced to denounce the war-crimes trials at Nuremberg by the sizable German-American population in Ohio. Legislators from New York, New Jersey, Pennsylvania, Massachusetts, and California—where large Italian-American minorities reside —were in the forefront of those who advocated lenient treatment of Italy at the end of World War II, who urged the United States to support Italian versus Yugoslavian claims to Trieste, and who advocated extensive American foreign aid to Italy. In these same states, along with Michigan and Wisconsin, there is also a large Polish-American element. Representatives and senators from these states have often been highly vocal in demanding a firm American policy toward Soviet Russia, especially as regards Russia's postwar machinations in Eastern Europe (18, pp. 22–23).

Another important problem toward which constituency pressure upon legislators has been intense is that of reciprocal trade and tariff legislation. By the end of Eisenhower's first term, considerable opposition to a continuation of foreign aid had developed within the Democratic-controlled Congress. In a number of instances, Democrats who had consistently voted for foreign assistance since the inauguration of the Marshall Plan now called for a re-examination of the policy with a view to a substantial reduction in foreign spending. One consideration motivating many legislators was the belief that foreign assistance was beginning to hurt American domestic industry. Thus American assistance to Japan, it was believed, had contributed to increasing Japanese industrial output, especially of textiles. As a result, producers in the United States faced serious competition. Japanese blouses and other textile goods made in Japan were flooding the American market. Vigorous protests were voiced in Congress against these Japanese imports. Democratic legislators from the South, where textile manufacturing has greatly expanded during the postwar period, were especially outspoken. Senator Olin Johnston (Democrat of South Carolina), for example, referred to June 15, 1955, when the United States and Japan signed a new trade agreement, as "the day the great Eisenhower giveaway administration sold the American textile industry and its thousands of workers down the river, and gave the Japanese textile industrialists a stranglehold on the American cotton textile market." Tariff reductions on Japanese printcloth were especially alarming to Senator Johnston, since 60 per cent of American-made printcloth was manufactured in his state. Representative Cleveland Bailey (Democrat of West Virginia) referred to the serious consequences for his district and the nation at large created by the increase in imports of Japanese glassware and pottery. He pointed out that "What little is left of West Virginia's glassware and pottery industry will be completely wiped out by imports from Japan, where the wage scale is 9 to 19 cents per hour compared to $1.72 in our West Virginia plants."

Republicans have supported the protest made by Democrats against tariff reductions on Japanese imports, despite the fact that a reduction in trade barriers has been a major plank in the Eisenhower administration's legislative program. On February 28, 1955, Senator Frederick G. Payne (Republican of Maine) called attention to the sharp decline in employment in the textile industry throughout the nation. He observed that in his state, four of the larger cities depended for one-third or more of their employment on textile manufacturing. Representative Edith Nourse Rogers (Republican of Massachusetts) has periodically voiced the same protest. On January 10, 1955, for example, she warned that continued tariff reductions might eventually bankrupt the

American textile industry. She informed the Administration that she did not "intend to stand by and see the great American textile industry ruined and used as a pawn for temporary political favor on the international chessboard of politics." [3]

An astute commentator on the legislative process, William V. Shannon, has written concerning the Senate: ". . . by its nature the Senate is not properly constituted to frame a national program. Senators are ambassadors of their states, advocates (and prisoners) of the local and regional interests of their diverse constituents." Writing in 1956 about the activities of Democratic majority leader Senator Lyndon Johnson of Texas, Shannon called attention to the importance of the oil and gas industry in Johnson's state and pointed out that he "cannot flout or ignore the incessant pressures of these powerful constituents and remain in office." Graphically depicting the problem being discussed here, Shannon continued:

It is difficult in the extreme to identify the oil and gas industry's particular interest with the nation's general interest. What is good for Superior Oil Company is not necessarily good for the United States. Indeed, the two interests at times seem diametrically opposed. In this power clash, Senator Johnson is trapped and compromised [20, pp. 195–98].

When foreign policy problems involve important domestic issues, the effort to resolve them must take one of two courses: either bipartisanship must be extended to the relevant domestic issues as well, or the partisanship in domestic issues must be extended to the foreign policy problems, thus obliterating bipartisanship.

[3] For texts of speeches by Senator Johnston, Representative Bailey, Senator Payne, and Representative Edith Rogers, see 8, pp. 8271–72, 426, 2208–9, and 202–3, respectively.

Decentralization of the American Party System

We have already referred to the extreme decentralization and the absence of discipline which characterize the American party system. It is manifestly impossible for the executive branch to consult with all members of Congress and all national party leaders in making important foreign policy decisions. Some selectivity is mandatory. The incumbent administration must reach agreement with at least the leaders of the opposition party; this agreement must then be translated into substantial minority party support in Congress. During the tenure of the Eightieth Congress (1947–48) the Republican congressional majority, under the leadership of Senator Vandenberg, was as a rule inclined to accept agreements worked out between Vandenberg and spokesmen for the Truman administration. The record of forty-seven unanimous votes by the Senate Foreign Relations Committee in the Eightieth Congress testifies to the fact that lack of party discipline did not seriously interfere with the attainment of bipartisan co-operation in the foreign policy field. But before and after the Eightieth Congress the lack of discipline within each party placed a serious barrier in the path of unified governmental policies. In the Great Debate of 1950–51 over American defense policy toward Europe, the Truman administration had substantial Republican support for its decision to defend Europe with ground troops, even though the most politically influential wing of the Republican party (the re-examinists, led by Senator Taft) could not be persuaded until after a period of several months to support the decision. Many of the difficulties of implementing the bipartisan principle after 1949 could be traced to increasing factionalism within the Republican opposition. "There was no one man or group of men recognized within the Republican Party," wrote Joseph C. Harsch, "as having the right to speak for the party in foreign policy.

On the contrary there are several rival groups unwilling to delegate such authority to any one person" (5, Apr. 26, 1950).

This problem did not disappear when the Republican party won the election of 1952. Traditionally, a party in opposition may be expected to suffer from factionalism more than the party in power, since it usually lacks both a recognized leader and a definite program. But during the first two years of the Eisenhower administration the principal threat to unity in foreign affairs came from the militants and irreconcilables within the President's own party, foremost among whom were Senators Joseph McCarthy of Wisconsin and William F. Knowland of California. The latter was in the anomalous position of being at the same time both the President's floor leader in the Senate and one of his most outspoken critics in foreign affairs. Before unified decisions could emerge under these circumstances it was necessary to have, in effect, a form of "tripartisanship": the President had first to persuade members of his own party to follow his leadership *before* he invited Democrats to do the same (17, Oct. 21, 1954, dispatch by Cabell Phillips). Ultimately, the cost of securing the consent of influential GOP leaders proved too high, since the price demanded was substantial modification of the President's foreign policy proposals, particularly in the direction of more militant anti-Communist policies in Asia. By 1955 the President had all but abandoned his efforts to unite extreme elements within the GOP behind policies supported by the moderate Republicans and a majority of Democrats in Congress. Thus, unlike the situation which confronted President Truman in 1947–48, President Eisenhower during 1953–54 possessed a numerical majority in Congress, but the core of support for his foreign policy program consisted on many occasions of a minority within his own party, joined by a majority of

Democrats (17, Apr. 3 and May 8, 1955, dispatches by William S. White).

The Majority Party and Bipartisanship

"Genuine bipartisanship," writes Cabell Phillips, "does not pay political dividends to either party" (17, Oct. 21, 1954). A basic assumption with protagonists of bipartisanship is that the sacrifices necessary to achieve unity in foreign affairs are borne equally by both parties. But if the postwar years provide a reliable test, this assumption is partially, and at times completely, erroneous. Different inducements may influence the majority and minority parties to work together in foreign affairs, and different considerations can lead one or both parties to decide to withdraw from continued bipartisan co-operation.

Turning first to the majority party, we may note that however persuasive the arguments in behalf of bipartisanship, the party in power cannot evade public responsibility for the success or failure of its policies. When the majority party collaborates with the opposition, it is, in effect, permitting the latter to share in the formulation of policy without at the same time requiring that it also accept responsibility for governing in the public interest. This difficulty becomes particularly acute when foreign policy failures have occurred, for the majority must then shoulder the blame for ineffective policy although it has permitted the opposition to participate in decisions that led to failures. This situation confronted the Truman administration after the collapse of Nationalist China in 1949. In reply to recurrent Republican allegations that China had never been included in the area of bipartisan consultation, Senator Connally replied for the Democrats:

Where, then, were the Senators who have been complaining in recent months about what happened in China and what the

State Department did or did not do? . . . Not a single one of those who are now attacking the State Department and its record in China ever proposed a different course, ever said a word, ever made a complaint . . . [7, Apr. 13, 1950, p. 5170].

If bipartisanship in practice means that the opposition party shares in the credit when a foreign policy is successful but divorces itself from blame when a foreign policy is unsuccessful, there is little incentive for the party in power to seek to employ the bipartisan principle.

Moreover, the majority party may abandon or curtail the application of the principle of bipartisanship if it suspects that the minority does not genuinely desire to co-operate in good faith. One factor explaining Senator Vandenberg's key role in the bipartisan process from World War II to 1950 lay in the fact that he had no apparent political ambitions aside from holding his seat in the Senate (21, Chap. 22). The Truman administration was rightfully convinced that he would not utilize information gained from bipartisan consultations for the advantage of the Republican party or for personal advancement. The Democrats did not have the same feeling about Senator Taft and other congressional leaders of the GOP.

Finally, the lack of a clear-cut definition of bipartisanship may, in the view of the majority party, work more to the credit of the opposition party than to the credit of the party in power. When foreign policy undertakings are successful, the opposition can claim (as Republicans claimed during the Truman administration, and Democrats have claimed since the Eisenhower administration took office) that effective foreign policy would not have been possible without the co-operation of the opposition party. On the other hand, when policies miscarry, the minority can claim that such policies were never part of the bipartisan approach, that the minority was not consulted in time to prevent the mistake, or that bipartisanship never assumed that the opposition party should take responsibility for unsuccessful policies. In any case, the vagueness of the term is a standing invitation to the minority party to share in the credit for foreign policy achievements but to escape the blame for policy failures.

The Minority Party and Bipartisanship

Rather different considerations may predispose the minority party against supporting the principle of bipartisanship. Foremost among these is the fear (voiced repeatedly by both parties when they have been in the opposition from 1945 to 1957) that collaboration with the incumbent administration deprives the opposition of its right to criticize existing policies and to propose alternatives. A substantial body of opinion has always existed in Congress that bipartisanship works a peculiar hardship upon the party out of power by depriving it of an obligation to insist upon full and frank debate on crucial international, and closely related domestic, issues.

Furthermore, an opposition party may lose its enthusiasm for bipartisan foreign policy because of the fact that public opinion almost invariably associates the party in power with successful policies in both foreign and domestic affairs. Normally the public does not inquire too deeply into the question of which party was in fact responsible for successful policies, or whether either party was responsible for them. Thus an administration may have worked closely with the opposition party to formulate foreign policy programs (as in the case of the Truman administration and its diplomatic undertakings toward Western Europe); or it may happen to be in power at a time when the nation benefits from fortuitous events abroad (as in the case of the Eisenhower administration and the evidence of disaffection in the Soviet satellites late in 1956 and early in 1957). In either instance the public usually does not hesitate to give the credit for favorable developments to the party in power.

The relevance of this fact to the point under discussion here is thus clear and significant: an opposition party stands to gain little political advantage from a bipartisan approach to foreign relations so long as the policies being pursued on this basis are successful policies. Neither Republicans during the Truman administration nor Democrats during the Eisenhower administration were able to translate their bipartisan co-operation into tangible political benefits strong enough to counteract the credit that accrued to these administrations for important achievements in the foreign policy field. Put in its simplest terms, an opposition party is in a perpetual quandary under a bipartisan approach to foreign affairs: either it co-operates with the party in power in behalf of sound policies and sees that party reap substantial political rewards, or it refuses to join in a bipartisan approach and then invites the accusation that it is insensitive to the need for national unity when serious diplomatic issues confront the nation.

From the point of view of the minority party, the greatest barrier to maximum two-party co-operation in the foreign policy field derives, however, from a sincere conviction that the policies of the incumbent administration are at variance with the national interest. The importance of this point was stressed by the GOP members of the House Foreign Affairs Committee in 1949:

We Republicans believe that our country should have a bipartisan foreign policy. It is more important, however, for our country's policy to be right than bipartisan. Unity solely for the sake of unity may be disastrous. History is strewn with the wreckage of countries that were united but on the wrong course.

Successful bipartisanship requires a certain minimum area of agreement between both parties concerning diplomatic objectives and means. Issues have arisen since the Second World War, and they will doubtless arise in the future, in which basic consensus was lacking. Compromise was not possible without a sacrifice of principle by one party or the other. One such issue has been the matter of tariff versus reciprocal trade. The difficulty of effecting a bipartisan solution to this and similar problems was well summarized by Walter Lippmann in 1954:

There are issues perhaps that can be postponed, perhaps evaded, perhaps bypassed, perhaps outlived. But if the issue has to be met, then there has to be a choice. It is impossible to work out a policy which at one and the same time opens and closes the American market, raises and lowers the tariff, expands American exports and restricts American imports. The search for an agreed policy in issues of this sort is the political equivalent of trying to square the circle.

"For issues of this kind," continued Lippmann—and he could just as easily have been referring to the Truman administration's policies toward the Far East, Palestine, and European defense, or the Eisenhower administration's diplomacy toward the Middle East—". . . the issues must be debated by those who have convictions and in the end there must be a count of the votes. For issues of this kind there is no substitute in a democratic society for debate and decisions" (12, Jan. 28, 1954).

6. The Environment of Bipartisanship

From time to time throughout this study, reference has been made to the importance of the atmosphere within which a bipartisan approach to foreign relations is required to operate. While such an approach usually envisions certain procedures designed to encourage collaboration between the parties in foreign affairs, procedures are not self-operating.

Before they can be used successfully, there must be a desire for unity on the part of the participants. A mere exchange of viewpoints between party leaders, for example, in no way guarantees that bipartisan agreements will emerge. Indeed, if such an exchange is entered into in a spirit of hostility and ill will, it may actually promote partisan discord in the field of foreign relations. Bipartisanship is heavily dependent upon the proper psychological environment.

In trying to determine the role of environment, it is difficult to differentiate between cause and effect. Circular reasoning becomes almost unavoidable, as when it might be said that the desire for unity will encourage effective use of existing procedures; yet success in using these procedures no doubt contributes to the desire for, and the belief in the possibility of attaining, that unity. While it would be bootless to speculate whether the atmosphere referred to here is essentially *cause* or *effect*—it is probably a little of both— the intimate relationship between it and the attainment of bipartisan co-operation can hardly be questioned or minimized. The decline of bipartisanship in the closing months of the Truman administration, for example, can be attributed in large measure to the intense partisan and personal animosities that came to characterize relations among many of the participants in the foreign policy process. The psychological environment was quite unfavorable to the realization of bipartisanship.

Experience since World War II makes it clear that the achievement of bipartisan co-operation is highly dependent upon amicable relations among key individuals. Lacking this relation, machinery and procedures are likely to accomplish very little. In the words of Joseph C. Harsch,

The machinery which put the Marshall Plan and the Atlantic Pact through Congress was basically the personal relationship which existed between two men—Arthur Vandenberg and

George C. Marshall at the Department of State. . . . They formed a close-working team which was able to take the prime measures of foreign policy out of the arena of domestic politics. Senator Vandenberg knew that George Marshall never would subordinate foreign policy to the Democratic Party, and Secretary Marshall knew that Senator Vandenberg would never subordinate foreign policy to the Republican Party. Bipartisanship in foreign policy had many components, but the central and activating component was the personal relationship between Vandenberg and Marshall [5, Apr. 23, 1951].

By contrast, Harsch described the situation prevailing after Vandenberg's retirement as follows:

Today our foreign policy is dominated by almost a total reversal of the condition which prevailed in the Vandenberg-Marshall period. Senator Taft has taken over the Vandenberg position among Senate Republicans. Dean Acheson is Secretary of State. . . . They do not agree on foreign policy purposes. They do not share a sense of the proper means. They do not trust each other to be non-partisan. Fairly or unfairly, the administration believes Senator Taft would scuttle a foreign policy for a Republican advantage any day. Conversely, Senator Taft and his associates completely lack confidence in Mr. Acheson's policies and political maneuvers. . . . The two men have become symbols of partisan battle, not partners in bipartisan foreign policy as were their predecessors [5, Apr. 23, 1951].

Two conditions above all others are likely to determine whether the requisite psychological atmosphere exists. The first is whether or not there exists a high degree of confidence on both sides in the judgment and competence of the major participants in the foreign policy process. Second, there must be a feeling of mutual trust and good faith. However dedicated to the bipartisan principle an incumbent administration may be, it is not likely to seek bipartisan agreements if it distrusts the motives of leading members of the opposition party or believes that they are not interested in reaching such agreements in good faith. Conversely, an opposition party is not likely to desire such agreements if it has little trust in executive policy makers.

An indispensable prerequisite of bipartisan foreign policy is the existence of a belief shared by policy makers that unity is necessary in foreign affairs and that sacrifices are necessary to attain it. For such a belief to exist, all the participants in the foreign policy process must be actuated by the same motives. They must be prepared to forego exploiting the political truce that prevails for partisan ends. Given such an atmosphere of good will and mutual dedication to the common goal, machinery and procedures established to facilitate co-operation between parties in foreign affairs may be utilized to maximum advantage. Otherwise, no significant or lasting unity in the foreign policy field is possible.

Summary

In this and the preceding chapter our central purpose has been to examine those factors—called here "determinants of bipartisanship"—that will produce co-operation or conflict between the two parties over foreign affairs. These factors relate to:

1. The connotations suggested by the term "bipartisanship."
2. The nature of the foreign policy problem toward which a bipartisan approach is being followed.
3. The President's position of leadership in the foreign policy field.
4. The organization and procedure of Congress.
5. The character and operation of the American party system.

6. The personal-psychological environment within which the bipartisan principle must be applied.

These six factors are intimately interrelated; and when we include the several subfactors listed under each of these six determinants, there is an almost infinite number of possibilities for their combination toward a particular foreign policy problem. Consequently, they must not be regarded in any sense as a formula by which the extent of co-operation between the parties can be predicted with precision. Instead, they have been offered herein as a means of clarifying the difficulties of approaching external problems upon a bipartisan basis. Such a clarification is a necessary preliminary to determining both the best means of avoiding failures and of evaluating the over-all utility of the bipartisan principle.

References

1. American Political Science Association, "Toward a More Responsible Two-Party System," *American Political Science Review,* Supplement to Vol. 44 (September, 1950).

2. Boorstein, Daniel, *The Genius of American Politics.* Chicago: University of Chicago Press, 1953. A penetrating study of the character of the American party system.

3. Brown, Ben H., Jr., "Congress and the Department of State," *Annals of the American Academy of Political and Social Science,* 289 (September, 1953), 100–107. Discusses the activities of the Office of Congressional Relations.

4. Cardozo, Michael H., "Committees Touching Foreign Relations Indirectly," *Annals of the American Academy of Political and Social Science,* 289 (September, 1953), 84–91.

5. *Christian Science Monitor.*

6. *Congressional Quarterly,* 1951, Vol. 7.

7. *Congressional Record* (daily edition).

8. *Congressional Record,* Vol. 101.

9. *Foreign Policy Bulletin,* April 22, 1949.

10. Green, James F., "The President's Control of Foreign Policy," *Foreign Policy Reports,* 15 (April 1, 1939), 10–20. A treatment of the means by which a president may evade legislative restraints on his power.

11. Griffith, Ernest S., "The Place of Congress in Foreign Relations," *Annals of the American Academy of Political and Social Science,* 289 (September, 1953), 11–21.

12. *Herald Tribune* (New York).

13. Kennan, George F., *American Diplomacy, 1900–1950.* Chicago: University of Chicago Press, 1951. A source of additional reading on the substance of American foreign policy in the postwar period.

14. Koenig, Louis W., *The Presidency and the Crisis.* New York: King's Crown Press, 1944. A readable treatment of President Roosevelt's management of foreign affairs before and during World War II.

15. Lippmann, Walter, *The Cold War.* New York: Harper and Brothers, 1947. Treats American foreign policy in the postwar period.

16. Morgenthau, Hans J., *In Defense of the National Interest.* New York: Alfred A. Knopf, 1951. Contains additional reading on American foreign policy in the postwar period.

17. *New York Times.*

18. "Power of Minorities in '46 Vote: Parties' Contest for Their Favor," *United States News,* 21 (October 18, 1946), 22–23.

19. Richards, James P., "The House of Representatives in Foreign Affairs," *Annals of the American Academy of Political and Social Science,* 289 (September, 1953), 66–72.

20. Shannon, William V., "The Power of the Senate," *The Commonweal,* 64 (May 25, 1956), 195–98.

21. Vandenberg, Arthur H., Jr. (ed.), *The Private Papers of Senator Vandenberg.* Boston: Houghton Mifflin Company, 1952.

22. Welles, Sumner, *Seven Decisions That Shaped History*. New York: Harper and Brothers, 1951.

23. ———, *Where Are We Heading?* New York: Harper and Brothers, 1946. This book and the one above furnish additional reading on the substance of American foreign policy in the postwar period.

24. White, William S., "Senator George—Monumental, Determined," *New York Times Magazine,* March 13, 1955, pp. 12, 42-47. An informative treatment of Senator George's role in the bipartisan process during the Eisenhower administration.

NINE

Bipartisanship: A Balance Sheet

In the infancy of the American Republic, the noted French-
man Alexis de Tocqueville wrote that

> it is most especially in the conduct of foreign relations that demo-
> cratic governments appear to me to be decidedly inferior to
> governments carried on upon different principles. . . . Foreign
> politics demand scarcely any of those qualities which a democ-
> racy possesses; and they require, on the contrary, the perfect use
> of almost all those faculties in which it is deficient [24, p. 138].

As we saw in Chapter 1, over a century and a half of American diplomatic history has amply vindicated De Tocqueville's perceptive judgment. Commentators upon American
foreign policy in more recent periods have also elaborated
upon the obstacles confronting the United States in the
conduct of its foreign affairs. Thus Graham H. Stuart has
written:

> In democracies . . . numerous checks are imposed upon auto-
> matic control of foreign relations by the head of the state. The
> result unfortunately is to make the conduct of foreign relations
> in a democracy both difficult and cumbersome. Perhaps in no
> country is this more evident than in the United States [23, p. 41].

Numerous factors in the mid-twentieth century have combined to persuade large numbers of citizens, party leaders, and public officials that the overriding need of the hour is for unity on the home front as an indispensable prerequisite for success in the foreign policy field. "The foreign policy of this country," the Conference of Governors resolved in 1947,

transcends in importance all partisan, personal, or political considerations and should be at all times an American foreign policy, representative of the best in America and representing the United States to the nations of the world as a country that seeks peace . . . [3, July 7, 1947].

Among the considerations that explain the unprecedented emphasis within recent years on the principle of bipartisanship are the recognition of numerous instances in American diplomatic history when partisan discord interfered with the making of consistent and effective foreign policy; the increased awareness that the constitutional division of authority between the President and Congress in foreign relations can breed governmental paralysis; the growing concern among policy makers and students of government with the impact of public opinion on foreign affairs; the widespread understanding that peace and security in international relations require long-range programs of economic and military assistance to other countries; and the comprehension that, in the age of hydrogen bombs and jet aircraft, decisions in foreign affairs must often be made quickly and yet decisively. Many citizens are convinced that disunity in the face of formidable external problems is a luxury that the nation cannot afford without serious jeopardy both to its own safety and to that of the non-Communist world as a whole.

How has a bipartisan approach to foreign relations actually fulfilled the need for which it was designed? Have the consequences of such an approach been, on balance, beneficial or detrimental? The purpose of this chapter is to examine these questions critically and comprehensively.

1. Assets of Bipartisanship

To persons familiar with the over-all development of American foreign policy since the Second World War, many of the assets of bipartisan foreign policy are self-evident and immeasurable. Others are perhaps less evident, and their long-range value to the American democracy may be open to serious question. We may characterize the advantages of bipartisanship in a general way by saying that without it the United States would have been unable to formulate most of the great milestones in its recent diplomacy, most notably the Greek-Turkish aid program, the Marshall Plan, the North Atlantic Pact, the program of arms aid to Europe, and a host of economic and military assistance programs to lesser countries. These undertakings were the foundation upon which the policy of containment rested in the postwar period. Without substantial bipartisan co-operation in their formulation, efforts to contain Communist expansionism would have collapsed, as John Foster Dulles has written, "like a house of cards if the governments of the still free peoples felt that there was such division within the United States that the policies . . . did not have assured continuity, at least in their broad outlines" (14, p. 121). To the individual who more than any other personified bipartisanship —Senator Vandenberg—collaboration between both of the parties makes two invaluable contributions to American foreign relations:

One: it permits our democracy to speak with a great degree of unity at critical moments when swift decision is vital and when we face totalitarian opponents who can command their own instant unity by police decree. Two: it leaves us free to change our national administration, if such be the peoples' desire ... without affecting the continuity of our foreign policy [25, pp. 450–51].

Such general evaluations can be open to few criticisms, even though they tell us little about the advantages of bipartisanship under specific circumstances. American diplomatic experience since World War II suggests that these advantages may be felt in five reasonably distinct, though closely related, areas.

Bipartisanship and Stability in Foreign Relations

First, co-operation between the parties in foreign affairs contributes to the stability of American foreign relations by fostering unity between the two branches of the government that share responsibility in foreign relations—the President and Congress. Although the American system of government continues to rest upon a constitutional doctrine of separation of powers, the unfortunate consequences of such a doctrine for foreign relations may be partially, and sometimes completely, overcome by a bipartisan approach. The postwar era has been relatively free of institutional conflicts within the government that jeopardized the nation's position in external affairs. When such conflicts have developed, as in the Great Debate over American defense strategy, they have usually resulted in an eventual clarification of foreign policy, even if their short-run impact was to foster instability and uncertainty.

The evidence from the case studies of important undertakings in American foreign policy presented earlier in this study strongly suggests that when programs have been formulated upon a bipartisan basis they are likely to receive wide support in Congress. The details of such programs may be changed, especially by groups such as the Appropriations committees, if they have not been included in preliminary consultations. Controversies may take place over the administration of such programs, as in the case of the Marshall Plan. In some instances, the Executive may be forced to make substantial concessions to win the necessary approval from Congress, as in the Mutual Defense Assistance Program. Still, throughout the postwar period, bipartisan collaboration has produced a remarkably impressive record of agreement between the White House and Congress upon the broad outlines of policy. In the absence of such agreement— especially during the periods 1947–48 and 1955–56 when control of the government was divided between the two parties—such creative and vital undertakings as the European Recovery Program and the Mutual Defense Assistance Program could not have been adopted.

We may summarize by saying that much of the credit for the united support that foreign policy decisions have received from both branches of the government in the postwar period must be attributed to a bipartisan approach to foreign relations.

Bipartisanship and the Continuity of Foreign Policy

Closely related to the value of bipartisanship in imparting stability to foreign policy decisions is its utility in promoting continuity to long-range undertakings in external affairs. It is in maintaining needed continuity that a democracy is at the greatest disadvantage when its major potential enemy is a totalitarian government. Many recent commentators on American foreign relations have emphasized the difficulty that any democratic government, not merely the United States, experiences in carrying through its commitments over long periods of time. George Kennan, for example, employs the following colorful metaphor:

... I sometimes wonder whether ... a democracy is not uncomfortably similar to one of those prehistoric monsters with a body as long as this room and a brain the size of a pin: he lies there in his comfortable primeval mud and pays little attention to his environment; he is slow to wrath—in fact, you practically have to whack his tail off to make him aware that his interests are being disturbed; but, once he grasps this, he lays about him with such blind determination that he not only destroys his adversary but largely wrecks his native habitat. You wonder whether it would not have been wiser for him to have taken a little more interest in what was going on at an earlier date and to have seen whether he could not have prevented some of these situations from arising instead of proceeding from an undiscriminating indifference to a holy wrath equally undiscriminating [**17**, pp. 66–67].

The pendulum-swings that have characterized our foreign policy at frequent intervals in the past cannot serve as a satisfactory basis for foreign policy for the leader of the free-world coalition in an era of cold war. Confronted by an ideological opponent ready to labor ceaselessly, patiently, and on many fronts in order to attain its philosophical goals, the United States has no option but to undertake enduring commitments and to give assurance that its commitments will be honored as long as necessary. Anything short of this risks diplomatic disaster and encourages Communist expansionism.

Threats to the continuity of American foreign policy arise primarily from two quarters: from the risk that Congress will initially refuse to support, or will subsequently repudiate, long-term foreign policy undertakings that the Executive deems vital to national security; and from the risk that a national election and the partisanship that invariably accompanies it may result in an abrupt and perhaps violent reorientation in foreign policy when a new administration takes control of the government. Bipartisanship, of course, does not eliminate either of these dangers completely. They cannot be eliminated, perhaps, without stripping Congress of any real jurisdiction over foreign affairs and without reducing political campaigns to shadowboxing between the major parties over frivolous and trumped-up issues. The risk that public policy may be changed—sometimes abruptly —is inherent in democratic government, and it cannot be removed without changing the nature of that government.

Nevertheless, bipartisanship can substantially reduce the risk that long-range foreign policy commitments will be capriciously abandoned or modified. Thus, with respect to the problem of European recovery, the fact that Congress cannot make appropriations for periods longer than one year constituted no particular barrier to drafting a program designed to extend for almost five years. Even though modifications were made by Congress in the ERP from year to year and budget requests were usually reduced somewhat below executive expectations, Congress annually approved the Marshall Plan until its objectives had been largely accomplished.

Several examples from postwar experience point to the success of the bipartisan approach in preventing disruption in foreign policy as a result of national elections. One of the earliest manifestations of bipartisanship, for instance, was the agreement between President Roosevelt and the 1944 GOP presidential candidate, Thomas E. Dewey, to exclude foreign policy issues from the election campaign in order not to interfere with the war effort. Similarly, during the Berlin blockade in 1948, Senator Vandenberg and other leading Republicans made it abundantly clear to the Soviet Union that a Republican victory would in no way weaken the determination of the United States to stay in Berlin and to maintain the airlift as long as necessary. In that same election, John Foster Dulles, Dewey's choice for Secretary of State in the event the Republicans won, was kept closely informed of developments in the foreign policy field so that needed continuity would be maintained (25, Chap. 23).

While this asset of bipartisanship should not be pressed too far—observers at home and abroad, for example, did expect that there would be a change in American Far Eastern policy had the GOP been victorious in 1948 [1]—it is true that when there is an evident need for continuity, bipartisan co-operation goes a long way toward assuring it.

BIPARTISANSHIP AS A DIPLOMATIC WEAPON

A third way in which the principle of bipartisanship in foreign affairs is valuable is that it serves as an effective tool in negotiations with other countries. A major weakness of democracies in foreign relations is in the danger that decisions made with other governments will be repudiated by the political opposition at home. Such an eventuality is inherent in any system of representative government, and there would appear to be no way of eliminating it altogether without destroying the representative character of the government itself. With totalitarian regimes, however, this problem does not normally exist. When diplomatic representatives of the Soviet Union negotiate, there is little or no possibility that their agreements will be altered by the Supreme Soviet or by Russian public opinion. The monolithic nature of the Soviet government effectively guarantees solidarity in negotiating with other countries.

On the other hand, bipartisanship has at times provided the United States with a means of forceful expression of a policy that is supported by both major political parties. In Chapter 2, reference was made to the importance of this

---

[1] Thus one observer wrote shortly after the election that "news of his [Dewey's] defeat at the polls created an atmosphere of the deepest gloom in Nanking" (9, p. 280).

point during the San Francisco Conference on International Organization, when Republicans and Democrats alike supported agreed-upon policies in their negotiations on the UN Charter. This public demonstration of American unity doubtless contributed greatly to strengthening the hand of the United States at the conference.

An even more graphic demonstration of the worth of bipartisanship in this connection was provided during negotiations between the wartime Allies over the Axis satellite peace treaties throughout the latter part of 1945 and 1946. Gradually, American foreign policy in this period changed to one of patience and firmness in dealing with the Soviet Union. Communist sources incorrectly attributed this new policy to pressures exerted upon the Truman administration by Republicans (particularly Senator Vandenberg) and by certain (unnamed) members of the American delegation to the foreign ministers conference. Repeatedly throughout successive sessions of the conference, however, Secretary Byrnes deliberately included Senators Vandenberg and Connally in negotiations in order to demonstrate the unity of the American delegation. After a brief interlude during May, 1946, negotiations over the Axis satellite treaties were resumed. Although he was reluctant to leave his pressing senatorial duties again, Senator Vandenberg informed Secretary Byrnes that he would once more participate in such negotiations if his absence should raise the "slightest doubt" concerning his own support of Secretary Byrnes or of established American foreign policy toward the treaties. At Byrnes's insistence, Vandenberg once more joined the American delegation to the foreign ministers conference in order to demonstrate that "patience and firmness" was a policy supported by Democrats and Republicans alike.

Prior to the Big Four Conference at Geneva in the late summer of 1955, the Eisenhower administration discussed problems to be considered at this conference with leading Democrats before Secretary of State Dulles left Washington for Geneva. Such prior consultations served notice upon foreign countries not to try to exploit political differences in the United States for their own diplomatic ends.

BIPARTISANSHIP AS AN ANTIDOTE TO EXTREMISM

The lack of strict party discipline within the United States and the freedom with which some members of Congress orate upon virtually any subject mean that the United States is sometimes embarrassed by extremist interpretations of its foreign policy. Foreigners who do not understand the intricacies of the American system of government sometimes fail to realize that many speeches on foreign affairs delivered by congressmen and other political leaders are designed for home consumption, to satisfy the demands of local constituents.

Forceful attacks by members of Congress, party leaders, and citizens outside the government upon American foreign policy sometimes create doubts abroad as to its integrity. A serious example of this in the postwar period was provided by the speeches of former President Hoover and Senator Taft made in late 1950 and early 1951 in the Great Debate over American defense strategy, particularly as regards Western Europe. Confusion was created abroad concerning the good faith of earlier declarations to defend Europe from aggression, as opposed merely to liberating her after attack. Several months were required before American defense policy was fully clarified.

An even more striking example of ill-timed speeches in the foreign policy field was furnished by the Wallace episode in 1946. In September, Secretary of Commerce Henry Wallace made a number of public statements attacking current foreign policy toward the Soviet Union and intimating that the Truman administration should exhibit greater friendliness toward its former ally. The timing of the Wallace attacks was particularly unfortunate, since they came in the same period as Secretary Byrnes's Stuttgart speech proposing a German-American nonaggression pact, a move obviously designed to gain the good will of the Germans and to strengthen the State Department's position in current negotiations with the USSR. The harm done by the Wallace speeches was effectively minimized by the firm stand taken in Europe by Secretary of State Byrnes, supported by Senators Connally and Vandenberg. In a release to the press, Vandenberg declared that

The authority of American foreign policy is dependent upon the degree of American unity behind it. Rightly or wrongly, Paris is doubtful of this unity this morning. Our bipartisan foreign policy during the last 18 months has had overwhelming bipartisan support. . . .

I am sure most Republicans, despite inevitable differences . . . [favor] a bipartisan foreign policy on a sound American basis which rejects dictatorship by anybody, which is neither hostile nor subservient to any other power on earth, and which defends human rights and fundamental freedoms.

But the situation equally requires unity within the Administration itself. We can only cooperate with one Secretary of State at a time [21, Sept. 15, 1946].

When Wallace continued to attack the Truman policy, Secretary Byrnes, joined by Senators Connally and Vandenberg, informed President Truman that if he did not accept Wallace's resignation, Byrnes himself would resign. President Truman backed Byrnes by accepting the "resignation" of Wallace, and in doing so offered dramatic evidence to the world that existing American foreign policy enjoyed the support of the Administration and of both political parties.

The Educative Value of Bipartisanship

An additional virtue of bipartisan foreign policy may be one that is less readily apparent than the advantages discussed above. This is the role of a bipartisan approach in educating members of the opposition party to the realities of international relations in the twentieth century.

No doubt a major factor in the decline of isolationist sentiment has come from the Democratic-Republican collaboration in meeting serious foreign policy problems. One of the key reasons Senator Vandenberg became the leading GOP spokesman in foreign affairs relates to the point being discussed here. As an expert on foreign relations from World War II to the time of his death, Vandenberg had few rivals in either party. His colleagues in Congress respected his judgment and his insight into international problems. His opinions carried great weight with members of Congress because they derived from a deep knowledge of, and wide experience with, foreign policy issues. Yet Vandenberg acquired this *expertise* comparatively late in his legislative career. He became well informed about foreign affairs largely because of the interest he developed in the subject after his "conversion" from isolationism during World War II and because of the opportunities afforded him by the Roosevelt and Truman administrations to broaden his knowledge and experience by negotiating with foreign governments and by working closely with the State Department at home. It is safe to say that without the postwar emphasis upon the principle of bipartisanship, Senator Vandenberg would never have acquired his deserved reputation as the leading authority within Congress on external affairs.

On the basis of his rich experience Vandenberg was able to justify his support of the Roosevelt and Truman administrations' major foreign policy undertakings with the most persuasive logic possible: a conviction that such under-takings were in accordance with the national interest and should, for that reason, be endorsed by both parties. Fre-quently throughout his legislative career, Senator Vanden-berg denied an accusation made by right-wing Republi-cans that bipartisanship required a kind of passive acquies-cence by the GOP in proposals submitted by the Truman administration. In 1947, for example, he informed the Senate that

Bipartisan foreign policy is not the result of political coercion but of non-political conviction. I never have even pretended to speak for my party in my foreign policy activities. I have relied upon the validity of my actions to command whatever support they may deserve [25, p. 351].

As we shall see in a subsequent portion of this chapter, it is possible to overemphasize the educative function of a bipartisan approach to foreign affairs. In a few cases, such as those of Senator Vandenberg, John Foster Dulles, John Sherman Cooper, and a handful of other Republicans, bi-partisanship offered an unparalleled opportunity to widen their perspectives in foreign affairs. For other Republicans the educative value does not appear to have been so marked. Depending upon their particular role in the bipartisan proc-ess, there may have in fact been a contrary result. We may anticipate a later portion of this chapter here by observing that to some degree, bipartisanship may have inculcated the view that the chief duty of an opposition party is to refrain from criticism, even constructive criticism, for fear that disunity at home would disrupt the stability and continuity of American foreign policy.

We may summarize our examination of the assets of bi-partisanship by concluding that on certain occasions it has proved invaluable through overcoming substantially the characteristics of the American politico-governmental system that have tended to foster disunity, instability, and inconsistency in the foreign policy field. When long-range commitments have been necessary in external affairs in recent years, the only possible basis for them has been collaboration between the two parties in their formulation and renewal from year to year.

Yet admitting the contributions that a bipartisan approach has made to American foreign relations since its inception during the Second World War, it is clear that the impact of bipartisanship upon the American politico-governmental system has not been wholly favorable. Bipartisanship may have counteracted certain evils while creating other evils. Most of its negative features have to date been ignored by public officials and students of government alike. The first step toward their elimination and a prerequisite to any well-balanced assessment of the pros and cons of bipartisanship would appear to be a critical evaluation of its negative features. The final portion of this study is devoted to such an evaluation.

2. *Liabilities of Bipartisanship*

BIPARTISANSHIP AND CONTROL OF FOREIGN RELATIONS

We may begin our analysis of the liabilities of bipartisanship by first inquiring: Does the bipartisan process transfer much of the decision-making process in foreign affairs from the Executive to Congress? If so, is this either consistent with the traditional constitutional pattern or presently desirable? That bipartisanship does encourage such a transfer seems undeniable. When prior consultation between spokesmen for each party is made the *sine qua non* of bipartisanship, it is but a step from this requirement to the demand that "Congress . . . take back the policy-making powers exercised today by the State Department without even a semblance of Senatorial review" (21, Feb. 13, 1947). If existing bipartisan procedures leave substantial numbers of legislators unsatisfied, what is more logical than to propose that these procedures be broadened to include more legislators?

Various suggestions have been heard in Congress since World War II, the general purport of which has been to require legislative concurrence in foreign policy decisions. Thus Senator Johnson (Democrat of Colorado) has proposed that a "continuous bipartisan advisory commission" be established among party members in Congress; such a commission would assure "a permanent foreign policy and other nations would know where we stand at all times" (15, Nov. 28, 1950). Recommendations of this sort are probably inevitable when there is an overriding concern for unity in the foreign policy field. It may be suggested, however, that their adoption might in the long run do vastly more harm to the nation's diplomatic interests than if there were no attempt at all to follow the bipartisan principle.

Attempts by Congress to intrude into the President's control of foreign relations may be experienced in an additional way: members of the opposition party (joined, on occasion, by members of the President's own party) may demand that he adopt their views as a price for continued unity in the foreign policy field, even though the President may have expressed his conviction that such views are contrary to the national interest. Considerable evidence exists that the postwar emphasis upon bipartisanship has encouraged such a phenomenon, but we shall examine only two instances. With regard to American foreign policy toward Nationalist China, an evident desire by the Truman administration to silence its critics led it, in the latter half of 1949, to abandon its announced policy of nonintervention in

Chinese affairs and, by early 1950, to sanction a new appropriation for the Chinese Government-in-Exile on Formosa.[2]

Palestine furnishes another example. The Truman administration's policy toward that country during 1947 and 1948 vacillated between support for the UN partition plan—the course generally favored in Congress—and a pro-Arab policy designed to protect American oil holdings in the Middle East—the course favored in the State and Defense departments. In each of these instances the attempt to make foreign policy by compromising two extreme viewpoints produced policies that no one was prepared to support with enthusiasm.

The net result of bringing more congressmen into consultation might be a kind of internal appeasement whereby the President is forced to accept proposals that he does not believe to be consistent with the national interest, in order to avert disunity within the government. Such appeasement would seem to have no more value for relations between parties or branches of the government than between states in international relations.

The liability of bipartisanship being discussed here is part of a larger problem dealt with by Walter Lippmann in *The Public Philosophy*. Lippmann is concerned with what he calls "an historic catastrophe." He defines this as the "breakdown in the constitutional order" in the Western democracies by which the two essential functions of the state—*governing* and *representing*—have become confused. The consequences of this confusion are felt most directly in foreign affairs. For, as Lippmann says,

the general rule is that a democratic politician had better not be right too soon. Very often the penalty is political death. It is

[2] For evidence of the change in the Administration's attitude toward China in this period, see the speech by Secretary of State Acheson on February 16 (12, pp. 427–30).

much safer to keep in step with the parade of opinion than to try to keep up with the swifter movement of events.

. . . .

Democratic politicians rarely feel that they can afford the luxury of telling the whole truth to the people. . . . The men under them who report and collect the news come to realize in their turn that it is safer to be wrong before it has become fashionable to be right. [Such politicians get ahead] only as they placate, appease, bribe, seduce, bamboozle, or otherwise manage to manipulate the demanding and threatening elements in their constituencies. The decisive consideration is not whether the proposition is good but whether it is popular . . . [18, pp. 15, 26–27].

It is possible to argue that Lippmann's diagnosis is exaggerated. What seems less debatable is that bipartisanship does result in greater legislative influence in foreign affairs, and that the burden of proof is upon those who would regard this trend, however necessary it may at times become, as a permanently desirable modification of our constitutional pattern in foreign relations. Even after the necessity for unity is conceded, Peter Drucker is correct when he argues that a "foreign policy can never be evolved by adding together particular interests—regional, economic, racial— or by finding a compromise among them; it must supersede them" (13, p. 659). In foreign affairs, if not in mathematics, the whole is different from the sum of its parts.

An additional consequence of bipartisanship for the control of foreign relations lies in the fact that many groups and agencies in the government may be *collectively* responsible for successes or failures of foreign policy undertakings, but none is *singly* responsible for them. Who, after all, is to blame for the inadequacies of American foreign policy toward China after 1945? The Democrats, since they controlled the White House? The Republicans, because they had a majority in Congress in the decisive period 1947 to 1949? Or were both parties responsible in equal measure? In this and similar cases of bipartisan co-operation, it is virtually impossible for the citizen to know who is accountable for failures in the foreign policy field.

BIPARTISANSHIP AND THE QUALITY OF STATESMANSHIP

Among protagonists of bipartisanship it has become a stock in trade to insist that the search for unity does not entail muzzling of the opposition party. While the sincerity of such views may be granted, there is no escaping the fact that under bipartisan foreign policy, decisions take on an aura of untouchability. There may be no deliberate effort to curb debate, but, to quote Samuel Grafton, the implication is unavoidable that "no legitimate controversies remain in the field, and that anyone who objects to the official line must be a bit of a creep" (20, Jan. 23, 1947). Frequently as he denied the charge that bipartisanship stifled constructive criticism in the foreign policy field, Senator Vandenberg nevertheless admitted "the inevitable fact that a unanimous bipartisan [Foreign Relations] Committee report . . . creates an impetus which discourages partisan attack." While "partisan attack" may be curtailed, Vandenberg continued, "factual attack" and "clarification" were encouraged (25, p. 550). This is a customary, and not altogether illuminating, distinction among disciples of bipartisanship.

Elsewhere we shall deal with the consequences that derive from the fact that debate may be restricted by appeals for unity in foreign affairs. Here we are concerned with the effect of restriction on the foreign policy decisions ultimately adopted. First, does the relative absence of penetrative debate foster a sense of false security, a feeling that "all is well" in external affairs? To quote again from Samuel Grafton, "The thought is that if both parties agree, there cannot be much to be concerned about" (**20,** Jan. 23, 1947). Something more than coincidence surely explains the fact that incisive debate within the government over Nationalist China's vulnerability to communism came only after the Nationalist armies had been put to rout and Chiang had fled to Formosa. At no time during the first half of 1949 was there a thorough bipartisan analysis of Nationalist China's problems. One cannot read the debate in the *Congressional Record* without being impressed by the prevailing spirit of optimism and complacency exhibited by Republicans and Democrats alike over Chinese affairs.

Why should optimism not have prevailed? The aid program of 1948 had been drafted through close co-operation between spokesmen for both parties from the executive branch and Congress. It was accepted as a bipartisan program. Who except a few individualists in Congress would rise to challenge its basic assumptions? Who would presume to dispute the collective wisdom of the State Department, committees of Congress, Senator Vandenberg, and others who supported the program? Who would willingly court the twofold charge that he was indifferent to the need for unity and that he alone could interpret the national interest correctly? Yet if China was to be saved at all, bold and imaginative measures were called for. These were not forthcoming. Indeed, they were not even suggested. And this fact may be to some extent attributable to the interparty co-operation that characterized debate over American foreign policy toward China.

The threat to American statesmanship posed in bipartisanship was well summarized by the late Harold J. Laski, who feared that bipartisanship could divide Congress

into a small group who really knows the facts behind the facts, and the larger body which must do the best it can with the material before it with constant feeling that it has become not a genuinely critical body but an organization which is not believed to "play the game" if it refuses to accept policies hammered out between the president and the inner bi-partisan group . . . [26, Jan. 29, 1949].

A danger closely akin to this is that bipartisanship may impart rigidity and inflexibility to foreign policy because of the difficulty of securing two-party agreement. This may be especially true if contemplated decisions are likely to prove controversial. If American foreign policy in the years after World War II suffered from a recurrent inability to adapt itself to rapidly changing events, part of the cause may be found in the prevailing emphasis upon bipartisanship. To operate with a modicum of success, a bipartisan approach to foreign affairs necessitates extended and intensive consultations between spokesmen for both parties. Consequently, the policy that ultimately emerges from this time-consuming process may already be outmoded by swiftly changing circumstances and may, for that reason, be less effective policy than if the executive branch had made the required decision unilaterally.

Finally, we must call attention to a tendency evident in the postwar period which may have in the end produced *less* unity in the foreign policy field. This was the widely prevailing belief that a bipartisan approach to foreign affairs can be tailored to fit almost any type of diplomatic problem. The well-nigh universal failure to recognize the limitations of such an approach has bred unrealistic expectations among policy makers, particularly those in Congress. When expectations are not fulfilled, the tendency is not to look for the explanation in the fact that the approach had only limited utility, but in the belief that motives on the other side were insincere or that there was insufficient bipartisan co-operation. One of the greatest barriers to bipartisanship derives from the fanciful hopes entertained by its friends. When unrealistic expectations are entertained, disillusionment, suspicion of executive policy makers, and an over-all spirit of acrimony between both parties inevitably follow in the wake of failure to realize them.

We may summarize this section by quoting from Joseph C. Harsch:

A bi-partisan foreign policy is bound to be a common denominator of the wishes of the two big parties. That restricts the flexibility and range of foreign policy, and tends to make it halting, slow and rigid, and it also tends to stifle criticism—which can sometimes be more useful if free from the responsibility involved in bipartisanship.[3]

BIPARTISANSHIP AND THE AMERICAN PARTY SYSTEM

"Now is the time," wrote Andrew Jackson to President-elect Monroe in 1816, "to exterminate the monster called party spirit." If this were accomplished, the new President could "eradicate those feelings, which, on former occasions threw so many obstacles in the way of government: and perhaps have the pleasure of uniting a people heretofore divided . . ." (5, p. 94). The ideal of government divorced from the blight of partisanship was not invented by modern American policy makers. The lines from Macaulay,

> Then none was for a party;
> Then all were for the state;

could serve as a motto for contemporary proponents of bipartisanship. James Madison (in *The Federalist,* No. 10) and George Washington (in his "Farewell Address") admonished the American Republic to shun "factions" and "parties."

The ideal is seductive. What patriot would not instantly

[3] State Department transcript of a monitored radio broadcast on the Columbia Broadcasting System, January 18, 1949.

agree that the welfare of the nation should be placed ahead of partisan advantage? Merely to ask the question in this form is to answer it, *since the question postulates false alternatives*. The pitfall contained in the question is exposed by Jennings when he writes that those who deplore partisanship in England "urge statesmen to 'pull together,' and not to have the bow side cry 'forward,' while the stroke side cries 'back.'" The difficulty with the metaphor, however, is that "there is no agreement as to who shall be cox" (16, p. 32).

As Jennings suggests, the crux of the difficulty inherent in efforts to eliminate partisan discords within a democratic government is precisely the question: In the absence of party conflict what groups will chart the course to be followed by the ship of state? Most individuals deprecate partisan excesses, especially when grave foreign policy issues confront the nation. But the chief obstacle to eliminating them is deciding how they can be avoided without serious limitation upon the parties themselves. Arguments advanced in behalf of bipartisan foreign policy usually presuppose that by some kind of unexplained process, the government will automatically follow the course best calculated to serve the public interest, if only partisanship can be avoided. The true patriot is therefore asked to choose between the interests of his party and those of his country. Most infrequently is there recognition among supporters of the bipartisan principle that parties, with all their faults, and democratic government are inextricably connected, and that occasional excesses by political parties are part of the price a democracy must pay for the freedom it prizes so highly.

This is not to romanticize the party system or to suggest that there are not well-known and serious abuses within it. Yet after the abuses have been catalogued, parties remain the most effective instrument for translating the popular will into governmental policy. Without parties, in the words of F. Scott Oliver, a democracy would degenerate into "an impotent babel of virtuous voices" (4, p. 36). Parties, writes another English scholar, Bulmer-Thomas, ". . . are an inevitable consequence of the fact that men form different judgements [*sic*] about the manner in which any given problem should be resolved." He concludes his perceptive study of the English party system with the thought that it "depends for its successful working on the realization by those engaged in it that parties are only instruments to serve a higher end" (8, pp. 298, 308).

If these observations seem unrelated to the specific context of bipartisanship in American foreign relations, they are repeated here only because persons who have developed an overriding concern for unity in foreign affairs have tended to generalize the admitted evils in American politics into a blanket indictment of the party system as a whole as it touches foreign policy questions. Taking as their reference point partisan animosity accompanying Senate consideration of the League of Nations issue following World War I, protagonists of bipartisanship have reached the general conclusion that partisanship can serve no useful purpose in the sphere of foreign relations. Since partisanship kept the United States out of the League of Nations (a development now conceded by many Americans to have been a tragic mistake), partisanship should be avoided altogether in external affairs. This is equivalent to reasoning that because Congress passes a bad housing law, it should be prevented from having anything to do with housing; or because juries sometimes decide cases unfairly, jury trials should be abolished. What is lacking in this argument in support of bipartisanship is a sense of historical and philosophical perspective concerning the contributions that parties make to democratic government. Abuses in the party system are

magnified, judged *in vacuo,* and condemned; contributions
—usually less dramatic in their manifestations, more long-
range, and more subtle in their effects—are virtually ignored.

What kind of party system is desired within the United
States? A committee of the American Political Science Association has answered: "An effective party system requires,
first, that the parties are able to bring forth programs to
which they commit themselves and, second, that the parties
possess sufficient internal cohesion to carry out these programs." The opposition party has a unique role: "to act as
the critic of the party in power, developing, defining and
presenting policy alternatives which are necessary for a true
choice in reaching public decisions" (1, pp. 17–18). The
committee makes no differentiation between internal and
external affairs.

Let us accept these criteria and ask how bipartisanship in
foreign affairs since the Second World War has affected the
American party system. First, bipartisanship, in the opinion
of leading Republicans and Democrats, has robbed each
party of much of its inimitable character, both in foreign
and domestic affairs. This conviction underlay Senator Taft's
lack of enthusiasm for the principle. Prominent Democrats
have also echoed this view, contending that too great an
emphasis upon unity has forced Democratic presidents to
modify the party's policies as a price for Republican co-
operation. Thus Ellis Arnall, former governor of Georgia,
wrote that "Acceptance of reactionary participation in the
making of foreign policy and the removal of foreign policy
improperly from the sphere of public discussion . . . was
forced on President Truman by well-meaning advisers of
both parties . . ." (2, p. 37). Impartial observers have
lamented the same development. The dilemma confronting
Democrats, wrote the London *Economist* after Truman's
victory in 1948, was to decide which policies "were those of

their own party, which had been genuinely agreed [to] with the opposition and which were mere concessions to the Republican die-hards in Congress" (22). Blair Bolles wrote in 1950 that a renunciation of bipartisanship by the Truman administration would "free Secretary Acheson from his present confused position over the degree of responsibility he owes to the Republican and Democratic parties, both of which he has tried to follow in opposite directions in dealing with Asia" (6, p. 2). If an evident weakness of the existing party system within the United States is, as D. W. Brogan has phrased it, that it is "difficult to pin responsibility on the 'party in power' and almost impossible to pin responsibility on the party not 'in power' . . ." (7, p. 87), then it is clear that bipartisanship aggravates an already serious weakness in the American government.

A related danger is that bipartisanship may devitalize the opposition party. Thus during 1949, one commentator writes, bipartisanship confined Republican opposition to the Truman administration's foreign policy measures "largely to the plane of generalities" (9, p. 500). Arthur Krock, of the *New York Times,* at length concluded that under the Truman administration the Republican party could not attack budgetary and tax proposals freely because bipartisanship

forces Republicans to consider tax increases in which they do not believe. This situation robs an opposition party of a definite program to deal with an alarming condition, and of an effective claim for being returned to office [21, Nov. 11, 1949].

There is some parallel between what can happen under a bipartisan approach to foreign affairs and a similar development in agricultural policy, as formulated by a leading farm interest group. The American Farm Bureau Federation has endeavored to elevate the question of government price supports for agricultural products "above politics." If such a movement is successful, McConnell writes, an important public issue will have become a "no-party policy. That is to say, it is superior to *either* party." He continues:

The presumption must exist that at its base lies a fundamental consensus that is not to be questioned. Does this consensus in fact exist in regard to parity, the core of the matter? Is the concept of parity . . . beyond criticism except by scattered discussion groups and the board of directors of the American Farm Bureau Federation? [19, p. 144.]

And we may ask, Is it to be supposed that a consensus *always* exists in foreign affairs, that there are no questions in the atomic age over which patriotic men may conscientiously differ?

Within a democratic society it is impossible to be precise about the degree to which partisan controversies are causes rather than reflections of divisions within the body politic. More often than not, the latter condition is true. Partisan differences, that is to say, are as a rule merely symptomatic of fundamental disagreements in the electorate over important public issues. The party system serves as a mechanism by which disagreements over policy are aired and by which policy is changed at periodic intervals to reflect the public will. Existing divisions in public opinion may be sublimated or otherwise repressed for a time; but if they are deep enough they will eventually break to the surface and may cause even sharper disagreements than before.

Bipartisanship thus may be utilized to achieve two results, either or both of which may at times be imperative when critical foreign policy issues arise: it may prevent substantial disagreement between the parties by seeking to have them collaborate in the formulation of policy, or it may cover up existing differences by fostering the impression that they do not exist or are inconsequential. In either case, however, and especially the latter, the long-range result of bipartisanship may be to intensify conflict between the parties and to turn this conflict into channels that make little contribution to strengthening governmental policy. Few students of American foreign policy would dispute the fact that in the postwar period a greater than average degree of personal animosity and friction has prevailed among policy makers in the government. Criticism frequently has not been directed at the merits of policy, but at individuals who were its architects. Decisions have been attacked through personal vendettas against Secretaries of State Marshall, Acheson, and Dulles; against Presidents Roosevelt, Truman, and (to a lesser degree) Eisenhower. The propensity of Congress to explain policy inadequacies by reference to "subversive groups in the State Department" who "sold China down the river" or "handed Eastern Europe to Stalin" may be traceable at least in part to an uncritical attachment to the principle of bipartisanship. When policy cannot be attacked for fear of causing disunity, and when (as in the case of China) opposition party members had themselves participated in framing the policy decisions, the attack is focused upon key individuals within the Administration. Thus William S. White wrote that the Democrats, who refrained from criticizing the Eisenhower administration's foreign policies for some sixteen months after the Republicans took office, were early in 1954 directing "loud and frankly partisan criticism" at Secretary Dulles' handling of foreign affairs. White continued: "Some of it is extraordinarily vehement simply because it issues from the throats of politicians long repressed" (21, May 9, 1954). Except when the nation is actually at war or when the danger of war is imminent, is it not better to have such criticism directed at the merits of policy and to have it expressed in time to influence the nature of policy finally adopted?

BIPARTISANSHIP AND EXECUTIVE LEADERSHIP IN FOREIGN AFFAIRS

Under the Truman administration a significant extension of legislative influence in the formulation and control of foreign relations accompanied efforts to apply the principle of bipartisanship to foreign affairs. Added to this were a number of well-publicized investigations of executive departments and policy makers, frequent public statements by leading congressmen concerning foreign policy, and numerous trips abroad by legislative committees and individual lawmakers. The cumulative effect of all this was further to expand the influence of Congress in external affairs to the point that legislative usurpation of executive functions was at times a genuine danger. After the Eisenhower administration took office in 1953 the opposite danger—virtually unrestrained executive supremacy in foreign affairs—emerged as a consequence of the desire to continue the practice of bipartisanship. Events early in 1955 illustrate the degree to which bipartisanship can strip Congress and the opposition party of any remaining influence over foreign policy. The salient facts, briefly, were as follows.

After the defeat of Nationalist China late in 1949, the Communist regime on the Chinese mainland had periodically expressed its determination to capture Formosa and certain offshore islands still under the control of Chiang Kai-shek's forces. During the Korean War, Formosa was under the protection of the American Seventh Fleet; but with the end of the war and the ensuing Communist victory in Indo-China, Red China appeared at last ready to launch an attack against these islands. Red China's increasing belligerence in the Formosa Straits posed a difficult choice for the Eisenhower administration. The Administration felt, on the one hand, that the Communist threat endangered the security of the United States and the free world. On the other hand, it was aware that the allies in the cold war and numerous spokesmen within the United States believed that Formosa was not worth protecting at the risk of a new world war. Consequently the White House was reluctant to commit itself publicly regarding whether or not it intended to defend Formosa from impending Communist attack. At the same time, the Administration apparently felt that a public declaration of some kind would deter Red China from an attack against these islands.

An apparent resolution of this dilemma was decided upon late in January. It lay in the President's asking Congress for a joint resolution approving "the use of the armed forces of the United States if necessary to assure the security of Formosa and the Pescadores." Such a resolution, in the President's view, would "clearly and publicly establish the authority of the President as Commander-in-Chief to employ the armed forces of this nation promptly and effectively. . . ." This would "reduce the possibility that the Chinese Communists, mistaking our firm purpose and national unity, might be disposed to challenge the position of the United States . . ." (11, Jan. 24, 1955, pp. 497–99). Resolutions were promptly introduced in both the House and Senate, and on the day after the President's speech of January 24, the House passed H. J. Res. 159 by the overwhelming majority of 409 to 3. As usual, Senate debate on the resolution was more protracted, but on January 28, S. J. Res. 28 was approved by a vote of 85 to 3. Seldom in American diplomatic history had there been so nearly unanimous a demonstration of unity in the face of a foreign threat. Here was bipartisanship par excellence. Supported by overwhelming votes in both houses, the President now possessed carte blanche to utilize the armed forces in the Formosa Straits as he might deem necessary to safeguard national security.

Yet it became apparent to observers in Washington during the course of the debate in Congress and in the days which followed that there existed fundamental differences of opinion, both within the President's own party and between the parties, over the proper course of action to be adopted toward the Formosa crisis. A significant number of Democrats and Republicans were known to oppose the retention of Formosa at the risk of a third world war. The resolution approved by Congress had not granted powers to the President to deal with a foreign policy crisis; what it had done was merely to reaffirm the President's authority to act to defend the security of the nation. At the time, this appeared to be a small enough price for Congress to pay in the interest of unity. Yet what the resolution did in effect was *to grant executive policy makers immunity from subsequent criticism* of the course of action ultimately adopted. During the Senate debate, the foremost opponents of the resolution were Senators Wayne Morse and Herbert Lehman, Democrats from Oregon and New York, respectively. Morse argued that he would always support the President when he acted as Commander in Chief, "unless a clear showing can be made that the President is following a course of action contrary to the security and welfare of the Nation, in which event a restrictive check should be put upon him by Congress." The President, said Morse, had the power to act to meet a threat to national security, but when he acted, "Congress has the duty to pass judgment upon the act, and proceed either to affirm, modify, or repudiate the President's course of action." What the President had asked for was, in essence, "a predated authorization of anything he may do under the resolution." Morse concluded that "the resolution should never have been introduced in the first place . . ."

(**11**, Jan. 26, 1955, pp. 634–35). Similarly, Senator Lehman contended that "if the President feels that certain action is necessary to defend the United States and the interests of the United States . . . let him take that action. That is his duty and his responsibility. It is then up to him to justify it to the Congress, to the country—and to history" (**11**, Jan. 28, 1955, p. 775).

The issue, in other words, was not whether the United States should or should not defend Formosa, but rather whether in merely requesting a prior authorization from Congress for the use of his powers—in the interest of demonstrating unanimity within the government—the President had not effectively silenced his critics in both parties. In the last analysis, Congress could not refuse to pass the requested resolution, for as Senator George contended in Senate debate, "If the Congress of the United States is willing to withhold moral support to the President . . . under existing conditions . . . what is the alternative? Let every member answer on his conscience, the question of what is his alternative" (**11**, Jan. 27, 1955, p. 716). In this case, asking was equivalent to receiving, since Congress could not fail to uphold the President without perhaps encouraging Red Chinese belligerence in the Formosa Straits area. Democrats, in William S. White's expressive phraseology, had been "tied to the President's Formosa policy with bonds as gossamer as the moonlight but as effective as steel" (**21**, Apr. 10, 1955). If it is true today, as numerous authorities on American foreign relations contend, that the only really effective restraints upon executive control of foreign relations are political restraints, and hence largely long range and indirect, even these are largely nullified when Congress for the sake of unity votes in advance to support the President's policy before it knows either what this policy is or before its probable consequences have been ascertained.

Retrospect and Prospect

Without recapitulating the major points made in this and preceding chapters, it might be profitable to review the over-all scheme of this study, to re-emphasize certain points made earlier, and to add others briefly in the interest of presenting as balanced a treatment of the subject as limitations of space permit.

In Chapter 1 an attempt is made to establish a historical background against which bipartisan efforts in the postwar era may be made more meaningful. Chapters 2 through 6 present case studies that illustrate how the bipartisan principle has been applied toward selected problems in recent American foreign relations. Chapters 7 and 8 analyze in more systematic detail the factors that will likely determine whether or not bipartisan co-operation is achieved. Finally, in this chapter we attempt to weigh the assets and liabilities of bipartisanship, with particular emphasis upon liabilities since they have not yet received the attention their seriousness deserves.

No doubt the cumulative effect of the last three chapters is to foster skepticism in the mind of the reader concerning the *possibility* and *desirability* of achieving bipartisan co-operation in foreign affairs. Such an impression is in part intentional; and in part it is simply inevitable, given the outline of the book. The last three chapters have stressed largely negative themes—i.e., difficulties in the path of, and liabilities accompanying, bipartisan foreign policy. No attempt has been made to accord equal space to the treatment of those factors that facilitate the accomplishment of, and the benefits to be derived from, co-operation between the parties in foreign relations.

But the reader may still legitimately ask this question: If the realization of bipartisanship is as difficult, and its effects at times as harmful, as Chapters 7 to 9 suggest, how is it that any bipartisan collaboration was achieved in the postwar period, and why do both parties continue to support the principle?

The answer is likely to be determined substantially by whether bipartisanship is interpreted broadly or narrowly. It may be thought of only in terms of an immediate end—policy supported by both political parties, or simply unity. By this definition any foreign policy undertaking approved (tacitly or explicitly) by both parties—or at a minimum a policy not opposed by one or both parties—would qualify as a bipartisan policy. Such a definition, however, is so all-inclusive as to be virtually worthless. Throughout this book, and specifically in Chapter 7, the term has been defined much more narrowly. It has been thought of as embodying not only an end to be attained (unity), but also the means by which it is to be attained. (Chapter 7 suggests four means that are fundamental.) Numerous policies could be cited that seemingly had the support of both political parties, but that were viewed by one party as outside the scope of bipartisan collaboration—e.g., policies toward Palestine, China, the Middle East, and Latin America in the postwar period.

If this more restricted definition of bipartisanship is accepted, then it is apparent that there have been relatively few genuinely bipartisan undertakings in American postwar foreign relations. Outstanding cases are the United Nations Charter, the Marshall Plan, the North Atlantic Pact, and certain lesser treaties such as those for the Axis satellites and Japan. Borderline cases would perhaps include the Greek-Turkish aid program, various developments in American relations with Nationalist China down to 1948, the program of arms aid for Western Europe, and attempts by the Eisenhower administration late in 1956 and early in 1957 to deal with the Middle East crisis.

It is possible, however, to underestimate the importance of the difficulties in the path of bipartisanship merely by referring to the few instances in which considerable bipartisan co-operation was achieved. For it must be recalled that in every one of these cases there existed an external threat of greater or lesser magnitude that made unity within the government mandatory. Obstacles to bipartisanship inherent in the American system of government and politics will, as Chapters 7 and 8 suggest, tend to be important in inverse proportion to the intensity of the threat confronting the nation from abroad. When no threat exists, or after an initial threat has receded, it is reasonable to expect that the barriers discussed in the previous chapters are likely to be more formidable than when the necessity for unity is universally admitted. A corollary of this general rule, which experience with bipartisanship since 1945 would seem to confirm, is that the difficulties described may be more relevant to the problem of maintaining co-operation between the parties over foreign affairs for long periods than to the more immediate issue of generating unity between them when urgent, and essentially short-run, foreign policy problems arise.

Whether policies continue to be viewed as bipartisan undertakings for months or years thereafter will depend upon still others factors, among which two are likely to be of fundamental importance. First, was the policy in question successful, or did it fail in attaining its major objectives? Second, does the nation continue to face the threat which originally prompted the co-operative policy, or perhaps a new threat, so that some kind of minimal bipartisanship is indispensable to national security? Of these two conditions, if the experience in trying to maintain bipartisanship toward Far Eastern and Middle Eastern affairs is a valid test, the former is perhaps of more crucial importance.

There are three additional reasons for enthusiastic and uncritical support for the bipartisan principle by political and governmental leaders within the United States. The first is that the term has become so nearly equated with the idea of patriotism that anyone who challenges its usefulness during periods of grave international crisis is likely to be regarded as indifferent to national security. Second, the liabilities of bipartisan foreign policy have to date been sensed only dimly, if at all. Finally, some of the harmful consequences of bipartisanship have not yet been fully felt. This is particularly true of the adverse influence of bipartisanship upon the political system. Years may be required before many of its important consequences can be systematically assessed.

Consider, for example, only one area in which subtle and long-range consequences from following the bipartisan principle may have been at work. This is the effect upon the Republican party of having collaborated with two Democratic administrations within the last decade in an effort to formulate acceptable foreign policies. Earlier in this chapter it was suggested that collaboration between the two parties helped to prepare at least certain leaders of the Republican party for a more enlightened role of statesmanship when the GOP gained control of the government. But what was the effect upon the rank-and-file Republican in Congress? It would be comforting to believe that the "educative effect" of bipartisanship was experienced by the Republican opposition as a whole. But it is at least a tenable position that until 1952 undue emphasis upon the bipartisan principle fostered the impression among Republicans in general that the chief duty of an opposition party is to refrain from criticizing the

Administration's foreign policies. Now self-restraint may be clearly a virtue when delicate matters of state confront the nation. But self-restraint is not, and cannot be, a substitute for foreign policy proposals; and practice in self-restraint can hardly be viewed as valuable preparation for responsible and imaginative leadership in the foreign policy field. Despite constant denials by Senator Vandenberg and other advocates of bipartisanship, it must be recognized that a devitalized opposition party will likely result when unity becomes the overriding concern.

Throughout this book our effort has been to explore the implications of bipartisan foreign policy for the United States. Yet as we reflect upon these implications, valuable insights can be gained from the experience of other countries in their attempt to maintain unity within the government in the face of grave external problems. Great Britain, for example, is often cited as a nation in which the bipartisan principle supposedly operates with almost complete efficacy. The fact often overlooked about British experience that has a direct bearing upon the value of bipartisanship for the United States is that the desire for unity has on occasion brought the British nation to the brink of disaster in international affairs. During the "appeasement era" of the 1930's, one commentator has written, the British Labour party

was too badly rent by its own quarrels . . . to be an effective opposition; most of its members, moveover, shared the cabinet's basic misunderstanding of realities in Europe. The most powerful critics were not Labourites but dissident Conservatives hobbled by party allegiance. Thus in the crucial area of foreign affairs the opposition lost its traditional role: it could not criticize the substance of policy, let alone offer an alternative, and it had no hope of turning out the government; the Prime Minister consequently had all too free a hand. Baldwin's successor, Neville

Chamberlain, used his freedom to the full. When in the spring of 1939 he at last admitted to the nation that his policy had failed, and reversed it almost overnight, he still retained office. In a period of normal parliamentary balance the admission of so gigantic a failure would have unseated the government and brought the opposition into office. But in 1939 there was no opposition worth the name, and it was sorely needed [27, p. 354].

Analogies between governments cannot be pressed too far. Nevertheless, Britain's diplomatic experience in the 1930's, when her appeasement policies at least had bipartisan support, offers a solemn warning concerning the danger of elevating the desire for unity into the *summum bonum*. The crux of the matter is that the nation's destiny in world affairs is much more likely to be determined by the soundness of its policies and the continued good health of its political institutions than by their mere bipartisan support. Unity is desirable only insofar as both political parties support policies that advance the country's diplomatic interests. Bipartisan co-operation in behalf of feeble and ineffective policies, on the other hand, is an almost certain road to diplomatic defeat.

Admitting the precedence of intelligent policy decisions over bipartisanship per se, and the liabilities inherent in such co-operation, it remains true that under certain circumstances there is no substitute for unity in the foreign policy field. This study has tried to suggest that such unity is more difficult to achieve than is generally admitted, and that the deleterious consequences of attaining it often outweigh its supposed advantages. When the alternatives before the country are either to practice bipartisan co-operation or to risk serious disunity in the face of a grave external threat, there can be little dispute over which alternative is to be preferred. Here the choice may lie, as it so frequently does in formulating governmental policy in all fields, in selecting the course of action that will prove least damaging to national security.

Nevertheless, it is imperative to remember the distinction between a positive good and a necessary evil. There can be little doubt that several of the assumptions supporting arguments for bipartisanship are at variance with other assumptions upon which democratic government and its inevitable handmaiden—a vital and dynamic party system—are founded. There seems no more reason to expect all patriots in a democracy to see eye to eye over foreign affairs than they do over domestic affairs. If the arguments usually advanced against enforced conformity of opinion in a democracy are valid, there is no reason to think they are any less valid when applied to the realm of foreign relations.

Is it, then, better to work for unity in foreign affairs by appeals to the spirit of bipartisanship, and by doing so to risk the evils outlined in this chapter? Or is it preferable to risk disunity in foreign affairs in order to escape these evils? No hard and fast rule can be laid down. Circumstances may compel the selection of now one, now the other, of these courses. One of the purposes of this study, however, is to emphasize that under certain circumstances the selection of the latter alternative is in fact the lesser evil.

The bipartisan principle should properly be viewed as a tool, on occasion an immensely valuable tool, to serve the nation's diplomatic interests. But however valuable it may be as a tool, it is nothing more than that. Since the end is effective diplomacy, circumstances may well dictate the use of other tools in place of a bipartisan approach. Two alternatives have already been suggested: vigorous presidential leadership when called for in foreign affairs, even at the expense of bipartisan co-operation; and clear statements of outstanding differences between the two political parties, when these differences are fundamental and cannot be reconciled. In the long run these may often advance the nation's interests in world affairs much more than bipartisanship.

When unity is required, it is likely to emerge and, what is perhaps more important, endure, as a result of the confidence of the American people in their elected leaders and in their belief that existing and proposed policies serve the best interests of the United States.

References

1. American Political Science Association, "Toward a More Responsible Two-Party System," *American Political Science Review,* Supplement to Vol. 44 (September, 1950).
2. Arnall, Ellis G., "The Democrats Can Win," *Atlantic Monthly,* **182** (October, 1948), 33–38.
3. *Baltimore Sun.*
4. Bassett, R., *The Essentials of Parliamentary Democracy.* London: Macmillan and Co., Ltd., 1937.
5. Binkley, Wilfred E., *American Political Parties.* New York: Alfred A. Knopf, 1945.
6. Bolles, Blair, "Should Bipartisan Foreign Policy Be Revived?" *Foreign Policy Bulletin,* **29** (March 31, 1950).
7. Brogan, D. W., *Politics in America.* New York: Harper and Brothers, 1954.
8. Bulmer-Thomas, Ivor, *The Party System in Great Britain.* London: Phoenix House, Ltd., 1953.
9. Campbell, John C., *The United States in World Affairs, 1948–49.* New York: Harper and Brothers, 1949.
10. *Congressional Quarterly,* 1955, Vol. 11. Pages 99–101 contain a convenient summary of the background to the Formosa crisis.
11. *Congressional Record* (daily edition).
12. *Department of State Bulletin,* **22** (January 16, 1950), 75–78.

13. Drucker, Peter F., "The American Political Tradition," *The Cambridge Journal,* 1 (August, 1948), 650–64.

14. Dulles, John Foster, *War or Peace.* New York: The Macmillan Company, 1950.

15. *Herald Tribune* (New York).

16. Jennings, W. Ivor, *The British Constitution.* London: Cambridge University Press, 1941.

17. Kennan, George F., *American Diplomacy, 1900–1950.* Chicago: University of Chicago Press, 1951.

18. Lippmann, Walter, *The Public Philosophy.* Boston: Little, Brown and Company, 1955. Chapters 1–5 discuss the difficulty that democratic governments experience in carrying through their commitments over long periods of time. This book will repay careful study by the student interested in the problem of too much legislative influence in foreign affairs.

19. McConnell, Grant, *The Decline of Agrarian Democracy.* Berkeley: University of California Press, 1953.

20. *New York Post.*

21. *New York Times.*

22. "No Voice in America," editorial in *Economist* (London), January 1, 1949.

23. Stuart, Graham H., *American Diplomatic and Consular Practice.* New York: D. Appleton-Century Company, 1936.

24. Tocqueville, Alexis de, *On Democracy in America,* ed. Henry S. Commager. New York: Random House, 1948.

25. Vandenberg, Arthur H., Jr. (ed.), *The Private Papers of Senator Vandenberg.* Boston: Houghton Mifflin Company, 1952. A lengthy account of the negotiation of the Axis satellite peace treaties is given in Chapters 15–16. Chapter 16 also contains a detailed account of the Wallace episode and its effect upon American foreign policy.

26. *Watertown Daily Times* (New York).

27. Willcox, William B., *Star of Empire.* New York: Alfred A. Knopf, 1950.

Bibliography

The titles listed below are designed to supplement the works upon which this study is based. The interested reader should utilize this bibliography in conjunction with other sources—especially primary sources—that are cited in the References at the end of each chapter.

Two recent books especially recommended to anyone desiring a deeper insight into the problem of conducting foreign affairs on a bipartisan basis are:

WESTERFIELD, H. B., *Foreign Policy and Party Politics*. New Haven, Conn.: Yale University Press, 1955. This book is a competent and thorough treatment of American foreign policy from World War II to the Korean War. Its writer is much more optimistic about both the possibility and desirability of bipartisan foreign policy than the author of this study.

YOUNG, ROLAND, *Congressional Politics in the Second World War*. New York: Columbia University Press, 1956. A scholarly and provocative treatment of a more limited period in American foreign policy. This book is especially valuable for an understanding of the emergence of bipartisan co-operation after the war.

1. American Foreign Policy, Particularly after 1945

BAILEY, T. A., *America Faces Russia: Russian-American Relations from Early Times to Our Day*. Ithaca, N.Y.: Cornell University Press, 1950.

———, *A Diplomatic History of the American People*. New York: Appleton-Century-Crofts, 1950. An immensely readable textbook, with emphasis upon the influence of parties and public opinion.

BEARD, C. A., *The Idea of National Interest*. New York: The Macmillan Company, 1934. In the midst of the postwar emphasis upon realism and idealism in foreign policy, this remains one of the most penetrating studies of the guiding principles of foreign affairs.

———, *President Roosevelt and the Coming of the War, 1941*. New Haven, Conn.: Yale University Press, 1948.

BEMIS, S. F., *A Diplomatic History of the United States*. New York: Henry Holt and Company, 1950. This is perhaps the most scholarly textbook on American diplomatic history.

BISSON, T. A., *America's Far Eastern Policy*. New York: Institute of Pacific Relations, 1945.

BROOKINGS INSTITUTION, *Major Problems of United States Foreign Policy*. Washington, D.C.: Brookings Institution, 1947, *et seq*. The annual volumes in this series contain well-organized and thorough analyses of outstanding problems in contemporary American foreign relations.

BROWN, W. N., *The United States and India and Pakistan*. Cambridge, Mass.: Harvard University Press, 1953. A brief, though competent, study of a frequently neglected aspect of American foreign affairs.

CHAMBERLAIN, LAWRENCE H., and SNYDER, RICHARD C., *American Foreign Policy*. New York: Rinehart and Company, 1948. Designed as a textbook, this work is valuable for its combination of explanatory and primary source materials.

Department of State Bulletin. Washington, D.C.: Government Printing Office. This journal appears weekly and provides an invaluable source for documentary materials and speeches by governmental officials.

Documents on American Foreign Relations. Princeton, N.J.: Princeton University Press for World Peace Foundation, 1939, *et seq.* This series is perhaps the best single source for documentary materials on American foreign affairs.

GRAY, GORDON, *Report to the President on Foreign Economic Policies.* Washington, D.C.: Government Printing Office, 1950.

HARRIS, S. E., *The European Recovery Program.* Cambridge, Mass.: Harvard University Press, 1948.

LATOURETTE, K. S., *The American Record in the Far East, 1945–51.* New York: The Macmillan Company, 1952. A penetrating treatment by a distinguished scholar on American Far Eastern policies.

LIPPMANN, WALTER, *The Public Philosophy.* Boston: Little, Brown and Company, 1955. This recent book by an astute observer would repay careful study by any student of American foreign relations.

———, *U. S. Foreign Policy: Shield of the Republic.* Boston: Little, Brown and Company, 1943.

McCLOY, J. J., *The Challenge to American Foreign Policy.* Cambridge, Mass.: Harvard University Press, 1953.

MARSHALL, C. B., *The Limits of Foreign Policy.* New York: Henry Holt and Company, 1954. The writer of this volume, for many years a State Department official, has given a perceptive analysis of the principles guiding American foreign policy.

MILLIS, WALTER (ed.), *The Forrestal Diaries.* New York: Viking Press, 1951.

PATTERSON, E. N. (ed.), "NATO and World Peace," *Annals of the American Academy of Political and Social Science,* 288 (July, 1953), 1–152.

PERKINS, DEXTER, *The American Approach to Foreign Policy.* Cambridge, Mass.: Harvard University Press, 1952.

———, *Hands Off: A History of the Monroe Doctrine.* Boston: Little, Brown and Company, 1942. This is probably the best available treatment of one of the leading principles of historic American foreign relations.

RAUCH, BASIL, *Roosevelt from Munich to Pearl Harbor.* New York: Creative Age Press, 1950.

TAFT, R. A., *A Foreign Policy for Americans*. New York: Doubleday and Company, 1951. A forceful statement by the late Senator Taft of the "re-examinist" position which he took during the Great Debate in 1950–51.

TAYLOR, ALLAN (ed.), *What Eisenhower Thinks*. New York: Thomas Y. Crowell, 1952.

The United States in World Affairs. New York: Harper and Brothers, 1947, *et seq*. This is an extremely valuable annual secondary source on American foreign relations.

VINACKE, H. M., *The United States and the Far East, 1945–1951*. Stanford, Calif.: Stanford University Press, 1952.

WILLIAMS, W. A., *American-Russian Relations, 1781–1947*. New York: Rinehart and Company, 1952.

WRIGHT, QUINCY, *A Foreign Policy for the United States*. Chicago: University of Chicago Press, 1947.

2. Foreign Affairs and the American System of Government

BINKLEY, W. E., *President and Congress*. New York: Alfred A. Knopf, 1947.

BOLLES, BLAIR, "Influence of Armed Forces on U. S. Foreign Policy," *Foreign Policy Reports*, 22 (October 1, 1946), 170–79.

——, *Who Makes Our Foreign Policy?* New York: Foreign Policy Association, 1947.

CHAMBERLAIN, L. H., *President, Congress, and Legislation*. New York: Columbia University Press, 1946.

COHEN, B. C., "Foreign Policy Making: Modern Design," *World Politics*, 5 (April, 1953), 377–92.

COLEGROVE, KENNETH, *The American Senate and World Peace*. New York: Vanguard Press, 1944.

CORWIN, E. S., *The President*. New York: New York University Press, 1948.

——, *Total War and the Constitution*. New York: Alfred A. Knopf, 1947.

DANGERFIELD, R. J., *In Defense of the Senate*. Norman, Okla.:

University of Oklahoma Press, 1933. A vigorous defense of the Senate's role in foreign affairs.

Dennison, E. E., *The Senate Foreign Relations Committee*. Stanford, Calif.: Stanford University Press, 1942. A valuable, though somewhat dated, monograph on one of the most important agencies concerned with foreign affairs.

Elliot, W. Y., *et al., United States Foreign Policy: Its Organization and Control*. New York: Columbia University Press, 1952.

Galloway, G. B., *Congress at the Cross-Roads*. New York: Thomas Y. Crowell, 1946.

Grassmuck, G. L., *Sectional Biases in Congress on Foreign Policy*. Baltimore: The Johns Hopkins Press, 1951.

Griffith, E. S., *Congress: Its Contemporary Role*. New York: New York University Press, 1952. A strong defense of the influence of Congress on domestic and foreign policy.

Hyman, Sidney, *The American President*. New York: Harper and Brothers, 1954. A highly readable and perceptive study of the presidency.

Kefauver, Estes, and Levin, Jack, *A Twentieth Century Congress*. New York: Duell, Sloan and Pearce, 1947. Senator Kefauver is a forceful advocate of closer executive-legislative relations in foreign affairs. Among his suggestions is a "question-and-answer period" in Congress for members of the executive branch.

London, Kurt, *How Foreign Policy Is Made*. New York: D. Van Nostrand Company, 1949.

McCamy, J. L., *The Administration of American Foreign Affairs*. New York: Alfred A. Knopf, 1950. This is easily one of the best single volumes on the administration of American foreign policy.

Nigro, Felix, "Senate Confirmation and Foreign Policy," *Journal of Politics,* **14** (May, 1952), 281–300.

Plischke, Elmer, *Conduct of American Diplomacy*. New York: D. Van Nostrand Company, 1950.

Pollard, J. E., *The Presidents and the Press*. New York: The

Macmillan Company, 1947. This work provides interesting insight into some of the extraconstitutional means by which presidents influence domestic and foreign policy.

Riddick, F. M., *The United States Congress*. Manassas, Va.: National Capitol, 1949. A comprehensive study of the organization and procedure of Congress.

3. Foreign Affairs, Politics, and Pressure Groups

Almond, Gabriel, *The American People and Foreign Policy*. New York: Harcourt, Brace and Company, 1950. This is one of the best studies available on the impact of public opinion on foreign affairs.

Binkley, W. E., *American Political Parties: Their Natural History*. New York: Alfred A. Knopf, 1943. Designed as a college textbook, this volume is a convenient one-volume study of American political history.

Bone, H. A., *American Politics and the Party System*. New York: McGraw-Hill Book Company, 1955.

Brogan, D. W., *Politics in America*. New York: Harper and Brothers, 1954. This book by a distinguished British observer contains many valuable insights into the operation and role of the American party system.

Cottrell, L. S., and Eberhart, Sylvia, *American Opinion on World Affairs*. Princeton, N.J.: Princeton University Press, 1948.

Key, V. O., *Politics, Parties and Pressure Groups*. New York: Thomas Y. Crowell, 1947. An outstanding textbook on American parties and pressure groups.

Lubell, Samuel, *Future of American Politics*. New York: Harper and Brothers, 1952.

——, *Revolt of the Moderates*. New York: Harper and Brothers, 1956. These two books by a shrewd observer will repay careful reading.

Markel, Lester, *et al.*, *Public Opinion and Foreign Policy*. New York: Harper and Brothers, 1949.

MASLAND, J. W., "Pressure Groups and American Foreign Policy Preceding Pearl Harbor," *Public Opinion Quarterly*, 6 (Spring, 1942), 115–23.

SCHATTSCHNEIDER, E. E., *Party Government.* New York: Rinehart and Company, 1942.

———, *Politics, Pressures, and the Tariff.* New York: Prentice-Hall, 1935. Professor Schattschneider is one of the foremost advocates of more centralized and highly disciplined American parties.

TURNER, H. A., *Politics in the United States.* New York: McGraw-Hill Book Company, 1955. A recent collection of readings (largely secondary) on the American party system.

Index

Crisis diplomacy, and bipartisanship, 112–13, 173–79
Czechoslovakia, Communist
coup in, 65

Democratic party
1956 platform of, 137
opposition of
to "adviser" to State Department, 167–68
to Middle East policy, 148–
49
support of Eisenhower by,
212–13
views of
on arms aid for Middle East,
133–34
on Jordan Valley project,
130
on tariff reductions, 208–10
Department of State; *see* State,
Department of
Destroyers, Anglo-American exchange of, 34
Dewey, Thomas E.
and bipartisan co-operation in
1948, 230–31
views of
on Palestine, 121–22
on UN Charter, 51
Domestic issues, and bipartisanship, 174–75, 205–11
Douglas, Paul H., 21–22
Dulles, John Foster
and Aswan High Dam, 145–
46
in elections of 1944, 51
role of, in bipartisan process,
166–68

Dulles—*continued*
and trip to Middle East, 128–
29
views of
on bipartisanship, 226
on NATO, 74

Eaton, Charles, 60
Economic Cooperation Administration, 66; *see also* Marshall
Plan
Egypt
and acquisition of Communist
arms, 141–44
ties of, with Communist bloc,
145–46
U.S. relations with, 137–48
Eisenhower, Dwight D.
appointment of, as com-
mander of NATO, 90
policy of
toward Formosa, 251–54
toward Middle East, 126–48
reports of, to Congress, 92–93
Europe, Western
defense of, 74–97
economic condition of, in 1947,
62
interim aid to (1947–48), 63
studies of economic need in,
62–63
European Recovery Program; *see*
Marshall Plan
Executive agreements, 15–16, 34
Executive-congressional relations;
see also Bipartisanship; Congress; Foreign policy, institutional conflicts in
and bipartisanship, 6–8

Harsch, Joseph C., 211–12, 218–19, 244
Hawaii, U.S. treaty with, 30
Hearings
  joint committee, 193
  of Senate Committee on Foreign Relations, 58, 64–65
Herter Committee, 63
Hoover, Herbert
  and conferences with Roosevelt administration, 39–40
  views of, on American defense policy, 88–89
Hopkins, Harry, 17–18
House of Representatives
  and aid to Greece, 60
  debate in
    on China aid bill, 105–6
    on Marshall Plan, 65–67
  powers of, in foreign affairs, 24
Hull, Cordell, 39–40
Hurley, Patrick J., 100–101

Ideology, in American politics, 196–97
India, U.S. assistance to, 192–93
"Interim appointments," in diplomatic field, 17
Interparty relations, 6–8
Isolationism, 33–34
Israel
  request of, for U.S. arms, 142–44
  U.S. policy toward, 126–31

Jackson, Andrew, 244
Japan, imports from, 208–10
Jay Treaty, 28–29

Jefferson, Thomas
  and Barbary pirates, 19–20
  and Louisiana Purchase, 29
Jennings, Ivor, 245
Johnson, Olin, 209
Johnson-Clarendon Convention, 36
Johnston, Eric, 129–30
Jordan Valley project, 129–30

Kennan, George, 228–29
Knowland, William, 197–98, 212
Knox, Frank, 36
Korean War, 87–88, 194–95
Krock, Arthur, 248

Laski, Harold J., 242–43
League of Nations, 38–39
Lehman, Herbert, 254
Lippmann, Walter, 217, 239–40
Lodge, Henry Cabot
  opposition of, to League of Nations, 38–39
  and peace treaty with Spain, 31
  and right of Senate in negotiations, 15
  and Treaty of Versailles, 32–33
Lovett, Robert, 75–77

McCarthy, Joseph, 212
McClellan resolution, 93
Mackinac Declaration, 50–51
McKinley, William, 37–38
Madison, James, 35
Majority party
  and bipartisanship, 213–15
  role of, in United States, 247–48
  and support for bipartisanship, 213–15

Manifest Destiny, 30–31
Mansfield, Mike, 135–36
Marshall, George
 letters of, approving Greek aid, 59–60
 speech of, at Harvard, 62
 testimony of
  on European defense, 93
  on Marshall Plan, 64
 views of, on China aid bill, 105
Marshall mission to China, 101–4
Marshall Plan
 bipartisanship toward, 61–72
 as example of bipartisan achievement, 67–72
Mexico, threat of war with, 20–21
Middle East
 bipartisanship toward, 116–55
 defense of, 131–37
 war in (1956), 146–48
Military establishment, control over, 18–23
Minority groups, and foreign affairs, 207–8
Minority party, and bipartisanship, 215–17
Morse, Wayne, 253–54
Mutual Defense Assistance Program, and bipartisanship, 81–87

Nasser, Abdel, 125, 142–43
National interest, and bipartisanship, 201–2, 244–45
Negotiations, and bipartisanship, 231–33
Nonpartisanship; see also Bipartisanship

Nonpartisanship—*continued*
 Secretary Hull on, 5n
 Senator Vandenberg on, 5n
North Atlantic Pact, bipartisanship toward, 74–81

Opposition party; *see also* Bipartisanship; Minority party; Political parties
 educative value of bipartisanship for, 235–37
 factionalism in, 211–12
 liabilities of bipartisanship for, 71–72, 248–49
 role of
  after diplomatic defeats, 111–12
  in the U.S., 248–49
Oregon Territory, 14–15, 35–36

Palestine
 and Israeli-Arab war (1948), 123–25
 partition of, 122–23
 refugees from, 124–25
Paris Peace Conference, 15, 47
Partisanship, in foreign affairs
 and annexation of Texas, 29–30
 and conflict over westward expansion, 36–38
 in election of 1944, 162
 and fisheries agreement of 1888, 30–31
 toward League of Nations, 26
 and Louisiana Purchase, 29
 as obstacle to bipartisanship, 198–202
 before World War II, 26–34
Party discipline, in United States, 197–98

Senate of the United States—*continued*
  power of, to confirm appointments, 16–18
  role of, in treaty making, 13–16
  and Texas treaty, 20–21
  and treaty with Spain, 31
  and Treaty of Versailles, 32–33
Seward, William H., 30
Shannon, William V., 210
Slavery issue, 29–30
Spanish-American War, 31
State, Department of
  and aid to Greece, 58
  and Office of Congressional Relations, 185–88
  studies by, of UN Charter, 45–46
Stevenson, Adlai E., 148–49
Stimson, Henry, 40
Stuart, Graham H., 224
Suez Canal
  Anglo-Egyptian dispute over, 139–41
  nationalization of, 145
Sumner, Charles, 36

Taber, John, 66
Taft, Robert A.
  and Department of State, 219
  and Greek aid, 60–61
  and MDAP, 83
  and NATO, 78
  opposition of, to bipartisanship, 247
  and U.S. defense policy, 89–92
  views of, on China policy, 181
Texas, annexation of, 29–30
Tocqueville, Alexis de, 224

Treaty of Versailles, 32–33
Treaty-making process, 13–16
"Tripartisanship," 212–13
Truman, Harry S.
  and European defense, 90–91
  and Korea, 21–22
  and Marshall Plan, 63–64
  and Palestine, 120–22
  and proposal of MDAP, 81
  and recognition of Israel, 124
"Truman Doctrine," 56

Union of Soviet Socialist Republics
  and conflict with West after World War II, 54–55
  and Middle East, 141–43
United Nations
  Charter of, 44, 52–53
  consensus between parties on, 50–51
  and Palestine, 122
United States v. *Curtiss-Wright Export Corporation* (1936), 179
Unpartisanship, 5n; *see also* Bipartisanship

Van Buren, Martin, 17
Vandenberg, Arthur H.
  and aid to Greece, 59
  and bipartisanship toward China, 102–3
  co-operation of, with Secretary Marshall, 218–19
  effect of bipartisanship upon, 235–36
  and Henry Wallace, 234
  illness and retirement of, 112
  and Mackinac Declaration, 50–51

Date Due